A Guide for Developing Interdisciplinary Thematic Units

Second Edition

Patricia L. Roberts

Richard D. Kellough

California State University, Sacramento

Merrill
an imprint of Prentice Hall
Upper Saddle River, New Jersey   Columbus, Ohio

Library of Congress Cataloging-in-Publication Data

Roberts, Patricia
  A guide for developing interdisciplinary thematic units / Patricia
L. Roberts, Richard D. Kellough. -- 2nd ed.
    p.   cm.
  Rev. ed. of: A guide for developing an interdisciplinary thematic
unit. c1996.
  Includes bibliographical references and indexes.
  ISBN 0-13-921164-0
  1. Interdisciplinary approach in education—United States.
  2. Lesson planning—United States.   I. Kellough, Richard D.
(Richard Dean)   II. Roberts, Patricia   Guide for developing
an interdisciplinary thematic unit.   III. Title.
  LB1570.R55   2000   99-25371
  375'.001—dc21   CIP

Editor: Debra A. Stollenwerk
Editorial Assistant: Penny S. Burleson
Production Editor: Mary Harlan
Design Coordinator: Diane C. Lorenzo
Cover Designer: Thomas Mack
Cover art: © Stephan Schildbach
Photo Coordinator: Sherry Mitchell
Production Manager: Pamela D. Bennett
Text Design and Production Coordination: Carlisle Publishers Services
Director of Marketing: Kevin Flanagan
Marketing Manager: Meghan McCauley
Marketing Coordinator: Krista Groshong

This book was set in 10/12 Palatino by Carlisle Communications, Ltd. and was printed and bound by The
Banta Company. The cover was printed by The Banta Company.

©2000 by Prentice-Hall, Inc.
Pearson Education
Upper Saddle River, New Jersey 07458

Earlier edition, entitled *A Guide for Developing an Interdisciplinary Thematic Unit*, ©1996 by Prentice-Hall, Inc.

Photo Credits: Scott Cunningham/Merrill, pp. 9, 14, 138; Barbara Schwartz/Merrill, p. 35; Mark Madden/KS
Studios/Merrill, p. 49; Anne Vega/Merrill, pp. 80, 82, 225; Tom Watson/Merrill, p. 137.

Printed in the United States of America

10 9 8 7 6 5 4 3

ISBN: 0-13-921164-0

Prentice-Hall International (UK) Limited, *London*
Prentice-Hall of Australia Pty. Limited, *Sydney*
Prentice-Hall of Canada, Inc., *Toronto*
Prentice-Hall Hispanoamericana, S. A., *Mexico*
Prentice-Hall of India Private Limited, *New Delhi*
Prentice-Hall of Japan, Inc., *Tokyo*
Prentice-Hall (Singapore) Pte. Ltd., *Singapore*
Editora Prentice-Hall do Brasil, Ltda., *Rio de Janeiro*

PREFACE

The purpose of this guide is to provide a practical and concise approach for (1) college and university students who are preparing to become competent school teachers, and (2) credentialed teachers who are interested in developing interdisciplinary thematic units. Teachers are becoming increasingly aware of the role of an interdisciplinary thematic unit for quality learning. Perhaps no single task will be more important in the future than that of improving our approaches to facilitating student learning. This guide provides one valuable approach and thus should serve as a supplement to what you learn (or have learned) in a general methods course. The sole purpose of this book is to provide guidance for developing interdisciplinary thematic units.

OUR BELIEFS

We believe the interdisciplinary thematic unit (ITU) is an instructional strategy that will help define a new expression of our professionalism. Certainly, developing and presenting an ITU in the classroom can be challenging—this approach often tests a teacher's dedication and ingenuity. Yet many educators hold the view that such units provide the most meaningful way to prepare students for the recreational, vocational, and everyday requirements of the 21st century. Perhaps one of the greatest challenges of the new century will be the reality of not only living life in the "fast lane," but also living life on a worldwide "information superhighway."

In the year 2000 and beyond, we believe that (1) life on the "superfacts freeway" will encompass students' interpretation of their own meanings through both assigned studies and self-selected independent inquiries; (2) education will consist mainly of inquiry-oriented processes that require students to ask questions and to develop their think-

ing skills through various approaches to research and the use of diverse resources; (3) action-oriented students will focus on pertinent questions and issues (concepts, generalizations, theories, principles) with not only local, regional, and state significance but also global importance; (4) there will be an increased emphasis on determining meaning from the interrelationships found in the content areas of various fields of study; and (5) integrated instructional experiences will equalize educational opportunities for all students.

We are confident that the interdisciplinary thematic approach can be useful in classrooms, though only if questioning is given the same priority that Albert Einstein gave it when reflecting on his own learning. "The most important thing is not to stop questioning," he wrote. "Curiosity has its own reason for existing. One cannot help but be in awe when one contemplates the mysteries of eternity, of life, of the marvelous structure of reality." We believe that the interdisciplinary thematic approach can provide students with a beginning toward that "marvelous structure of reality."

Unfortunately, we are beginning to hear voices—and not merely from disgruntled critics—critical of the basic characteristics and ways of education. If we are to improve our educational approaches significantly in the years ahead, then all of us must join in making that effort. Strong action will be necessary at all educational levels. Presenting interdisciplinary thematic units in the classroom can be part of that action. In addition, private citizens and voluntary groups must join in partnerships to support the effort, including businesses and industries, labor and farm organizations, and scientific, health, and educational institutions. Basically, every part of our society has a responsibility. It is important, too, that the quality of our educational approaches continues to be seen as both a national and an international concern.

To reverse a perceived deterioration in education is now a major national goal, involving all segments of society. It will not be enough to simply cope with educational problems as they individually rise to a clear community concern about a particular problem's effect on our children's progress. As part of addressing current educational concerns, we believe that the educational progress of the future leaders of tomorrow can be assisted by an inclusion of interdisciplinary thematic units throughout the curriculum. This guide supports that proposition.

HOW THIS BOOK IS ORGANIZED

This guide is intended for a teacher interested in offering, assessing, and evaluating an integrated curriculum through the inclusion of interdisciplinary thematic units of instruction. Its focus and organization is designed for teacher preparation at the college and university level, for in-service seminars and workshops at the district level, and for independent use. Through its five chapters, you will find helpful guidelines and ideas to assist you in developing your own thematic units, capable of being vehicles to foster interdisciplinary awareness. As a pre- or post-credentialed teacher, the following contents may be of interest to you.

- Questions and activities for class discussions and individual inquiries appear at the conclusion of each chapter.
- Suggested readings at the end of each chapter offer additional sources to increase your understanding of selected subject matter.
- Pages of the guide are perforated for easy removal of material.
- An appendix of planning masters, a glossary, and indexes of children's literature, names, and subject headings, provide further reference material/aids.
- Albert Einstein's sayings at the beginning of each chapter are documented in *The Importance of Albert Einstein* (Lucent Books, Inc., 1994) by Clarice Swisher.

Chapter 1 presents an explanation of the integrated curriculum and its potential advantages and limitations. It explains the concept of the interdisciplinary thematic unit and foundation theories that support its development and implementation. Chapter 2 presents an overview of the development of themes and of selecting, scoping, and sequencing learning activities for an ITU. Chapter 3 provides guidelines and exercises to guide you in developing objectives and the types of learning activities for an ITU. Chapter 4 addresses the assessment component of student learning. After instruction in Chapter 5 on the development of your lessons for the ITU you are asked to complete the development of your own ITU. Additionally, although space in this book is limited, Chapter 5 has three complete (or nearly complete) sample ITUs for your perusal.

NEW TO THIS EDITION

This book was essentially rewritten from the first page to the last. The primary reason for the rewrite was the request by nearly every reviewer for more content in a book that would not grow in size. That became our challenge.

Ways that this edition differs from the first include the following:

- a section for further reading at the end of every chapter
- guidelines for lesson planning (Chapter 5)
- addresses of relevant Internet websites (all chapters)
- increase of specific examples throughout (all chapters)
- more on assessment (Chapter 4), including more sample checklists, rubrics, use of portfolios, and new content on preparing assessment items
- relevant questions for discussion at the end of each chapter
- strong connections between each chapter via summaries
- discussions on national standards, constructivism, the online classroom, and increased use of technology
- examples of writing objectives in the cognitive, affective, and psychomotor domains
- rewritten exercises designed to help you assess and reflect continually on your progress in understanding an approach to developing an interdisciplinary thematic unit. Because it is unlikely that all exercises could be appropriate to your teaching situation, you, your peers, and the instructor can select the exercises to be done.

In summary, *A Guide for Developing Interdisciplinary Thematic Units* is intended as a starting point for caring teachers who find themselves challenged by students who face a world with many complex concerns. These students are in need of problem-solving skills that may best be developed through the most meaningful kinds of learning, such as can be offered through the use of ITUs in an integrated curriculum. Although even the most dedicated educators cannot determine the future of students in their charge, they can provide positive role models as adults who offer and maintain interdisciplinary teaching and learning. Furthermore, teachers can enhance their curricula by accepting the students' input and placing carefully planned activities into units that will guide the students toward developing the problem-solving skills and knowledge necessary for surviving and thriving in not only today's changing times but also in the years ahead. This guide is a teacher-to-teacher discussion toward that end.

ACKNOWLEDGMENTS

Many people have helped and encouraged us during the development of the second edition of this guide. For the features that are good, credit them; for those that are not so good, blame us. We want to express our warmest appreciation to the teachers who provided us with samples of materials they have developed and whose names are acknowledged in the guide.

We also want to thank the following colleagues who served as reviewers, who provided thoughtful, positive, and succinct suggestions for improvement that we hope they will agree are reflected well in this edition.

Swen H. Digranes, Northeastern State
    University
Maureen Gillette, College of St. Rose

Bob Hoffman, San Diego State University
Betty J. Krenzke, Concordia University
Connie H. Nobles, Southeastern Louisiana
    University
Vesna Ostertag, Nova Southeastern University

Additionally, we continue to respond to the other reviewers and users of this guide and have made changes as a result of their feedback. Those who have provided contributions, for which we are very grateful, include JoAnne Buggey, University of Minnesota; Barbara Kacer, Western Kentucky University; Cynthia G. Kruger, University of Massachusetts–Dartmouth; Cynthia E. Ledbetter, University of Texas at Dallas; and Linda Levstik, University of Kentucky.

Further, we want to express our sincere appreciation to our friends at Merrill/Prentice Hall, especially to Debbie Stollenwerk, our editor, who encouraged us to write this guide and who provided intelligent technical suggestions and unfaltering emotional support throughout its development.

For the members of our families, we have appreciation beyond words. Writing this book was a time-consuming process and they understood.

P.L.R.
R.D.K.

BRIEF CONTENTS

CONTENTS

CHAPTER 3

Developing Objectives and Learning Activities   65

CHAPTER 4

Assessment of Student Learning   111

CHAPTER 5

Completing Your ITU: Lesson Planning and Sample Units   147

Appendix: Planning Masters   249

CHAPTER 1

Introduction to an Interdisciplinary Thematic Unit

Out there is this huge world which exists independent of us human beings and which stands before us like a great eternal riddle, at least partially accessible to our inspection and thinking.

—Albert Einstein

INTERDISCIPLINARY THEMATIC UNIT FOR INTERMEDIATE GRADE STUDENTS: *EXPLORATIONS*

Christine Pappas, Barbara Z. Kiefer, and Linda S. Levstik selected the theme of exploration (see *An Integrated Language Perspective in the Elementary School: Theory into Action,* Longman, 1990) as a way to launch an across-the-curriculum interdisciplinary study for fourth- and fifth-grade students. This thematic unit was adjusted to meet local requirements as part of regional studies in the fourth grade and part of a national history study in the fifth grade. The unit was broad and planned around exploring time, the arts, science, history, and language. During a 20-day thematic unit on exploration, team teachers began the unit with a broad overview of different ways exploration occurs. To begin, the students explored other people's lives by reading poetry, biography, autobiography, and historical fiction, writing a fictionalized biography, role-playing, and performing other related activities.

Then the students were asked to intensively study the concept of exploration and use primary source materials, additional role play, and reflective inquiry. Problem solving was included through math and art activities, student writing, and experiments. Some classes were shortened when art, music, physical education, and library periods were scheduled. The unit met state requirements for reading and language arts with language activities integral to the whole curriculum. The students shared their work with peers and participated in other creative and factual activities from the theme. These activities were related to the following disciplines:

- *English.* The students discussed word origins, made dictionaries of word origins, collected regional expressions, learned sign language, and created metaphors and similes. They wrote journals about journeys they had taken or wished they had taken.
- *Expressive arts.* The students made a time line of the history of selected musical instruments, listened to recordings of styles of music developed over time, explored different art mediums, and suggested dance steps to reflect the theme of exploration.
- *History.* The students made a time line around the classroom and placed noteworthy explorations on it. They also collected information

for a comparison chart to show positive and negative effects of explorations.

- *Language arts.* The students role-played a discussion at an early explorer's settlement about how to deal with the native people nearby. Then the students reversed the situation and played their roles from the native people's perspective.
- *Science.* The students explored the concept of time by displaying ways that time can be measured, by researching a time line of important explorations and discoveries in medicine in the last 200 years, and by inviting an astronomer to class for a question-and-answer period about explorations and discoveries in another study area—time and space.
- *Social science.* The students researched the past by studying the forms of government that various explorers brought to the worlds they explored. They researched the present by exploring contemporary careers when visiting selected worksites and conducting an inventory of needed skills. Further, the students discussed important topical issues such as good government and freedom.

A primary responsibility of a teacher is to provide learning experiences that result in the students' creation of new schemata and the modification of existing schemata.[1] The educators mentioned previously who offered the thematic unit on exploration for fourth- and fifth-grade students provided situations intended to modify their students' existing schemata about the concept and to stimulate the organization of new schemata. As you read and study this chapter, bits and pieces of new information are stored in your short-term memory, where the new information is rehearsed until ready to be stored in long-term memory. If the information is not rehearsed, it has been essentially meaningless and will eventually fade from your short-term memory. If it is rehearsed and made meaningful through connections with other stored knowledge, then this new knowledge is transferred to and stored in your long-term memory, either by adding to existing schemata or by forming new schemata. The format for this guide is designed to facilitate your rehearsal of new information and build new understandings or rebuild previous ones about interdisciplinary thematic teaching.

KNOWLEDGE AND MEANINGFUL LEARNING

It has become quite clear to many teachers that to be the most effective in helping students develop meaningful understandings (and hence their motivation to learn), much of the learning in each discipline can be made more effective and longer lasting when that learning is integrated with the whole curriculum and made meaningful to the lives of the students. This approach appears more successful than simply teaching unrelated and separate disciplines at the same time each day. **Meaningful learning,** then, is defined as learning that results when the learner makes connections between a new experience and prior knowledge and experiences that were stored in his or her long-term memory.

If learning is defined only as being the accumulation of small parts of information, we can say we already know how small parts are learned and how to teach this accumulation. The accumulation of tiny pieces of information, however, is at the lowest end of a spectrum of types of learning and leads to what is sometimes referred to as **procedural knowledge.** In contrast, learning that is most meaningful and longest lasting and includes higher levels of thinking is referred to as **conceptual knowledge.** To support the development of conceptual knowledge, research results indicate using (1) a curriculum in which disciplines are integrated, and (2) instructional techniques that involve the learners in social interactive learning such as problem-based and project-centered learning, cooperative learning, peer tutoring, and cross-age teaching.

MULTILEVEL INSTRUCTION

As you know from your study of the works of Piaget,[2] Bruner,[3] Caine and Caine,[4] Dunn,[5] Gardner,[6] Sternberg,[7] and others, students in your classroom have their own independent ways of knowing and learning; and they also may be at different stages (and substages) of cognitive development. It is important to know how each student best learns and where each student is developmentally, that is, to individualize both the content and the methods of learning. In doing so, it is helpful to use **multilevel instruction** (or **multitasking**). Multilevel instruction is when different students or groups of students are working at different tasks to accomplish either the same or different objectives. An example is the classroom scenario shown in Figure 1.1.

When integrating student learning, multitasking is an important and useful, perhaps even necessary, strategy. Project-centered teaching, often a valuable instructional component of interdisciplinary thematic instruction, is a method that easily allows and provides multilevel instruction. Multilevel teaching occurs when several levels of teaching and learning are going on simultaneously. When using multilevel instruction, individual students and small groups will be doing different activities at the same time to accomplish the same or different objectives. While some students may be working independently of the teacher, others may be receiving direct instruction from the teacher—perhaps in a traditional mode to obtain procedural knowledge.[8]

An important responsibility for the teacher when using multilevel instruction is being certain, to the extent possible, that students share their learning in a way that all students have equal opportunity to learn the procedural and conceptual knowledge expected. To that end, you can use strategies such as frequent checks for comprehension, weekly sharing, and student presentations about any culminating experiences of the unit.

INTEGRATED CURRICULUM AND RELATED TERMS

When learning about integrated curriculum, you might be confused by the plethora of terms that are used, such as integrated studies, thematic instruction, holistic education, multidisciplinary teaching, integrated curriculum, interdisciplinary curriculum, and interdisciplinary thematic instruction. In essence, regardless of which of these terms is being used, the reference is to the same thing—plans for teaching by relating disciplines.

FIGURE 1.1 Classroom Scenario: Using the Theory of Learning Capacities (Multiple Intelligences) and Multilevel Instruction

During 1 week of a 6-week thematic unit on weather in a seventh-grade classroom, students concentrated on learning about the water cycle. For this study of the water cycle, the teacher divided the class into several groups of three to five students per group. Each group worked simultaneously on six projects to learn about the water cycle. One group of students designed, conducted, and repeated an experiment to discover the number of drops of water that can be held on one side of a new penny versus the number that can be held on one side of a worn penny. Working in part with the first group, a second group designed and prepared graphs to illustrate the results of the experiments of the first group. A third group of students created and composed the words and music of a rap song about the water cycle. The students in a fourth group incorporated their combined interests in mathematics and art to design a project, collect the necessary materials, and create a colorful and interactive bulletin board about the water cycle. A fifth group read about the water cycle in materials the students researched from the Internet. Finally, a sixth group created a drama about the water cycle. On Friday, the groups shared their projects with the whole class.

Curriculum and Instruction

Originally derived from a Latin term referring to a race course for the Roman chariots, the term **curriculum** still has no widely accepted definition. As used for this text, curriculum is that which is planned and encouraged for teaching and learning. This includes both school and nonschool environments, overt (formal) and hidden (informal) curriculums,[9] and broad and narrow notions of content—its development, acquisition, and consequences. **Instruction** is the planned arrangement of experiences to help a learner develop understanding and to achieve a desirable change in behavior. Because it is not always easy to determine where the term *curriculum* ends and *instruction* begins, in regard to integrated curriculum, there is basically no difference. The terms integrated curriculum and integrated instruction both refer to expected learning experiences.

Integrated Curriculum Defined

The term **integrated curriculum,** or any of its synonyms mentioned previously, refers to a way of teaching and a way of planning and organizing the instructional program so the discrete disciplines of subject matter are interrelated in a design that (1) matches the developmental needs of the learners[10] and (2) helps connect the students' learning in ways that are meaningful to their current and past experiences. In that respect, integrated curriculum is the antithesis of traditional, disparate, subject matter–oriented teaching and curriculum designations.

Integrated Curricula Past and Present

The reason for the various terminology related to integrated curriculum is, in part, because throughout most of the history of education in this country, educators' efforts to integrate student learning have provided numerous labels. Without fully reviewing that history prior to today's times, in some form or another, the most recent popularity stems from the late 1950s, initiated by some of the discovery-oriented, student-centered projects supported by the National Science Foundation. These projects include *Elementary School Science* (ESS), a hands-on and integrated science program for grades K–6; *Man: A Course of Study* (MACOS), a hands-on, anthropology-based program for fifth graders; and *Environmental Studies* (name later changed to *ESSENCE*), an interdisciplinary program for use at all grades, K–12, regardless of subject matter orientation.

Today's interest in curriculum integration is also generated from several inextricably connected sources: (1) the success at curriculum integration that has been enjoyed by middle-level schools since the beginning of the middle school movement in the 1960s,[11] (2) the literature-based, whole-language movement in reading and language arts that began in the 1980s,[12] (3) the diversity of children in the regular classroom coupled with growing acceptance of the philosophy that a certain percentage of school dropouts is not a viable assumption,[13] (4) the needs of the workplace, advances in technology, and a concomitant trend of integrating vocational education with academic education in secondary schools,[14] (5) the challenges students will face in the 21st century, the application of information technologies to K–12 education in the United States, the recent recommendations of the President's Committee of Advisors on Science and Technology (PCAST) to strengthen the use of technology in America's schools,[15] and (6) the recent research in cognitive science and neuroscience demonstrating the necessity of helping learners establish bridges between school and life, knowing and doing, and content and context, with a parallel rekindled interest in constructivism as opposed to a strictly behaviorist philosophical approach to teaching and learning.[16]

THEORETICAL ORIGINS OF INSTRUCTIONAL STYLES AND THEIR RELATION TO CONSTRUCTIVISM AND INTEGRATED CURRICULUM

In a broad sense, **behaviorism** is a theory that equates learning with predicted changes in observable behavior. **Constructivism** is a theory that holds that learning entails the construction or reshaping of mental schemata and that mental processes mediate learning. Whereas behaviorists are concerned with behaviors that are overt, constructivists are interested in both overt and covert behaviors.[17] Perhaps the following will help clarify how learning theory affects changes to curriculum and instruction.

Constructivism and the integration of curriculum are not new to education. The importance of the constructivist and curriculum integration approaches are found, for example, in the writings of John Dewey[18] and Arthur W. Combs.[19]

Instructional styles are deeply rooted in certain theoretical assumptions about learners and their development. Although it is beyond the scope of this guide to explore those assumptions in depth, three major theoretical positions with research findings suggest different ways of working with children, each based on certain philosophical and psychological assumptions. These theoretical positions are as follows:

- **Romanticism-maturationism.** Tied to the theoretical positions of romanticism-maturationism is the assumption that the learner's mind is neutral-passive to good-active, and the main focus in teaching should be the addition of new ideas to a subconscious storage of old ideas. Key persons include Jean J. Rousseau and Sigmund Freud; key instructional strategies include classic lecturing with rote memorization.

- **Behaviorism.** Tied to the theoretical position of behaviorism is the assumption that the learner's mind is neutral-passive with innate reflexes and needs, and the main focus in teaching should be on the successive, systematic changes in the learner's environment to increase the possibilities of desired behavior responses. Key persons include John Locke, B. F. Skinner, A. H. Thorndike, Robert Gagné, and John Watson; key instructional strategies include practice reinforcement as in workbook drill activities and programmed instruction.

- **Cognitive-experimentalism.** Tied to the theoretical position of cognitive-experimentalism (including constructivism) is the assumption that the learner is a neutral-interactive, purposive individual in simultaneous interaction with physical, biological environments. The main focus in teaching should be on facilitating the learner's gain and construction of new perceptions that lead to desired behavioral changes and ultimately to a more fully functioning individual. Key persons are John Dewey, Lev Vygotsky, Jerome Bruner, Jean Piaget, and Arthur W. Combs; key instructional strategies include discovery, inquiry, project-centered teaching, cooperative and social-interactive learning, and interdisciplinary instruction.

With a diversity of students, a teacher must be eclectic to be most effective, and have a strong emphasis toward cognitive-experimentalism-constructivism because of this theory's focus on divergence in learning and on the importance given to learning as a change in perceptions. Learning as a change in perceptions utilizes at appropriate times the best of strategies and knowledgeable instructor behaviors, regardless of whether individually they can be classified within any style dichotomy such as "direct or indirect," "formal or informal," or "traditional or progressive."

An integrated curriculum approach may not necessarily be the best approach for every school, nor the best for all learning for every student, nor is it necessarily the manner by which every teacher

should or must always plan and teach. As evidenced by practice, the truth of this statement becomes apparent.

CURRICULUM INTEGRATION: SUMMARY OF PURPOSES

To summarize, the major purposes of curriculum integration include the following:

1. To introduce curriculum in a more comprehensive manner and not teach separate subjects each day
2. To involve students in direct, purposeful, and meaningful learning
3. To promote students' understanding that learning is interrelated, that knowledge across disciplines is inextricably interconnected, and that the process of learning, as in life, is whole and connected rather than a series of specific and unrelated pieces of knowledge, subjects, topics, and disparate skills
4. To assist students in following individual interests through individualized and personalized instruction
5. To provide opportunities for students to learn what they need and to be motivated to learn rather than learn only what a particular curriculum dictates
6. To facilitate students' learning together (i.e., to integrate affect with cognition)
7. To facilitate students in their becoming independent problem solvers

THE SPECTRUM OF INTEGRATED CURRICULUM

To facilitate the students' content learning along with their experiences, a teacher's efforts will fall at various places on a spectrum or continuum, from the least integrated instruction (Level I) to the most integrated (Level V), as illustrated in Figure 1.2.[20] To distinguish the levels, we use the factors of student input and decision making and the blending of disciplines.

The diagram in Figure 1.2 should not be interpreted as going from worst-case scenario (far left) to best-case scenario (far right), although some people may interpret it as such. In reality, there are various interpretations to curriculum integration, and on the basis of many factors each teacher must make an individualized decision about its use. Figure 1.2 is meant solely to show how efforts to integrate fall on a continuum of sophistication and complexity.

FIGURE 1.2   Continuum of Curriculum Integration

Level I	Level II	Level III	Level IV	Level V
Least integrated	Material blended from various disciplines	Material kept in separate disciplines	Few distinct discipline boundaries	Most integrated No discipline boundaries

Level I

Level I is the traditional organization of curriculum and classroom instruction, during which teachers plan and arrange the subject-specific scope and sequence in the format of topic outlines. If there is an attempt to help students connect their learning and their experiences, then it is up to individual classroom teachers to do it. A student who moves during the school day from classroom to classroom, teacher to teacher, subject to subject, from one topic to another is likely learning at a Level I instructional environment. A topic in science, for example, might be "earthquakes." A related topic in social studies might be "the social consequences of natural disasters." These two topics may or may not be studied by a student at the same time. Such a traditional approach is common in elementary school teaching, where the children receive subject-specific instruction at precise times during the school day (e.g., if it is a Tuesday at 8:00 a.m., it must be reading). But even then, this type could be called a Level I approach to curriculum integration when what the children are doing in reading is related in a way they understand with one or more additional disciplines, such as social studies or science.

As an example, consider children in kindergarten through second grade who are reading or listening to the story, *Francis, The Earthquake Dog*, written by J. R. Enderle and S. G. Tessler and illustrated by B. Scudder (Chronicle Books, 1996). This story is about a young boy and a dog based on fact that reflects some of the disastrous consequences of an earthquake (social studies) and can lead to a study of causes of tremors (science). In San Francisco in 1906, young Edward saves a stray terrier from being hit by a vegetable cart and takes him to his father, a chef at the St. Francis Hotel. The earthquake begins that evening and even while he and his father look for shelter in the tent city at Golden Gate Park, Edward worries about the dog. When the two return to the hotel, they hear barking from under the ruins and discover the lost terrier.[21] After the story, the children relate their reading to a discussion about whether the solution of a tent city used for the homeless in 1906 could work today and what assistance, if any, is provided for animals during natural disasters. They get involved in a project to learn what to do during an earthquake in their area and report ways to be prepared to survive for several days without government and agency help after a major quake. The children suggest several questions to answer through study: (1) What food, clothing, and first-aid materials could be made available for their families? (2) What preparations could be made for animal companions? (3) What resource personnel could be contacted for information about earthquake preparedness programs sponsored by city, county, and state agencies in the area?

Level II

If the same students are learning English/language arts, or social studies/history, or mathematics, or science, using a thematic approach rather than a topic outline, then they are learning at Level II. Even if various disciplines are still taught at specific times of the school day (e.g., reading at 8:00, mathematics at 9:00, and so on, many elementary school teachers can individually base much or all of the learning day (or several days) around a central theme. When so doing, they are teaching at Level II integration.

At the intermediate and secondary grade levels, at Level II integration, themes for one discipline (e.g., social studies or history) are not necessarily planned and coordinated to correspond or integrate with themes of another (e.g., mathematics) or to be taught simultaneously.

Topic versus Theme.   The difference between what is a topic and what is a theme is not always clear. Whereas "earthquakes" and "social consequences" are topics, "natural disasters" could be the theme (or educational umbrella) under which these two topics could fall. In addition, as implied in the preceding section, themes are likely to be longer in duration than topics. For the purposes of this guide, a **theme** is the point, the message, or the idea that underlines a study. The theme may explain the significance of the study (e.g., Nature can affect people in a disastrous way), or it may communicate to the student what the experience means (e.g., People should be prepared to respond to nature's disasters). In some instances, the theme may represent in whole or in part a problem to be solved, in which case it may be a **problem-centered interdisciplinary thematic unit (ITU)** (e.g., What can people do more effectively to respond to nature's disasters?). Many topics comprise an ITU, which is organized around a theme. Sometimes the theme of a study becomes clearer to students when an overall guiding question is presented and discussed, such as "What happens in our society after natural disasters?" At Level II, the students may have some input into the decision making involved in planning themes, topics, and content from various disciplines.

Some educators say that the integrated curriculum of the 21st century will be based on broad, unchanging, and unifying concepts (that is, on conceptual themes).[22] If so, it would be a recycling of an approach of the 1960s, such as professed by Jerome Bruner and implemented in some of the National Foundation–sponsored curriculum projects of that era. In fact, action has already begun in that direction, for example the National Standards for Science Education for grades K–12 (national standards are discussed in Chapter 2) are centered around unifying conceptual and procedural schemes, such as "systems, order, and organization," and "form and function."[23]

Level III

When the same cohort of students is learning two or more core subjects (English/language arts, social studies/history, mathematics, and science) around a common theme, such as "natural disasters," from one or more teachers, they are then learning at Level III integration. At this level, teachers agree on a common theme, then they *separately* deal with that theme in their individual subject areas, usually at the same time during the school year. So the content that the student is learning from a teacher in one class is related to and coordinated with the content that the student is concurrently learning in another or several other classes. Some authors may refer to Levels II or III as coordinated or parallel curriculum.[24] At Level III, students may have some input into the decision making involved in selecting and planning themes and content.

Level IV

When teachers and students clearly collaborate on a common theme and its procedural and conceptual content and when discipline boundaries begin to disappear as teachers teach about a common theme—either solo as in a self-contained classroom or as an **interdisciplinary teaching team**—Level IV

integration is achieved. For example, at Indian Trail Junior High School (Addison, Illinois), working with the same cohort of students, a team of teachers from English, mathematics, physical education, science, and social studies implement a 5-day unit titled "Inspector Red Ribbon." The unit begins with a video showing a prom night automobile accident. Students have 5 days to review the evidence, investigate further, recommend an indictment, and present their conclusions at a mock press conference. During those 5 days in each of their classes, the students work on the case.[25]

In longer-term thematic studies at the Illinois Mathematics and Science Academy, sophomores study the critical decisions that have driven American development, and seniors at the academy investigate dilemmas resulting from modern advances in science and technology.[26]

Level V

A Level V integrated thematic approach[27] is evident when teachers and their students have collaborated on a common theme and its content, discipline boundaries are truly blurred during instruction, and teachers of several grade levels and of various subjects teach toward student understanding of aspects of a common theme.

Because this guide has been prepared to assist you in developing an interdisciplinary thematic unit, it is important that you periodically assess at which level you would feel comfortable implementing an integrated curriculum in a classroom. The initial self-assessment provided by Exercise 1.1 will not only help you become more knowledgeable about what is involved in teaching an ITU, but also will help you better understand what your professional relationship with other teachers and with the students might be like. Now do Exercise 1.1 on page 21.

ROLE OF THE TEACHER IN AN INTEGRATED CURRICULUM

When initiating an integrated curriculum, you will want to provide a warm, friendly, and accepting environment in which the students can freely engage in learning activities that are developmentally appropriate—that relate to their interests, needs, and abilities. It may well be that the diversity of the student cohort will dictate the level of integration of the curriculum.[28]

In this integration, a single theme can be the organizational focus of both the language activities and the various content areas (disciplines such as math and science). To do this, you can provide ways for students to study a topic in depth (conceptual knowledge) and to develop a variety of skills (procedural knowledge) in the process. Accordingly you will want to have an assortment of classroom learning materials available for the students to touch, manipulate, explore, and experiment. You can take advantage of all the school-based learning related to the activities. Through it all, you can act as a catalyst who stimulates the learning of the students as they explore issues that are meaningful to their lives. Here are some examples:

- If students are studying ancient Greece, how does a community of that time compare with their own neighborhood community of today?
- If students are studying early newcomers in the colonies in land now America, how were newcomers of that time treated as compared with newcomers today?
- If students are studying changes during the seasons, how does a current season and its changes compare with a past season and its changes? What issues related to seasonal changes and their lives can be explored?

As students explore and make comparisons, they will stimulate one another and that will help you, too, continue to be a learner.

Diversity and Multiculturalism

Most teachers realize that today's students comprise a great diversity of individuals, with a full range of cultural, ethnic, and economic heritage and first languages. They realize that America's people are multi-everything—multilingual (features of language), multiethnic, and multicultural (our features of customs, religion, traditions, history)—and that the students in their classrooms represent the changing demographics of our pluralistic nation.

With this diversity, every teacher should want to improve the quality of human relations in the classroom to foster an appreciation in students for the multiethnic composition of our society at large and our communities in general. Every teacher should want to help students become aware of who they are as unique individuals and who they are as Americans—for they all have had an American experience to relate to others. Thus, an interdisciplinary thematic unit can be a useful vehicle for improving the quality of human relations in the classroom, especially when it includes projects designed to provide a multicultural perspective. Such projects can help students understand the idea of *e pluribus unum* ("out of many, one"), en-

riching their sense of the tremendous variety of American experiences and what being an American means to each individual American.

Several projects are shown in Figure 1.3, which focus on diversity and multiculturalism. Ironically, to show the many interdisciplinary possibilities, the different areas had to be subdivided for the purposes of discussion instead of being melded and integrated into a whole.

Effective Teacher Defined

Researchers emphasize the qualities of effective teachers—especially those who work with culturally diverse students.[29] Being effective is defined as (1) having teaching behaviors that engage the students in learning that produces rates of academic learning as high as or higher than the rates reported in previous research on effective teaching, and (2) being seen as effective in delivery of instruction and organization by other teachers and school personnel as well as by students and parents.[30]

Effective Teacher Qualities

Effective teachers of culturally and linguistically diverse students are those who

- Believe that classroom practices that tend to validate the diverse cultural and linguistic heritage of students are important ways of fostering self-esteem in students (including their feelings and emotions)
- Believe that multicultural awareness enriches the lives of all students (e.g., learning about Latino culture not only benefits Latino students but also helps develop a sensitivity to another culture in other students (feelings and emotions)
- Communicate clearly when giving directions and presenting new information (skills)
- Demonstrate the ability to communicate rationales for instructional techniques and participate in staff development through courses and workshops (knowledge)
- Demonstrate specific instructional skills (e.g., organize instruction so it is meaningful to students), incorporate hands-on (that is, doing it) and minds-on (that is, thinking about what is being done) learning, use patterned books for reading, plan lessons around individual skills, encourage collaborative and cooperative interactions among students, and use a thematic curriculum in consultation with the students (skills)
- Engage students in instruction by pacing instruction appropriately, by involving the students in the lessons through collaborative and cooperative

learning, by monitoring the progress of each student, and by providing prompt feedback (skills)

- Mediate instruction for limited-English-proficient (LEP) students by alternately using both the students' native language and English for instruction, thus providing clarity (skills)
- Seek help from others and provide help when asked; describe themselves as confident, creative, energetic, resourceful, and collaborative; and often spend their own money to get the material needed for meaningful learning activities (disposition)
- Specify expected outcomes and demonstrate high expectations (although not necessarily identical expectations) for all students (attitude and skills)

Various teacher interactions, a number of which are shown in Figure 1.4 (on page 12), can be suitably integrated into an interdisciplinary thematic unit. (Planning Master 1.1 will be helpful in preparing an overhead transparency for a group discussion.) What other interactions for the classroom teacher would you add to the diagram? What examples would you place under the headings?

Class Management in an Atmosphere of Active Inquiry

When children are actively learning, they are exactly that—active; and when children are active, they can be noisy, even boisterous. Most certainly they are noisier than when in the traditional classroom, where all students are seated with their chairs facing the front of the room in which the teacher spends much of the time doing direct, teacher-centered instruction. When actively learning via a student-centered, project-oriented ITU, however, the movements and noise made by students are more likely to be educational and productive. When a student's movement or noise is not necessary or enhancing to the learning activity, then—just as when using any other type of instructional strategy—you must implement your usual management plan (perhaps a peer conflict resolution meeting) or remind the students of procedures and, if necessary, apply the established consequences of not following those procedures.

To successfully implement an ITU may require a shift in your concept of classroom management and control, and perhaps even that of the school administrator. Integrated studies require students to take more responsibility for their own learning and for their own conduct. Much less class time is spent in teacher-centered, worksheet-oriented, and textbook-oriented instruction. Thus, for teachers who have difficulty sharing authority with their students, an approach that incorporates active inquiry means

A diverse group of students work together in a warm, friendly, and accepting environment.

confronting in new ways what has traditionally been referred to as control and discipline. An emphasis on student initiative and responsibility produces a much greater frequency of those teachable moments that mean so much to both students and adults. Because ITUs usually take on a life of their own, students also assume responsibility for their own academic lives more willingly. They enjoy having the trust and independence to be more responsible for themselves and their learning.[31]

ROLE OF THE STUDENTS IN AN INTEGRATED CURRICULUM

In an integrated curriculum, the emphasis should be on the cooperation, responsibility, and initiative that students demonstrate both in the activities and throughout the learning process. This emphasis should be central to the students' involvement in and responsibility for their learning. For example, in various learning activities, students will be expected to work with others in partnerships and small groups. Membership and roles within groups will vary, depending both on the activity and on each student's interest. As part of that interest, an individual student can "reserve" a particular topic of study. The student then searches for answers to questions that he or she has asked in consultation with the teacher. The student's search may include moving around the classroom, asking questions, consulting others, and referring to a variety of data sources.

Various student interactions, a number of which are shown in Figure 1.5, can be suitably integrated into an interdisciplinary thematic unit. (Planning Master 1.2 will be helpful in preparing an

FIGURE 1.3   Activity Web for Fostering Human Relations Through an ITU Approach

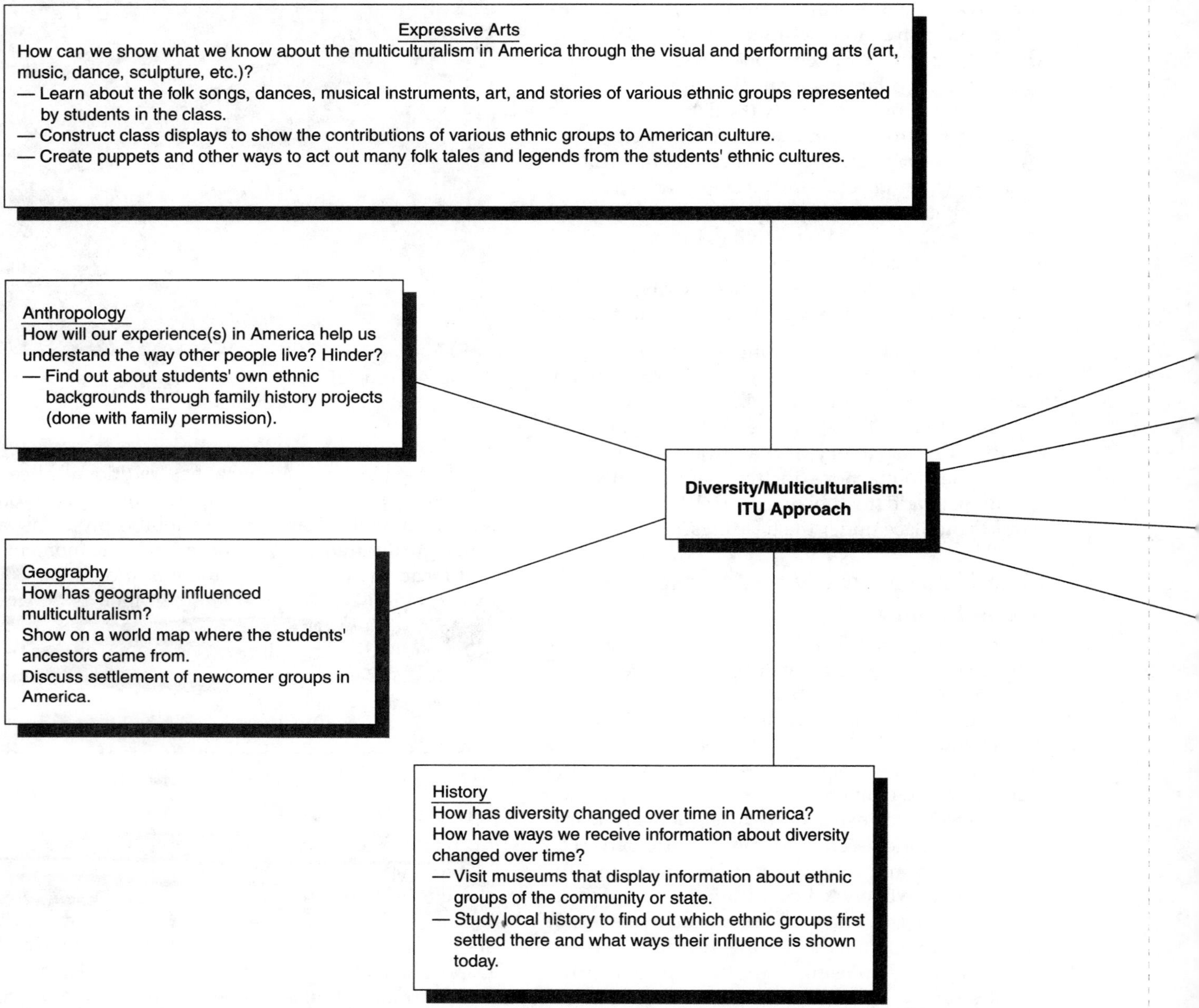

Expressive Arts
How can we show what we know about the multiculturalism in America through the visual and performing arts (art, music, dance, sculpture, etc.)?
— Learn about the folk songs, dances, musical instruments, art, and stories of various ethnic groups represented by students in the class.
— Construct class displays to show the contributions of various ethnic groups to American culture.
— Create puppets and other ways to act out many folk tales and legends from the students' ethnic cultures.

Anthropology
How will our experience(s) in America help us understand the way other people live? Hinder?
— Find out about students' own ethnic backgrounds through family history projects (done with family permission).

Diversity/Multiculturalism: ITU Approach

Geography
How has geography influenced multiculturalism?
Show on a world map where the students' ancestors came from.
Discuss settlement of newcomer groups in America.

History
How has diversity changed over time in America?
How have ways we receive information about diversity changed over time?
— Visit museums that display information about ethnic groups of the community or state.
— Study local history to find out which ethnic groups first settled there and what ways their influence is shown today.

overhead transparency for group discussion.) What other student interactions would you add to the diagram? What examples would you place under the headings?

ROLE OF THE SCHOOL FOR OPTIMAL CURRICULUM INTEGRATION

For years, teachers of elementary schools have at some level used integrated instruction, especially those teaching in self-contained classrooms for all or most of the school day. Most teachers of middle-level and secondary schools, until recently, have not had the advantage of meeting their students for long blocks of time. As many teachers have discovered, the traditional scheduling of instructional periods of 45 to 60 minutes each (a common schedule for the upper grades), is not conducive to the most effective implementation of interdisciplinary thematic instruction. To restructure schools to deliver quality learning to all students, nontraditional scheduling has been a major part of that effort.

Economics
What work in the economy is done by people to develop and bring information to us?
— Make a class book of people in an ethnic group who have made contributions in the community. Include their achievements and, if possible, invite them to the classroom.

Mathematics
How can we express what we know about multiculturalism through mathematics?
— Detect a pattern in terms of the dominance of ethnic groups with names in your area's telephone directory.
— Compare data with that found in a directory (available at a large library) of an area in another part of your state.

Political Science
How have people organized themselves to provide information about government and politics?
— Collect news articles about the position of an ethnic group in a conflict situation.

Science
How have scientists from diverse groups contributed to our way of life?
— Ask students to research inventors from diverse groups.
— Invite scientists from various groups to class to discuss their inquiries and accomplishments.

Sociology
In what ways in the community can we participate to resolve a real problem related to diversity?
— Ask students to research contemporary groups with ethnic memberships.
— Discuss the purposes and contributions of members of multicultural groups.
— Invite members of various ethnic groups to class to discuss cultural roots, language, and customs.
— Take field trips to businesses, city council meetings, county supervisor meetings and state legislatures, or attend service group meetings that focus on selected ethnic groups.
— Take field trips to investigate the quality of the local water works or the use of pesticides.
— Organize "Stop the Violence" or "Stop the Hate Crimes" forums.
— Make a calendar of holidays for the school year that are observed by students in the class.
— Elicit suggestions from students about ways to foster better human relations in the classroom, implement them, and hold ongoing discussions through regular class meetings and forums.

Sometimes, however, it may appear that more energy is devoted to organizational change (how the curriculum is delivered) than to school curriculum (what is taught). Note that the two are inseparable. School organization has a direct effect on what students learn, evident in the fact that educators spend much valuable time trying to restructure their schools to effect the most productive delivery of the curriculum—both the planned and the hidden curricula. Although constant change can be unsettling and even distracting to a classroom teacher, many researchers conclude that rather than reaching some organizational plateau, exemplary schools are those that establish and maintain a climate of constant modification; they are in a continual process of inquiry, reflection, and change.[32]

Organizational Change for Optimal Curriculum Integration

Organizational changes are referred to as **school restructuring,** a term that has a variety of connotations, including not only curriculum integration but also nontraditional scheduling, site-based management,

FIGURE 1.4   Visual Web of Teacher Interactions

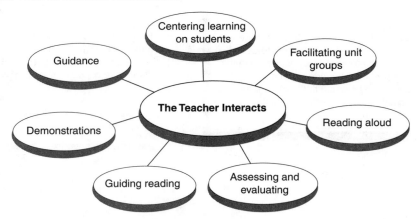

FIGURE 1.5   Visual Web of Student Interactions

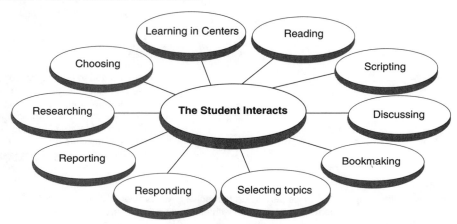

collaborative decision making, school choice, personalized learning, and collegial staffing. School restructuring has been defined as "activities that change fundamental assumptions, practices, and relationships, both within the organization and between the organization and the outside world, in ways leading to improved learning outcomes."[33] No matter how school restructuring is defined, educators agree on the following point: The design and functions of schools should reflect the needs of young people of the 21st century, rather than the needs of the 19th century.

The redesigning of schools into "houses," each with an interdisciplinary team of teachers plus additional support personnel, represents a movement that is becoming increasingly common across the country. This movement is from what has been referred to as a "system of schooling" rooted in the "Industrial Age" toward a design more in touch with the emerging demands of the new millennium,

or the "Information Age."[34] With this redesign, the intention is that schools will better address the needs and capabilities of each unique student.

Block Scheduling

To allow for more instructional flexibility and to accommodate mutual planning time for teachers, increasingly more schools are using some form of block scheduling, an arrangement when for at least part of the school day, blocks of time ranging from 70 to 140 or more minutes replace the traditional structure of 45- to 60-minute classes. Even small schools (with enrollment less than 400 students[35]) are meeting pressures to expand curriculum options through integrated curriculum and block scheduling. The possible variations are nearly limitless.

Advantages and Limitations of Block Scheduling. Consistently reported in the research about schools using block scheduling, where students and teachers work together in longer but fewer classes at a time, are (1) greater satisfaction among teachers and administrators, and (2) improvement in both behavior and learning of students. Students to do more writing, pursue an issue in greater depth, enjoy classes more, feel more challenged, and gain deeper understandings. In addition, learning time is optimized when between-class time is reduced, instruction is coordinated, scheduling is flexible, and teaching colleagues collaborate on instruction. With teachers teaching fewer students in fewer courses, instruction can be significantly greater with more students taking advanced courses, the student-teacher interaction can be more productive, and the school climate has fewer discipline problems. Because planning periods are longer, teachers have time to plan and interact with parents. Further, teachers get to know the students better and are therefore able to respond to a student's needs with greater care.[36] In evaluations of schools using block scheduling, it was found that more course credits were completed, students had equal or better mastery and retention of materials, and there was an impressive reduction in suspension and dropout rates.[37]

Nontraditional school schedules also have problems. Some that may arise from block scheduling are (1) content coverage in a course may be less than that which was traditionally covered, (2) a mismatch may result between content actually covered and that expected by state-mandated tests, and on the dates those tests are given to students, and (3) community relations problems may occur when students are out of school and off campus at nontraditional times. In short, even considering the problems, little doubt remains that longer blocks of instructional time with students is a positive factor that contributes to their meaningful learning and, correspondingly, supports the use of interdisciplinary thematic instruction.

ROLE OF MODERN TECHNOLOGY AND COMMUNITY RESOURCES IN AN INTEGRATED CURRICULUM

Students cannot use what is unavailable to them. Interdisciplinary thematic instruction can consume many hours of precious preinstructional time to ensure that materials, equipment, and other resources that students will need for their learning will be available to them. As one teacher exclaimed after her first year of using ITUs, "I never worked so hard in my life; I never enjoyed teaching so much."

Community members, geographic features, buildings, monuments, historic sites, and other places in the local area constitute one of the richest instructional laboratories that can be imagined. To take advantage of this accumulated wealth of resources, and to build school-community partnerships, you should start a computer file of community resources. For instance, you might include files about the skills of the students' parents and other family members, noting which ones could be resources for the study occurring in your classroom. You might also include files on various resource people who could speak to the class, on free and inexpensive materials, on sites for field trips, and on what other communities of teachers, students, and adult helpers have done. (Chapter 2 discusses more about the community as a resource.)

Vehicles for Obtaining and Sharing Ideas and Information

Example 1. What began as an isolated, single-grade, telecommunications-dependent project for sixth graders at West Salem Middle School (Wisconsin) eventually developed into a longer-term, cross-grade interdisciplinary program of students and adults working together to design and develop a local nature preserve.[38] Sixth graders began their adventure by interacting with explorer Will Steger as he led the International Arctic Project's first training expedition. Electronic on-line messages via the Internet allowed students to receive and send messages to Steger and his team in real time. Students delved into the Arctic world, researching the physical environment and the intriguing wildlife, reading native stories and novels about survival, keeping their own imaginary expedition journals, learning about the impact of industrialized society on the Arctic, and conversing with students from around the world. But something very important was missing—a connection between the students' immediate environment and the faraway Arctic.

The team of sixth-grade teachers brainstormed ideas to establish this connection and develop an interdisciplinary approach to the study of a nearby geographical feature—the local 700-acre Lake Neshonoc, an impoundment of the LaCrosse River, a tributary of the Mississippi River. Special activities, including an all-day "winter survival" adventure, gave students a sense of what the real explorers experience. Students learned about hypothermia, winter trekking by cross-country skiing, and how to build their own snow caves.

West Salem Middle School's focus became the lake. Although many students had enjoyed its recreational opportunities, they had never formally studied it. The Neshonoc Partners, a committee of parents, community leaders, teachers, students, and environmentalists, was established to assist in setting goals, brainstorming ideas, and developing the program for a year's study. Students showed immediate interest in becoming actively involved in the project. A second committee involving parents, students, and the classroom teacher met during lunchtime on a weekly basis to allow for more intensive discussions about the lake and the overall project.

For several weeks, students learned about the ecosystem of Lake Neshonoc through field experiences led by local environmentalists and community leaders. Guest speakers told their stories about life on the lake and their observations about the lake's health. Student sketchbooks provided a place to document personal observations about the shoreline, water testing, animal and plant life, and the value of the lake. From these sketchbooks, the best student creations were compiled to create books to share electronically with students who have similar interests in schools from Russia, Canada, Missouri, South Carolina, Nevada, Wisconsin, and Washington, D.C. The opportunity to share findings about their local watershed sparked discussions about how students can make a difference in their own communities. Comparative studies gave students a chance to consider how other watersheds are impacted by humans and nature.

West Salem students also worked with the local county parks and recreation department to assist in developing a sign marking the new county park where a nature sanctuary would reside. Students brainstormed design ideas and then constructed a redwood sign with the help of a local technical educational teacher. Today the sign is a symbol of the

partnership that has been established between the students and the community. It is a concrete reminder that together everyone can work for the common good of the community and the environment. Students celebrated the study of the lake with a closure. Steger, with community leaders, parents, school board members, and staff, commended the students for what is sure to be the start of a long and enduring relationship—a partnership created out of common respect and appreciation for the value of the ecosystem.

Example 2. A school in Hamburg, Germany, provides yet another example. Arctic Yearbook is an international, cross-curriculum project for secondary-level students of English as a foreign language (EFL). In Hamburg, teachers of biology, math, history, German, and English work with a common cohort of secondary school students, using as a central theme the development of plankton. The goal is to gradually enlarge the students' perspective from the school's own pond to the Elbe River, to the North Sea, and to the Northern Atlantic Ocean. The plan involves communicating with the Bremerhaven-based Alfred Wegener Institute, which is conducting research near Greenland, and establishing telecommunications with the institute's research vessel, *Polarstern*. During the thematic study the students will develop their understandings in biology, math, history, and language.

As shown in the preceding examples, teachers who are looking to make their classrooms more student centered, collaborative, interdisciplinary, and interactive are increasingly turning to telecommunications networks.[39] These webs of connected com-

For students, use of the computer can be motivating, exciting, and effective as an instructional tool.

FIGURE 1.6   Sample Internet Sites for Teachers and Students

Ask Dr. Math (http://forum.swarthmore.edu/dr.math.dr-math.html). This location is for students and teachers to get answers to questions pertaining to mathematics.

Beyond the NEA Handbook: Documenting Electronic Sources on the Internet (http://falcon.eku.edu/honors/beyond-mla). This paper written by Andrew Harnack and Gene Kleppinger of Eastern Kentucky University (Richmond) should be useful to all teachers, but especially to those teaching English (see also entry *Citing Internet Addresses*).

The Bulletin of the Center for Children's Books (edfu.lis.uiuc/edu/puboff/bccb). This information is updated monthly with an accompanying "Bulletin Dozen," a theme-based list of children's books.

The Children's Literature Web Guide (www.ucalgary.ca/dkbrown/index.html). This site is by David K. Brown, University of Calgary, with a section "Authors on the Web" and e-mail links directly to authors.

Citing Internet Addresses (http://www.classroom.net/classroom/CitingNetResources.html). This reference also is useful for teachers and students.

Classroom Connect (http://www.wentworth.com). Provides resources for teachers; links to schools.

Co-Vis Project (http://www.nwu.edu/mentors/welcome.html). This site can match mentors with students to work on long-term projects in science.

Electronic Emissary (http://www.tapr.org/emissary). This University of Texas at Austin program can match K–12 teachers with experts in science, mathematics, and engineering.

ENC (http://www.enc.org). The Eisenhower National Clearinghouse for Mathematics and Science Education provides resources, activity guides, and links to schools.

ERIC Documents Online (http://edrs.com). This site is used for searching ERIC documents.

FedWorld (http://www.fedworld.gov). This subject index to the U.S. government also permits access to information from government agencies and departments.

Global School House (http://www.gsh.org). This site provides classroom-tested ideas and lesson plans.

Globe Program (http://www.globe.gov). An international environmental science and education partnership is shown at this site.

Kathy Schrock's Guide for Educators (http://www.capecod.net/schrockguide/). This location resources information for research on education.

Language and Literacy Project (http://www.uis.edu/cook/langlit/index.html). This University of Illinois (Springfield) site is a source of resources on language and literacy.

Learn the Net (http://www.learnthenet.com). This site is a place to learn how to use the Internet.

Library of Congress (http://www.lcweb.loc.gov/homepage/lchp.html). This site includes the National Digital Library with life history manuscripts from the Federal Writers' Folklore Project, Civil War photographs, early motion pictures, legal information, and research sources.

Middle School Home Pages Around the World (http://www.deltanet.com/hewes/middle.html). Connect with middle school home pages to learn what other middle-level schools are doing.

Newspapers in Education (http://www.ole.net/ole/). This location is the Detroit News–supported site for information about education.

Peter Milbury's School Librarian Web Pages (wombat.cusd.chico.k12.ca.us/pmilbury/lib.html). This site is for school library resources with a list of additional sites for K–12 librarians and teachers.

School Match (http://schoolmatch.com). This site is a free directory of all U.S. schools.

School Page (http://www.eyesoftime.com/teacher/index.html). This site is a teacher's resource exchange.

Teachers Network (http://www.teachnet.org). This site is a teacher's exchange.

puters allow teachers and students from around the world to reach each other directly and gain access to quantities of information previously unimaginable. Students using networks learn and develop new inquiry and analytical skills in a stimulating environment, and perhaps gain an increased appreciation of their roles as world citizens. Sample web sites and addresses are shown in Figure 1.6 and at the end of each chapter in this guide. A sample lesson plan illustrating student use of the Internet is shown in Figure 5.2 and suggested web sites are also found in the margins of the units in Chapter 5.

INITIATING AN INTERDISCIPLINARY THEMATIC UNIT

When initiating an interdisciplinary thematic unit, you will want to plan parts of the unit in advance, during the preactive phase of your planning and decision making; however, the unit will develop as the students' study evolves, as their interests become known and their input is included. Now turn your attention to the following section and review decision making and thought processing as phases of instruction.

Decision-Making and Thought-Processing Phases of Instruction: Collaborative Decision Making

You have probably heard that during any single school day, a classroom teacher makes hundreds, perhaps thousands, of decisions. It has been said that a teacher makes 3,000 nontrivial decisions every day.[40] Some of those decisions will have been made prior to meeting the students for instruction, others will be made during instruction—by the teacher and also collaboratively with the students—and yet still others are made later as the teacher reflects on the instruction for that day.

Thus, instruction can be divided into four decision-making and thought-processing phases: (1) the planning or preactive phase, (2) the teaching or interactive phase, (3) the analyzing and evaluating or reflective phase, and (4) the application or projective phase.[41] The preactive phase consists of all those intellectual functions and decisions you will make prior to actual instruction. The interactive phase includes all the decisions made during the immediacy and spontaneity of the teaching and learning. Decisions made during this phase are likely to be more intuitive, unconscious, and routine than those made during the planning phase. The reflective phase is the time you will take to reflect on, analyze, and judge the decisions and behaviors that occurred during the interactive phase as a result of this reflection. Decisions are made—individually or collaboratively with your students—to use what was learned in subsequent instructional actions. At this point, you are in the projective phase, abstracting from your reflection and projecting your analysis into subsequent instructional activities. When teaching an integrated curriculum, you will want to involve your students in all phases of decision making and thought processing.

Essential Steps in Developing an ITU

The essential steps in developing an ITU, which are discussed in more detail in later chapters, include the following:

1. **Theme.** Select a general theme; finalization of the theme title and its topics will be done in collaboration with your students and any members of your teaching team. When in collaboration with members of a teaching team and it is your first time at curriculum integration, your team should probably "think small," that is, not try to accomplish too much.

2. **Overview.** Write the unit overview (summary), goals, and if appropriate, major concepts to be addressed, as well as instructional objectives to the extent possible. Some of these will change and new ones can be added as the unit develops during implementation.

3. **Instructional resources.** Anticipate and locate instructional resources that might be needed, including technological and community resources. Student input will be needed about this as the unit develops.

4. **Organization of the subject matter.** Select and organize the subject matter, including writing some questions, and then develop potential experiences and activities (e.g., constructing, discussing, drawing, evaluating, experimenting, inquiring, listening, observing, organizing, performing drama roles, problem solving, sharing, field trips). These experiences and activities will develop further as you build upon the curiosity of the students about the theme when starting the unit.[42]

5. **Classroom environment.** Plan and arrange the classroom environment with materials that will interest and stimulate the students to want to know more about the theme. The classroom is your place of work and the students' place of learning. Involve your students in this atmosphere.

6. **Unit finale, closure, or culminating activity.** If appropriate for the group, plan a finale to close the unit in collaboration with the students, and engage them in summarizing what they have learned with other students or with their parents or other community members. The finale can include both written and oral presentations with visuals done by the students.

7. **Assessment.** Plan assessment procedures that include (1) diagnostic assessment (preassessment) at the start of the unit to discover what students already know or think they know about some of its content; (2) formative assessment, which is an ongoing daily assessment to determine

how students are doing; and (3) summative assessment to discover what, in fact, was learned from the unit.

Advantages and Limitations of an Integrated Curriculum

Many researchers and educators emphasize that using the interdisciplinary thematic unit is a highly effective, meaningful, and authentic educational approach, but like any other instructional approach it may well have limitations.[43]

Advantages. Some advantages as seen from the point of view of research and implementation include the following:

1. Advocates emphasize that traditional curriculum has been largely a fragmented set of subjects as teachers present them, and as knowledge of the learning processes increases, integrative curriculum makes sense and is being employed more often. As one example, teachers at Willamette Primary School (West Linn, Oregon) use inquiry, project-centered investigations as the basis for integrated curriculum. Additionally, teachers at Gladstone High School (Portland, Oregon) integrate English and science to create a "philosophy of care" for students to help them better understand both disciplines. Further, teachers at Hudson's Bay High School (Vancouver, Washington) created a school-within-a-school to integrate the learning of mathematics, science, and English. Advocates of such programs argue that integrative curriculum helps make learning more natural and helps students to bridge their understandings.[44]

2. Advocates applaud the educational variety that is central to an integrated curriculum and that is developmentally appropriate for the learning of youth—no two days are ever the same, and the curriculum changes depending on the students. Students become active.

3. Advocates applaud the idea that students become active participants in their learning, not simply passive listeners. All levels of abilities can be acknowledged. The curriculum is carefully planned, but it remains flexible and somewhat open ended. Supporters emphasize that interdisciplinary thematic instruction enables teachers to serve a large and diverse number of students and use students' classroom research to determine changes in approach that will enhance learning. In effect, students are empowered with responsibility for their own learning.[45]

4. Some advocates mention that teachers will be able to pass on the success of their research to others more quickly.

5. Supporters emphasize that the teacher can easily elicit the students' ideas as the primary focus of the study and can lead students into their own explorations, as the teacher stays within the curriculum mandates of the school, district, and state.

6. Advocates seem to agree that teachers and students can best meet their varied needs in different environments through ITUs. Indeed, it is argued that the more diverse the students, the more integrated the curriculum should be.

7. The use of an integrated curriculum can attract support and needed resources from the school, the district, and from outside the district. For example, the New York State New Compact for Learning requires schools to do interdisciplinary, community-based instruction.[47]

You may want to add your own points to the previous ones made by educators who say yes to the use of an interdisciplinary thematic unit as an approach to teaching and learning.[48]

Limitations. Now consider the points of those educators who say no. Following are some limitations educators have considered:

1. Not all educators believe there is adequate time or resources to plan and implement an ITU. One common problem that often arises in developing an ITU is finding common planning time for members of a teaching team. To counter this, many schools today provide a common planning time to members of an interdisciplinary teaching team, in addition to teachers' individual preparation periods.

2. Not all educators are comfortable with the idea that there is no precise manual of instructions to follow that could provide the themes, connections, metaphors, stories, and other materials to help integrate the learning;[49] that there is additional distractive movement and noise that might be detrimental to the learning of some students; and that assessment strategies are difficult to design.[50]

3. Not all educators believe that an ITU approach is effective in the classroom with all students. According to the analysis published in an ERIC document, "Findings on the effectiveness of integrative education are inconclusive."[51] Similarly, another problem could arise when a predeveloped ITU is used in which the students have no, or only limited, opportunity to participate. Such a unit

might positively affect the learning of only a few students and be a waste of valuable instructional time for others.

4. Not all educators believe that an ITU approach contributes to research, because the student population in any one classroom or cohort may not be representative and thus the benefits seemingly accrued would not be transferable to other groups of students.

5. Not all educators believe that an ITU is easy to implement (and, indeed, they are correct, but nobody ever said that good teaching is easy). With additional student movement and noise, successful class management and control may become difficult.[52] An ITU might be difficult to plan and implement because of restraints on resources and time generated from the home, the community, the classroom, the school, and the district. For example, there is no agreed upon structure, scope and sequence, content, or time regulation for study across the disciplines through the grade levels. Also, there are still many classrooms with no access to the Internet, and when schools acquire that access, computer use may be limited to only a few students at a time, unless, of

course, the classroom has the necessary equipment such as a light pad to project the computer screen onto a larger screen. Finally, working with the Internet can be very time consuming.

6. Not all educators believe that the approach would be accepted by a majority of students, parents, and teachers. For example, an ITU would require much time in teacher preparation and a willingness and interest by all in its implementation. Additionally, a teacher should understand the theory and philosophy behind such an instructional approach to implement the interdisciplinary aspect effectively.

7. Not all educators believe that teachers know where the students are in terms of knowledge and skills, that some teachers lack the imagination to predict how students at different grade levels could benefit through an ITU. Not all educators believe that the students who are empowered with more direction for their own learning will challenge their own assumptions to gain accurate procedural and conceptual knowledge. As a consequence, those students will retain inaccurate knowledge and be limited in their skills.

SUMMARY

This chapter has provided an introduction to developing an interdisciplinary thematic unit (ITU) and has addressed not only the levels of curriculum integration but also some of its possible advantages and limitations. To provide a foundation for using an ITU, a brief review of the history of curriculum integration, related theory, and recent applications

was provided. Questions for discussion, suggestions for further reading, and selected Internet sites are provided at the end of this chapter. To further reflect upon the content of this chapter, turn your attention to Exercises 1.2 through 1.4 on pages 23 through 28.

QUESTIONS AND ACTIVITIES FOR DISCUSSION

1. What classroom observations and experiences have your peers had related to the use of integrated instruction and ITUs? Ask them to share their observations with you in small-group or whole-class discussions. Take notes on the discussion and, with the group members, suggest any guidelines for teaching with ITUs you infer from those notes.

2. What questions do you have about developing ITUs? Offer your questions to peer volunteers to develop a question map on the board, on an overhead transparency, or on a large sheet of butcher paper. Copy the final question map and use one of the questions to start your own individual inquiry about ITUs. Report what you find to others in a group meeting.

3. Some critics have serious concerns about the kinds of thematic units discussed in much of the literature currently available. For example, one concern is that the in-depth studies on ITUs may be about topics that are neither meaningful nor personally and academically powerful to learner and teacher. If this concern is expressed by a parent or school board member, in what way(s) would you assure that person that the selected topic(s) has personal and academic value for the students?

4. What do you consider the three most important factors that would influence your teaching with an integrated thematic unit? Explain.

5. For a specific grade level, identify three or four classroom management problems commonly experienced by teachers. Do you believe teaching an integrated curriculum using ITUs would cause an increase, a decrease, or any changes in the types and frequencies of common management problems experienced by teachers of that grade level? Share your response with others in your class.

6. Why do you suppose past attempts at integrated instruction did not survive the test of time? Take one of those efforts, research it, and share your findings with your classmates.

7. Review the text section on the summary of purposes for curriculum integration. Do you disagree with any of those? Are there other purposes you would add? Explain your answer.

8. With regard to the qualities of an effective teacher listed in this chapter, identify those with which you feel most competent and least competent. Compare your lists with those of your classmates. Plan a personal or a group strategy for sharing competencies and becoming more competent in areas where you feel weakest.

9. Explain how the roles of students are distinctly different when learning by ITUs compared with learning in a more traditional mode. Are there any similarities? If so, identify them.

10. Explore the Internet on the topic of curriculum integration (or related topics as decided by your class) and share with others in your class any useful websites you discover.

11. Identify one of the limitations of integrated instruction as discussed in this chapter and find out how that limitation has been resolved by schools and teachers who are deeply committed to and successful with curriculum integration. Share your findings with others in your class.

12. Because longer blocks of instructional time with students appear to be a positive factor that facilitate students' meaningful learning, research the concept of a modified block schedule (also called split-block periods) or a flexible block schedule. A modified block schedule is a combination of both traditional, 40-minute periods and longer blocks of time. A flexible block schedule often includes a seven-period day with all classes meeting for varied time periods on different days during the week. Report your findings to the group.

13. From your point of view, in what way would you expand on the educational assumptions for using an integrated curriculum in the classroom? Additionally, how would you explain to a parent the philosophical underpinnings of thematic approaches for learning and teaching? How would you briefly explain the research base you know about to support thematic learning? How could you find out more about some responses to these questions?

14. Team up with a partner and prepare two lists, one headed "Behaviorism" and the other "Constructivism." On the lists, record the similarities and differences between the two theories of learning. Compare your lists with two other partners in your group.

15. Work with your instructor and your group to prepare a schema map about teaching, a concept relevant to you as a prospective teacher or a newly practicing one. This can be a visual diagram, perhaps a web design, to show a mental construct about how you organize your perceptions of knowledge and situations about teaching. After you have prepared your map, what questions do you have about its preparation?

EXERCISE 1.1

Reflecting upon the Levels in the Spectrum
of Integrated Curriculum

Instructions.   The purpose of this exercise is to share with others (perhaps in small groups according to grade levels) your reflections about the levels at which you see yourself teaching in the spectrum of integrated curriculum.

1. At which levels do you see yourself teaching? Why?

2. Which levels do you see yourself avoiding? Why?

3. What types of professional relationships do you see yourself having with other teachers and with the students?

Notes during group discussion:

EXERCISE 1.2

Brainstorming Ideas Related to an ITU

Instructions.   With others in a small group, brainstorm ideas related to an interdisciplinary thematic unit and offer suggestions. Your purpose is to develop a list of topics related to a theme or topic of your choice. Remember, there are no right or wrong ideas—all are accepted. Consider the suggestions in the following schematic web to keep the brainstorming alive if the ideas should lag.

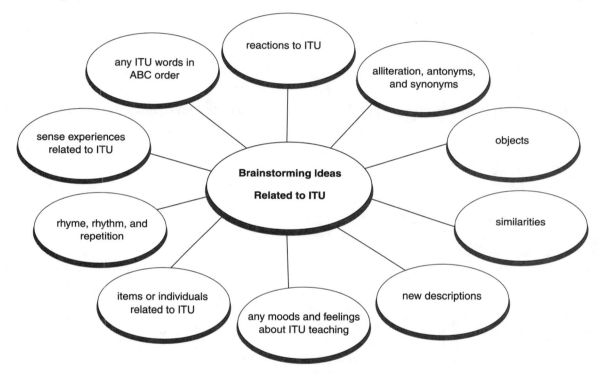

Involve two volunteers from the group to record your group's ideas on a chart or on a transparency that can be shown to others in the class on the overhead projector. You can organize the ideas in a web or other format if you wish. Follow these steps in completing the exercise:

1. Suggest ways to categorize ideas about developing an interdisciplinary thematic unit and then suggest a theme and headings for the categories you see in the web included in this exercise.

2. Individually, locate one professional article about an interdisciplinary thematic unit and read it, perhaps one mentioned in the notes or suggested readings in this chapter. Take notes.

3. Return to your small group and add any information to the web that you gained from the article.

4. Meet back with the whole group and report on the group's ideas about the interdisciplinary thematic unit. Note the similarities and the differences in the schemata among the groups. Use the space that follows for your notes if needed.

EXERCISE 1.3

Discovering Informational Sources about ITUs

Instructions.   You have an important responsibility to be knowledgeable about an integrated curriculum before you develop an interdisciplinary thematic unit for your students. What informational sources stand out as useful in your mind? Your educational purpose for this exercise is to record what will help you in developing an interdisciplinary thematic unit around a theme you have selected. Share what you have found with others in your class. One of your sources might be just the source someone else needs to develop and implement a unit. To begin your search, you may want to select from the "For Further Reading" section in this chapter or do searches on the Internet, perhaps via the addresses listed in Figure 1.7. Look for material that will help you develop and implement a thematic unit of your choice.

1. Source: _____

_____

_____

Reason selected: _____

_____

_____

2. Source: _____

_____

_____

Reason selected: _____

_____

_____

3. Source: _____

_____

_____

Reason selected: _____

_____

_____

4. Source: _____

_____

_____

Reason selected: _____

_____

_____

5. Source: _____

_____

_____

Reason selected: _____

_____

_____

6. Source: _____

_____

_____

Reason selected: _____

_____

_____

7. Source: _____

_____

_____

Reason selected: _____

_____

_____

8. Source: _____

_____

_____

Reason selected: _____

_____

_____

EXERCISE 1.4

Interviewing a Teacher about Interdisciplinary Thematic Units

Instructions: For this exercise, interview one or more elementary, middle, or high school teachers. Perhaps you will want to interview one who is new to the education profession and then interview one who has been in teaching for 5 years or more. As an option, you may want to interview a person who is teaching in elementary school and one who is teaching either at a middle school or a high school. For this exercise, you should make blank copies of this form. Use the questions to guide the interview, and then report back to the whole group.

1. How long have you been an employed teacher?

_____

_____

_____

2. In what ways have you used (or do you use) interdisciplinary thematic units?

_____

_____

_____

3. If you have used ITUs, was it individually or as a member of a team? Explain.

_____

_____

_____

4. Why are you using (not using) interdisciplinary thematic units?

_____

_____

_____

5. What training about interdisciplinary thematic units did you have?

_____

_____

_____

6. What initial advice in terms of preparing an interdisciplinary thematic unit can you offer me?

_____

_____

_____

7. In what ways do you use community resources? Technology?

_____

_____

_____

8. In what ways do you attend to the importance of diversity and multiculturalism in your classroom?

_____

_____

_____

9. What do you like most about teaching with an interdisciplinary thematic unit? What do you like least?

_____

_____

_____

10. What other specific advice do you have for those of us developing and preparing to implement interdisciplinary thematic units?

_____

_____

CHAPTER NOTES

1. A schema (plural; schemata) is a mental construct by which the learner organizes his/her perceptions of situations and knowledge. Note the difference in schema maps and concept maps in J. D. Novak, "Concept Maps and Venn Diagrams: Two Metacognitive Tools to Facilitate Meaningful Learning," *Instructional Science*, 19(1), 29–52 (1990).

2. J. Piaget, *To Understand Is to Invent* (New York: Grossman, 1973).

3. J. Bruner, *Actual Minds, Possible Worlds* (New York: Cambridge University Press, 1986).

4. R. N. Caine and G. Caine. *Making Connections: Teaching and the Human Brain* (Arlington, VA: Association for Supervision and Curriculum Development, 1991).

5. R. Dunn, *Strategies for Educating Diverse Learners*, Fastback 384 (Bloomington, IN: Phi Delta Kappa Educational Foundation, 1995).

6. For Gardner's distinction between "learning style" and the "intelligences," see H. Gardner, "Reflections on Multiple Intelligences: Myths and Messages," *Phi Delta Kappan*, 77(3), 200–203, 206–209 (November, 1995); or H. Gardner, "Multiples Intelligences Perspective," and Chapter 5 of N. Colangelo and G. A. Davis (eds.), *Handbook of Gifted Education, 2nd Edition* (Needham Heights, MA: Allyn & Bacon, 1997).

7. R. Sternberg, *Metaphors of Mind: Conceptions of the Nature of Intelligence* (New York: Cambridge University Press, 1990).

8. See, for example, Airasian, P. W. and Walsh, M. E. "Constructivist Cautions," *Phi Delta Kappan*, 78(6), 444–49 (February, 1997).

9. The hidden curriculum is defined as the accepted or implied values and attitudes and the unwritten rules of behavior students must learn to participate and to be able to succeed in school. See K. Ryan, "Mining the Values in the Curriculum," *Educational Leadership*, 51(3), 16–18 (November, 1994).

10. See the following: Chp. 1 in *Secondary School Teaching: A Guide to Methods and Resources; Planning for Competence* by Richard D. Kellough and Noreen G. Kellough (Columbus, OH: Merrill, 1999); Chp. 2 in *Middle School Teaching: A Guide to Methods and Resources, 3d Edition* by Richard D. Kellough and Noreen G. Kellough (Columbus, OH: Merrill, 1999); "Meeting the Challenge" in *A Resource Guide for Elementary School Teaching, 4th Ed.* by Richard D. Kellough and Patricia L. Roberts (Columbus, OH: Merrill, 1998), pp. 20–3.

11. See, for example, C. K. McEwin et al., *America's Middle Schools: Practices and Progress: A 25 Year Perspective* (Columbus, OH: National Middle School Association, 1996).

12. During the past 50 years, various movements and approaches have been used to try to find the most successful approach to teaching English and the language arts movements with names such as *whole language, integrated language arts, communication arts and skills, literature based,* and so forth. Whatever the cognomen, certain common elements and goals prevail: student choice in materials to be read; student reading and writing across the curriculum; time for independent and sustained silent reading in the classroom; use of integrated language arts skills across the curriculum; use of nonprint materials; use of trade books rather than textbooks and basal readers.

13. See W. Malloy, "Essential Schools and Inclusion: A Responsible Partnership," *Educational Forum, 60*(3), 228–236 (Spring, 1996).

14. See W. Schwartz, *Preparing Middle School Students for a Career* (New York: ERIC Clearinghouse on Urban Education, 1996); Southern Regional Education Board. 1995 Outstanding Practices: High Schools That Work (Atlanta, GA: Author, 1995); and B. A. Lankard, *Restructuring and Vocational Education: Trends and Issues Alerts* (Columbus, OH: ERIC Clearinghouse on Adult, Career, and Vocational Education, 1996).

15. In *Report to the President on the Use of Technology to Strengthen K–12 Education in the United States* by David E. Shaw, Chair, Panel on Educational Technology (Washington, DC: President's Committee of Advisors on Science and Technology, 1997). The Panel concluded that systematic research on educational technology will prove necessary to ensure the efficacy and cost-effectiveness of technology use in K–12 schools in the U.S.

16. See G. Solomon, "Of Mind and Media," *Phi Delta Kappan, 78*(5), 375–380 (January, 1997); and J. Abbott, "To Be Intelligent," and C. R. Pool "Maximizing Learning: A Conversation with Renate Numerla Caine," *Educational Leadership, 54*(6), 6–10 and 11–15 (respectively [March, 1997]).

17. See J. G. Brooks and M. G. Brooks, *In Search of Understanding: The Case for Constructivist Classrooms* (Arlington, VA: Association for Supervision and Curriculum Development, 1993).

18. J. Dewey, *How We Think* (Boston, MA: Heath, 1933).

19. A. W. Combs (ed.), *Perceiving, Behaving, and Becoming: A New Focus for Education* (Arlington, VA: 1962 ASCD Yearbook, Association for Supervision and Curriculum Development, 1962).

20. The section entitled "The Spectrum of Integrated Curriculum" was developed by Richard D. Kellough and appears in a similar form in several Prentice Hall books. See those by Kellough and by Roberts in the readings at the end of this chapter.

21. Patricia L. Roberts, *Literature-Based History Activities for Children, Grades 1–3* (Needham Heights, MA: Allyn & Bacon, 1998), p. 154.

22. See, for example, E. M. Lolli, "Creating a Concept-Based Curriculum," *Principal, 76*(1), 26–27 (September, 1996); and H. L. Erickson, *Stirring the Head, Heart, and Soul: Redefining Curriculum and Instruction* (Thousand Oaks, CA: Corwin Press, 1995).

23. J. S. Bruner, *Process of Education* (Cambridge, MA: University Press, 1960).

24. National Research Council, *National Science Education Standards* (Washington, DC: National Academy Press, 1996), p. 104. Also see B. Tucker et al., "Integrating Middle School Curriculum: A Two-Tiered Development Model," *Research in Middle Level Education Quarterly,* 19(1), 43–58 (Fall, 1995).

25. K. Rasmussen, "Using Real-Life Problems to Make Real-World Connections," *ASCD Curriculum Update* (Summer, 1997), pp. 4–5.

26. See W. J. Stepien et al., "Problem-Based Learning for Traditional and Interdisciplinary Classrooms," *Journal for the Education of the Gifted,* 16(4), 338–357 (Summer, 1994); and W. Stepien and S. Gallagher, "Problem-Based Learning: As Authentic as It Gets," *Educational Leadership,* 50(7), 25–28 (April, 1993).

27. For detailed accounts of teaching at this level, see C. Stevenson and J. F. Carr (eds.), *Integrated Studies in the Middle Grades* (New York: Teachers College Press, 1993).

28. E. Garcia, *Understanding and Meeting the Challenge of Student Cultural Diversity* (Boston: Houghton Mifflin, 1994).

29. See C. Dwyer, *Language, Culture, and Writing* (Berkeley, CA: Center for the Study of Writing, University of California, 1991); and A. M. Villegas, *Culturally Responsible Pedagogy for the 1990s and Beyond* (Princeton, NJ: Educational Testing Service, 1991).

30. There are many recent publications with specifics about the characteristics of effective teaching. See, for example, C. Danielson, *Enhancing Professional Practice: A Framework for Teaching* (Alexandria, VA: Association for Supervision and Curriculum Development, 1996).

31. Many resources are available to help the teacher who wants to establish a cooperative, responsible classroom environment. See, for example, Chapter 11 of P. R. Burden, *Classroom Management and Discipline: Methods to Facilitate Cooperation and Instruction* (New York: Longman, 1995); and Chapter 20 of M. Hunter, *Enhancing Teaching* (New York: Macmillan College Pub. Co., 1994).

32. See, for example, S. S. Parks and S. Hirsh, *A New Vision for Staff Development* (Alexandria, VA: Association for Supervision and Curriculum Development, 1997), p. 46; and the final chapter of S. N. Clark and D. C. Clark, *Restructuring the Middle Level School: Implications for School Leaders,* Middle Schools and Early Adolescents Series (Albany, NY: State University of New York Press, 1994).

33. D. T. Conley, "Restructuring: In Search of Definition," *Principal,* 72(3), 12 (January, 1993).

34. J. Villars, *Restructuring Through School Design,* Fastback 322 (Bloomington, IN: Phi Delta Kappa Educational Foundation, 1991), p. 41.

35. C. Roelike, *Curriculum Adequacy and Quality in High Schools Enrolling Fewer Than 400 Pupils* (Charleston, WV: ERIC Clearinghouse on Rural Education and Small Schools, 1996).

36. S. Willis, "Are Longer Classes Better?" *ASCD Curriculum Update,* 35(3), 3 (March, 1993).

37. J. M. Carroll, "Organizing Time to Support Learning," *The School Administrator,* 51(3), 26–28, 30–33 (March, 1994).

38. J. Wee, "The Neshonoc Project: Profiles in Partnership," *World School for Adventure Learning Bulletin* (Fall, 1993), pp. 2–3. Adapted and used by permission.

39. See, for example, J. A. Levin and C. Thurston, "Research Summary: Electronic Networks," *Educational Leadership,* 54(3), 46–50 (November, 1996) and other articles in that theme issue titled "Networking."

40. C. Danielson, *Enhancing Professional Practice* (1996), p. 2.

41. A. L. Costa, *The School as a Home for the Mind* (Palatine, IL: Skylight Publishing, 1991), pp. 97–106.

42. See, for example, M. R. Davenport et al., "Negotiating Curriculum (Integrating Curriculum)." *Reading Teacher,* 49(1), 60–62 (September, 1995).

43. For a description of the origin, development, student activities and projects, and "pluses" and "minuses" of using an integrated history/geography, English curriculum, see J. Coate and N. White, "History/English Core," *Social Studies Review,* 34(3), 12–15 (Spring, 1996). In the same issue, see also a description of an integrated curriculum approach to world history/language arts in L. Doig and J. Sargent, "Light, Camera, Action."

44. J. Braunger and S. Hart-Landsberg, *Crossing Boundaries: Explorations in Integrative Curriculum* (Portland, OR: Northwest Regional Educational Lab, 1994).

45. See J. M. Low and W. Shironaka, "Letting Go—Allowing First-Graders to Become Autonomous Learners," *Young Children,* 51(1), 21–115 (November, 1995); and R. Novick, *Developmentally Appropriate and Culturally Responsible Education: Theory in Practice* (Portland, OR: Northwest Regional Educational Laboratory, 1996).

47. P. Impson et al., "Interdisciplinary Education—You Bet It Can Work!" *NASSP Bulletin,* 79(569), 32–37 (March, 1995).

48. See also A. Hall, "Using Social Studies as a Basis for Interdisciplinary Teaching," *State of Reading,* 2(1), 23–28 (Spring, 1995); T. Shanahan (ed.) et al., "Avoiding Some of the Pitfalls of Thematic Units (Integrating Curriculum)," *Reading Teacher,* 49(8), 718–719 (May, 1995).

49. See C. B. DeCorse, "Current Conversations, Teachers and the Integrated Curriculum: An Intergenerational View," *Action in Teacher Education,* 18(1), 85–92 (Spring, 1994); and D. L. Kain, "Recipes or Dialogue? A Middle School Team Conceptualizes 'Curricular Integration'," *Journal of Curriculum and Supervision,* 11(2), 163–187 (Winter, 1996).

50. See, for example, B. Borwood, "Energy and Knowledge: The Story of Integrated Curriculum Packages," Pathways: *The Ontario Journal of Outdoor Education,* 7(4), 14–18 (January, 1995).

51. D. Walker, *Integrative Education,* ERIC Digest, Number 101 (Eugene, OR: ERIC Clearinghouse on Educational Management, 1996).

52. You may be interested in C. White, "Making Classroom Management Approaches in Teacher Education Relevant," *Teacher Education and Practice,* 11(1), 15–21 (Spring/Summer, 1995).

FOR FURTHER READING

Arredondo, D. E., & Rucinski, T. T. (1996, Spring). Integrated curriculum: Its use, initiation and support in midwestern schools. *Mid-Western Educational Researcher, 9*(2), 37–41, 44.

Clark, J. H., & Agne, R. M. (1997). *Interdisciplinary high school teaching: Strategies for integrated learning.* Boston: Allyn & Bacon.

Coate, J., & White, N. (1996, Spring). History/English core. *Social Studies Review, 334*(3), 12–15.

Dickinson, T. S., & Erb, T. O. (Eds.). (1996). *We gain more than we give: Teaming in middle schools.* Columbus, OH: National Middle Schools Association.

Kellough, R. D. (1996). *Integrating language arts and social studies for intermediate and middle school students.* Upper Saddle River, NJ: Merrill/Prentice Hall. 1996.

Kellough, R. D. (1996). *Integrating mathematics and science for intermediate and middle school students.* Upper Saddle River, NJ: Merrill/Prentice Hall.

Kellough, R. D. (1996). *Integrating mathematics and science for kindergarten and primary children.* Upper Saddle River, NJ: Merrill/Prentice Hall.

Kohn, A. (1996). *Beyond discipline: From compliance to community.* Alexandria, VA: Association of Supervision and Curriculum Development.

Lauritzen, C. et al. (1996, February). Contexts for integrating curriculum. *Reading Teacher, 49*(5), 404–406.

Nagel, N. G. (1996). *Learning through real-world problem solving: The power of integrative teaching.* Thousand Oaks, CA: Corwin Press.

Nowicki, J. J., & Meehan, K. F. (1997). *Interdisciplinary strategies for English and social studies classrooms: Toward collaborative middle and secondary teaching.* Boston: Allyn & Bacon.

Prescott, C. A. (1996). *Education and work: Toward an integrated curriculum framework. A report on the integrated system for workforce education curricula project.* Waco, TX: Center for Occupational Research and Development.

Roberts, P. L. (1996). *Integrating language arts and social studies for kindergarten and primary children.* Upper Saddle River, NJ: Merrill/Prentice Hall.

SELECTED INTERNET ADDRESSES

Angola High School, Angola, Indiana
(http:neptune.esc.k12.in.us/steuben/semsd/block/ahsdks.html)
High school site that implemented a 4×4 block schedule in 1995; other information on scheduling at (http://www.wr.cc.mn.us/kwe/block.html).

Association for Supervision and Curriculum Development
(http://www.ascd.org)
Organization that provides ongoing insights on schooling and educational change.

Watson High School, Colorado Springs, Colorado
(http://www.classroom.net.classweb/myhome.html)
Site for high school use of 4×4 block schedule since 1990–91 which consists of a school year of three 12-week trimesters and a day that is divided into five 70-minute class periods.

INDIVIDUAL NOTES

CHAPTER 2

Initiating an Interdisciplinary Thematic Unit

*For this delicate little plant (curiosity of inquiry), aside from
stimulation, stands mainly in need of freedom; without this it goes
to wrack and ruin without fail.*

—Albert Einstein

INTERDISCIPLINARY THEMATIC UNIT FOR HIGH SCHOOL STUDENTS: CIVILIZATIONS—*HEART OF A JAGUAR* AND MAYAN CULTURE

Steve and Jo Ellen Ham, high school teachers in Winnetka, Illinois, selected the theme of culture as a way to introduce an integrated unit about the Mayan people for high school students (see "Maya Emersion: An Integrated Cultural Unit Based on *Heart of a Jaguar* by Marc Talbert" by Jo Ellen Ham and Steve Ham in *SIGNAL Journal*, 21(3), 15–6, Summer, 1997).

This thematic unit incorporated various teaching ideas to accompany the historical fiction novel, *Heart of a Jaguar*, by Mark Talbert. Set in a village in the Yucatán peninsula near Chichén Itzá, this story is about a Mayan boy, Balam, who struggles to achieve manhood and, during a drought, participates in the fasts, prayers, and rituals that must be done to appease the gods and bring rain to his village. To begin, the students saw portions of a video on the Maya (*Maya: Lords of the Jungle* [PBS Home Video A1660]). Then the students were asked to begin an intensive study about the concept of cultural emersion with an announcement that proclaimed an emergency alert. The alert declared that the entire class would become time travelers in a week's time to Mexico back to the year 1200

A.D. They would arrive in the Yucatan region during the last years of the ancient Maya and would face some threatening situations such as droughts and invasions. The students would have exactly 1 week to prepare so they could survive this experience. They would have 1 week to learn anything they think would help them survive in a society which would be both primitive and different from their own. The preparation activities were related to several disciplines:

- *Expressive arts*. The students listened to the five-line poem, *Journey of the Nightly Jaguar*, by Burton Albert and illustrated by Robert Roth (New York: Atheneum, 1996).
- *History*. The students brainstormed related topics with the teacher and got acquainted with resources in class and in the library. They searched for entries found in the bibliography in *Heart of a Jaguar* and referred to a Mayan dictionary at the back of the book. They also searched the Internet for resources about Mayan culture.
- *Geography*. Pictures of the environment were placed on the classroom walls and students were asked to label them and write explanations as part of their research.
- *Language arts*. The students selected Mayan names and practiced on Mayan pronunciations (e.g., *yax* meaning "dark blue-green forest leaves" and *hahah* for "rain"). They also located and read

paragraphs rich in sensory language, and transformed the paragraphs into a poetic format.
- *Literature*. The students shared Mayan stories related to the folkloric beliefs. Two examples were *People of Corn: A Mayan Story*, retold by Mary-Joan Gerson and illustrated by Carla Golembe (New York: Little, Brown, 1995), and *The Turtle's Shell* and *The Gift of Corn* (Mexican Fine Arts Center Museum, 1852 W. 19th Street, Chicago, IL 60608). *People of Corn* is a story that tells how people were created from corn and *The Gift of Corn* and *The Turtle's Shell* are two Aztec legends in English/Spanish text.
- *Social studies*. The students divided into research teams with individuals on each team assigned a topic to report back to their whole team. The students researched the past—they studied the crops, diet, food preparation, local animals, hunting techniques, family structure, social structure, and the governing units. They also researched the present by discovering ways that ancient Mayan practices and beliefs and modern Spanish influences blend together in the lives of today's young people. Further, they discussed their understandings of the Mayan culture, different kinds of violence in other cultures, the possibility of one's actions through the window of another culture with different cultural values, and the issue of becoming oversensitized to violence.

As an example of an interdisciplinary unit, *Heart of a Jaguar* gives yet another indication of the power such a unit can hold: The two teachers initiated the unit in a way that develops in students an awareness and appreciation for a particular topic and then, like the students of West Salem Middle School (see Chapter 1) they get involved in various ways.

In Chapter 1 you were introduced to the purposes of integrating the curriculum, the levels of curriculum integration, theories that support curriculum integration, some applications, and the importance and value of using technology and the community as resources. In addition, you were introduced to what experts consider to be advantages and limitations of engaging the students of today's diverse and multicultural classrooms with learning experiences by way of curriculum integration and interdisciplinary thematic instruction.

In this chapter you will be asked to suggest examples of ways to initiate units—perhaps as the Hams did in the chapter-opening vignette. Specifically, the roles of the teacher and the student are considered. In one exercise, you are asked to select a theme for a unit, formulate questions to guide the study, and select resources related to those questions. In another exercise you will collect information related to the scope and sequence of a unit in a classroom of your choice.

SELECTING A THEME FOR AN INTERDISCIPLINARY THEMATIC UNIT

You will recall, as defined in Chapter 1, a theme title is or should be more than simply a topic—it is the essence (point), the communication (message), or

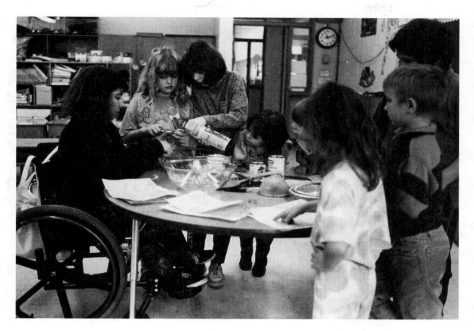

Students might study some themes on an ongoing basis, such as the value of cooperation. These students have found ways to work well together on an activity related to an ITV.

the idea (concept, precept, pattern, design) that underlines a study. When working within an integrated curriculum, students might study a theme on an ongoing basis—a long-term thematic study as exemplified by the West Salem Middle School and the Illinois Mathematics and Science Academy examples presented in Chapter 1.

Rationale for Selecting a Theme

Sometimes themes are selected by the teacher or by a teaching team before meeting the students for the first time. Other times, they are selected by the teachers in collaboration with students. As we will be emphasizing, even when the theme is preselected with guidance from the teacher, students still should be given major responsibility for deciding the final theme title, topics, and corresponding learning activities. Integrated thematic instruction works best when students have ownership in the study, when they have been empowered with major decision-making responsibility. See Figures 2.1 and 2.2 for examples of selected theme words and sentences.

A theme also can provide an emotional dimension to the unit that goes beyond the information related to the study of a topic. For instance, the theme might be the acceptance of one's self or others, growing up, overcoming fear, or overcoming prejudice. It might be based on justice, integrity, or ethical principles. It can also be an inspiration or a sharing of human emotions (i.e., a sharing that gives students respect for life that includes the lives of animals, plants, and humans).

When suggested by students, themes often relate to such ideas as "friendship is important," "fears can be overcome," "self-understanding can be developed," "families are important," and "prejudice is harmful." Other themes might focus on ideas such as the benefits from cooperation, of valuing education, of accepting others, of giving and receiving support from others, of having a moral code to guide one's actions, and of establishing a positive relationship with an adult—with a significant and caring other.

Criteria for Theme Selection

The basis for theme selection should satisfy two criteria: The theme should (1) fit within the expected scope and sequence of mandated content, and (2) should be of interest to the students.

Regarding the first criterion, many teachers have told us that when they and their students embarked on an interdisciplinary study, they did so without truly knowing where the study would go or what the learning outcomes would be—and they were somewhat frightened by that fact (we learned this ourselves when we were classroom teachers). When the unit was completed, however, their students had learned everything (or nearly everything) that the teachers would have expected them to learn had the teachers used a more traditional content-centered approach. And, it was more fun!

The second criterion is easy to satisfy, as it will most assuredly be when students are truly empowered with major decision-making responsibility for

FIGURE 2.1   Sample Theme Words

activists	cooperation	innovations
addresses (speeches)	crusades	inspirations
administrations	cultures	inventions
adventures	declarations	issues
adversaries	democracies	journeys
aeronautics	demonstrations	justice
agreements	departures	lodgings
ambitions	depths	machines
arbitrations	deprivations	migrations
aristocracies	determinations	minorities' rights
beginnings	dictators	modern society
blockades	dignity	nationalism
bonanzas	dilemmas	nations
boundaries	diplomacy	navigations
boycotts	disasters	needs
bravery	discoveries	neighborhoods
breakthroughs	diversity	nonviolence
buildings	dynasties	oppressions
business	emancipations	ordeals
calamities	emigrations	patterns
campaigns	encounters	prejudice
celebrations	environments	pollution
changes	escapes	problems
citizenship	explorations	resistance
clothing	extinctions	resources
colonizing/colonies	families	searches
companionships	fighters	segregation
conservation	freedoms	self-awareness
constitutions	gateways	settlements
contributions	governments	social groups
controversies	hardships	survival
courage	heritages	symbols (freedom)
conflict with climate	heroes	transportation
conflict with self	hibernations	others suggested by students
conflict with others	independence	

what and how they learn. So, once a general theme is selected (one that satisfies the first criterion), its final title, subtopics, and corresponding procedural activities should be finalized in collaboration with the students.

In some schools, a general theme is preselected and identified for each grade, one that can be considered from the perspective of the past, the present, and the future and one that reflects the school's educational goals (see Figure 2.3). A common example is the theme of "self" for first grade. Just a few sample themes that have been commonly used for various grades are "change and continuity," "communities," "communication," "families," "environments," "heritage," "self-awareness," "symbols of freedom," "systems and interactions," and "transportation."

Useful Documents as Resources for Theme Selection

As just implied, frequently a teacher or teaching team will identify a theme for a unit from the review of school, district, and state documents, or the national curriculum standards. Because these documents usually have been thoughtfully prepared by experienced experts with their knowledge of the

FIGURE 2.2   Sample Theme Sentences

Change can be beneficial.

Cultures can clash.

People can be courageous and clever.

People can be independent and resourceful.

Laws and rules affect our families.

People are interdependent.

People can overcome handicaps.

People are sensitive to nature.

People have conflicts with themselves.

People have conflicts with the climate.

People have conflicts with others.

People remember their loved ones and preserve their memory.

People search for freedom.

War costs humans in different ways.

The weak and strong can help each other.

Others suggested by students.

developmental needs of students at various ages well in mind, such documents are valuable in developing interdisciplinary thematic units that are appropriate for a certain place in the scope and sequence of the instructional program (see, for example, Figure 2.3).

THE NATIONAL CURRICULUM STANDARDS: A REVIEW OF THEIR HISTORY AND STATUS

Curriculum standards define what students should know (content) and be able to do (process and performance). At the national level, curriculum standards did not exist in the United States until the 1990s, except for those developed and released for mathematics education in 1989 (which are being revised as this text goes to press).[1] When in the early 1990s support for national goals in education was endorsed by the National Governors Association, then President George Bush immediately formed the National Education Goals Panel. Shortly thereafter, the National Council of Education Standards

FIGURE 2.3   Sample Sequential Grade Level Themes for Social Studies and History

Kindergarten:	Awareness of Self in a Social Setting
1st Grade:	The Individual in Primary Social Groups (e.g., Understanding School and Family Life)
2nd Grade:	Meeting Basic Needs in Nearby Social Groups (e.g., The Neighborhood)
3rd Grade:	Sharing Earth's Resources with Others (e.g., The Community)
4th Grade:	Understanding Human Life in Varied Environments (e.g., The Region)
5th Grade:	Understanding People of the Americas (e.g., The United States and Its Close Neighbors)
6th Grade:	Understanding People and Cultures (e.g., The Eastern Hemisphere)
7th Grade:	Understanding a Changing World of Many Nations (e.g., A Global View)
8th Grade:	Building a Strong and Free Nation (e.g., The United States)
9th Grade:	Understanding Systems that Make a Democratic Society Work (e.g., Law, Justice, and Economics)
10th Grade:	Understanding Origins of Major Cultures (e.g., A World History)
11th Grade:	The Maturing of America (e.g., History of the United States)
12th Grade:	Selections usually made from (1) Issues and Problems of Modern Society and (2) Introduction to the Social Sciences

and Testing recommended that national standards for subject matter content in K–12 education be developed for all core subjects—the arts, civics/social studies, English/language arts/reading, geography, history, mathematics, and science.

Initially, funding for the development of standards was provided by the U.S. Department of Education. In 1994, Congress passed the Goals 2000: Educate America Act, later amended in 1996, with the Appropriations Act (see Figure 2.4; also see goals panel website at (<http://www.negp.gov>). This development encouraged states to set standards. Long before this time, however, national organizations devoted to various disciplines were working on defining and developing standards.

The National Curriculum Standards Recommendations

The national curriculum standards represent the collective thinking by expert panels to responses from teachers in the field about what are the essential elements of a basic core of subject knowledge that all students should acquire. They serve not as national mandates but rather as voluntary guidelines to encourage curriculum development to promote higher student achievement. It is the discretion of state and local curriculum developers to decide the extent to which the standards are used. Strongly influenced by the national standards, nearly all 50 states are developing state standards, such as New York State's *Learning Standards for Health, Physical Education, and Home Economics* (Albany, NY: New York State Education Department, revised edition, 1996), and *Language Arts Standards and Performance Objectives,* which includes standards for reading and writing (1996) and standards for listening, speaking, viewing, and presenting (1997), adopted by the Arizona State Board of Education. Many districts and schools are developing standards of their own.

By 1992, more than 40 states, usually through state curriculum frameworks, were following the 1989 standards for mathematics education to guide what and how mathematics is taught and how student progress is assessed. A summary of recommendations for mathematics instruction is shown in Figure 2.5. The essence of many of these recommendations—a thematic, hands-on, inquiry-oriented, performance-based approach to learning less but learning better—can also be found in the standards that were subsequently developed for other disciplines (see Figures 2.6 and 2.7).

Standards by Content Area.   In addition to standards for mathematics, the following list describes standards development for other content areas of the K–12 curriculum. Although space in this book is too limited to give adequate attention to all the standards, you can access any of the standards via the

FIGURE 2.4   Goals 2000: The National Educational Goals

By the year 2000 . . .
- All children in America will start school ready to learn.

- The high school graduation rate will increase to at least 90%.

- All students will leave grades 4, 8, and 12 having demonstrated competency over challenging subject matter including English, mathematics, science, foreign languages, civics and government, economics, the arts, history, and geography, and every school in America will ensure that all students learn to use their minds well, so they may be prepared for responsible citizenship, further learning, and productive employment in our nation's modern economy.

- The nation's teaching force will have access to programs for the continued improvement of their professional skills and the opportunity to acquire the knowledge and skills needed to instruct and prepare all American students for the next century.

- U.S. students will be first in the world in mathematics and science achievement.

- Every adult American will be literate and will possess the knowledge and skills necessary to compete in a global economy and exercise the rights and responsibilities of citizenship.

- Every school in the United States will be free of drugs, violence, and the unauthorized presence of firearms and alcohol, and will offer a disciplined environment conducive to learning.

- Every school will promote partnerships that will increase parental involvement and participation in promoting the social, emotional, and academic growth of children.

FIGURE 2.5 Summary of Recommendations for Mathematics Instruction

Increased attention to:
- The active involvement of students in constructing and applying mathematical ideas
- Problem solving as a means as well as a goal of instruction
- Effective questioning techniques that promote student interaction
- The use of a variety of instructional formats (e.g., small groups, individual explorations, peer instruction)
- Student communication of mathematical ideas orally and in writing
- The establishment and application of the interrelatedness of mathematical topics
- The systematic maintenance of student learnings and embedding review in the context of new topics and problem situations
- The assessment of learning as an integral part of instruction

Decreased attention to:
- Teacher and text as exclusive sources of knowledge
- Rote memorization of facts and procedures
- Extended periods of individual seatwork practicing routine tasks
- Instruction by teacher exposition
- Paper-and-pencil manipulative skill work
- The relegation of testing to an adjunct role with the sole purpose of assigning grades

Internet, such as by http://www.mcrel.org or http://putwest.boces.org/standards.html or by contacting the organizations or associations listed.

Arts (visual and expressive). Developed jointly by the American Alliance for Theater and Education, the National Art Education Association, the National Dance Association, and the Music Educators National Conference, the National Standards for Arts Education was published in 1994. Contact Music Educators National Conference (MENC), 1902 Association Drive, Reston, VA 22091.

Economics. Developed by the National Council on Economic Education, standards for the study of economics were published in 1997. Contact National Council on Economic Education (NCEE), 1140 Avenue of the Americas, New York, NY 10036.

English/language arts. Developed as a joint project by the International Reading Association and the National Council of Teachers of English, standards for English/language arts education were published in 1996. Contact National Council of Teachers of English (NCTE), 1111 Kenyon Road, Urbana, IL 61801 (see Figure 2.6).

Foreign languages. Standards for Foreign Language Learning: Preparing for the 21st Century was published by the American Council on the Teaching of Foreign Languages in 1996. Contact American Council on the

Teaching of Foreign Languages (ACTFL), Six Executive Plaza, Yonkers, NY 10701-6801.

Geography. Developed jointly by the Association of American Geographers, the National Council for Geographic Education, and the National Geographic Society, standards for geography education were published in 1994. Contact National Geographic Society, PO Box 1640, Washington, DC 20013-1640.

History/civics/social studies. The Center for Education and the National Center for Social Studies developed standards for civics and government, and the National Center for History in the Schools developed the standards for history, all of which were published in 1994. Contact the Center for Civic Education, 5146 Douglas Fir Road, Calabasas, CA 91302-1467, or the National Center for the Social Studies, 3501 Newark Street, NW, Washington, DC 20016-3167, or the National Center for History in the Schools, University of California at Los Angeles, 231 Moore Hall, 4005 Hilgard Avenue, Los Angeles, CA 90024. The history standards are also printed in *OAH Magazine of History, 9*(3), 7–35 (Spring, 1995).

Health. The Joint Committee for National School Health Literacy developed standards that were published in 1995. Contact the American Alliance for Health, Physical Education, Recreation and Dance (AAHPRD), 1900 Association Drive, Reston, VA 22091.

FIGURE 2.6   Recommendations for English/Language Arts Instruction

Increased emphasis on:
- Adjusting spoken and written language vocabulary and style to communicate effectively with audiences and for different purposes
- Applying knowledge of language structure, language conventions of spelling, capitalization and punctuation, media techniques, figurative language, and genre to create and critique
- Applying strategies to comprehend, evaluate, and appreciate texts; draw on prior experience, their interactions with others, their knowledge of word meaning and other text, their word identification strategies, and their understanding of sound-letter correspondence, sentence structure, context, and graphics
- Conducting research on issues and interests by generating ideas and questions and by posing problems; gathering, evaluating, and synthesizing data from a variety of sources such as print and nonprint texts, artifacts, or people, and communicating their discoveries in ways that suit their purpose and audience
- Participating as knowledgeable, reflective, creative, and critical members of a variety of literacy communities
- Reading a range of literature in many genres to build an understanding of human experience
- Reading a range of texts—fiction, nonfiction, classic, and contemporary works—to acquire new information to respond to the needs and demands of society and the workplace; read for personal fulfillment and to build an understanding of themselves and of the cultures of the United States and the world
- Respecting diversity in language use, patterns and dialects across cultures, ethnic groups, geographic regions, and social roles
- Using different writing process elements (e.g., narrative writing, procedural writing) to communicate with different audiences for a variety of purposes
- Using spoken and written language for the purposes of enjoyment, persuasion, exchanging information, and learning about a particular topic of interest; develop competence in English and understanding of content across the curriculum
- Using a variety of resources such as databases, computer networks, libraries, or videos to gather and synthesize information and to create and communicate knowledge

Decreased emphasis on:
- Unclear goals of teaching (i.e., goals that lack meaning)
- Single-discipline learning
- Traditionally distinct content areas
- Teacher always as the center of classroom interaction

Physical education. In 1995, the National Association of Sport and Physical Education (NASPE) published *Moving into the Future: National Standards for Physical Education.* Contact NASPE, 1900 Association Drive, Reston, VA 22091.

Science. With input from the American Association for the Advancement of Science and the National Science Teachers Association, the National Research Council's National Committee on Science Education Standards and Assessment developed standards for science education which were published in 1995.

Contact National Science Education Standards, 2102 Constitution Avenue, NW, Washington, DC 20418 (see Figures 2.7[2] and 2.8[3]).

Technology. With initial funding from the National Science Foundation and the National Aeronautics and Space Administration, and in collaboration with the International Technology Education Association, standards for technology education are being developed with an anticipated release date of 1999. Contact Technology for All Americans Project, 1997 South Main Street, Suite 701, Blacksburg, VA 24061-0353.

FIGURE 2.7   Recommendations for Science Instruction

Increased emphasis on:
- Understanding and responding to individual student's interests, strengths, experiences, and needs
- Selecting and adapting curriculum
- Focusing on student understanding and use of scientific knowledge, ideas, and inquiry processes
- Guiding students in active and extended scientific inquiry
- Providing opportunities for scientific discussion and debate among students
- Continuously assessing student understanding
- Sharing responsibility for learning with students
- Supporting a classroom community with cooperation, shared responsibility, and respect
- Working with other teachers to enhance the science program

Decreased emphasis on:
- Treating all students alike and responding to the group as a whole
- Rigidly following curriculum
- Focusing on student acquisition of information
- Presenting scientific knowledge through lecture, text, and demonstration
- Asking for recitation of acquired knowledge
- Testing students for factual information at the end of the unit or chapter
- Maintaining responsibility and authority
- Supporting competition
- Working alone

Although there has been ongoing debate about their eventual value, it is anticipated that by the dawn of the new millennium these standards will be in place and have a positive effect upon the academic achievement of students in the public schools of the United States.

THE PROCESS OF SELECTING A THEME

For selecting a theme, the process differs somewhat depending on whether you are working independently or as a member of a team.

Selecting a Theme when Working Independently

If you are working solo, you might want to first list all the possible themes and topics that you can find in existing documents that were discussed in the preceding section. As you make the list, note any of the themes and topics that might be relevant to your goals. Then decide on a theme that can be correlated with each subject area without violating the educational plans for which you are responsible during

the academic year. Sometimes you may have to select content from two or more units that you have planned previously; at other times, you may want to integrate some content from previous units. If a theme for the ITU under consideration is not yet apparent, now is the time to select one, using the topic(s) you (perhaps with your students) have earmarked in your list. Critique your selected theme by examining it for various characteristics. See the questions in Figure 2.9 as guides for this critique (see also Planning Master 2.1). Later, in collaboration with your students, you will refine and finalize the theme title.

Selecting a Theme when Working as a Member of a Teaching Team

Often a team of two or more teachers collaborate in teaching an interdisciplinary thematic unit. When working on particular units, teaching teams sometimes invite temporary members such as specialty teachers and experts from the community. In the primary grades, teams of teachers may collaborate on a grade-level unit, or teams from more than one grade level may collaborate on a sequence of related units

FIGURE 2.8 Sample Recommendations for Science Learning

Increased emphasis on:
- Understanding scientific concepts and developing abilities of inquiry
- Learning subject matter disciplines in the context of inquiry, technology, science in personal and social perspectives, and history and nature of science
- Integrating all aspects of science content
- Studying a few fundamental science concepts
- Implementing inquiry as instructional strategies, abilities, and ideas to be learned
- Activities that investigate and analyze science questions
- Investigations over extended periods of time
- Process skills in context
- Using evidence and strategies for developing or revising an explanation

Decreased emphasis on:
- Knowing scientific facts and information
- Studying subject matter disciplines (physical, life, earth science) for their sake
- Separating science knowledge and science process
- Covering many science topics
- Implementing inquiry as a set of processes
- Activities that demonstrate and verify science content
- Investigations confined to one class period
- Process skills out of context
- Getting an answer

for several or all grades at that school. At middle-level schools and high schools, interdisciplinary teaching teams will consist of teachers from two or more disciplines.

First Step: Decide How Team Will Work Together. The first step is for the team members to discuss how unit development will proceed as a collaborative endeavor. All team members—and guest members, if desired—are encouraged to participate as equally as possible. Usually a team leader is selected for the school term or only for the development of this particular unit. If team members do not have a common planning time during the daily school schedule, then the team will need to decide how frequently and when it will meet. Ideally, during development and implementation of an ITU, interdisciplinary teams share a minimum of 6 hours of common planning time each week.

Second Step: Decisions about Student Learning Expectations. The second step is for the team to arrive at a consensus about what the students should achieve from the interdisciplinary unit of study, in terms of both conceptual and procedural knowledge. To set goals, the team will probably discuss some of the subject-specific frameworks, goals, objectives, curriculum guides, textbooks, supplemental materials, and units that are already in existence. The discussion among team members should also focus on what each member will contribute to the development and implementation of the unit and to the accomplishment of the unit's educational goals. Taking this step will help clarify the scope and sequence of the unit, so that all members of the team will have an understanding of what can and cannot be done. Be realistic—talk about any limitations and constraints you see in this undertaking. Taking time to play the part of educational "troubleshooters" will enable the team to identify various stumbling blocks before those potential problems impede the progress of the unit, which will make implementation of the ITU go more smoothly. For instance, early in ITU development members may want to clarify the purpose of working together, write a mission statement for the team, and make suggestions for turning that statement into a working plan.

FIGURE 2.9 Critiquing a Theme

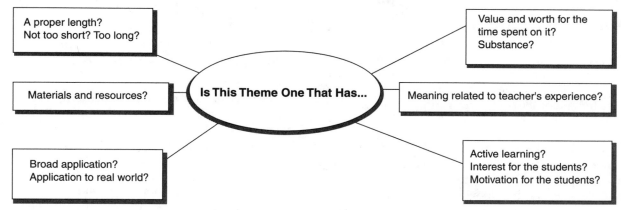

Third Step: Share Materials and Brainstorm Ideas.

An ITU pulls material from across the curriculum, and therefore the team will need to review information that each team member presents from his or her subject area. Together, members should list possible topics that can be found from existing curriculum documents. Meanwhile, new ideas will emerge as brainstorming is inevitable. Remember that dialogue and compromise are essential—a give-and-take is needed in these discussions because some themes and topics will correlate with certain subject areas better than with other areas. Also keep in mind that for team teachers, the goal is to find a theme or topic that works for everyone. All team members will want a theme that relates well with each subject area and that will not disturb (too much) the educational plans that individual team teachers already have in place for the academic year (refer to Figures 2.1 and 2.2 earlier in the chapter).

In some cases, the team may have to select content from units that one or more teachers have planned previously. In other cases, the team may have to merge some content from previous units. At this point, if a theme for the ITU has not yet become apparent, although it probably has, the time has come to derive a theme from the topic(s) that team members have put forward.

Themes Are (or Should Be) Forever Evolving

Although the unit may evolve from parts of previously implemented units of instruction, the most effective ITUs are often those that are the most current. This fact means that ever-changing global, national, and local topics provide a smorgasbord from which to choose, and teaching teams must constantly be aware of the changes in the world, the society, and the interests of students to update old plans and develop new and exciting ones.

Communications with Other Teams

One teaching team's units should not conflict with another's at the same or another grade level. If a school has two or more second-grade teams, for example, the teams may want to develop units on different themes and share their products. Furthermore, a middle school team may want to share its units with high school teams and perhaps with affiliated elementary schools. The lines of communication within, between, and among teams and schools are critical to the success of integrated curriculum and interdisciplinary thematic instruction.

Once selected, a theme should be critiqued by examining it for various characteristics. The questions in Figure 2.9 may be of help in this critique. For additional insight into the process of selecting a theme for an ITU, now do Exercises 2.1 and 2.2 on pages 53 through 58.

GIVING THE ITU A NAME

Giving the unit a name should be done in collaboration with your students. Before selecting a theme title discuss with students ways the unit will be meaningful to the members of the class and the school, and how it will be integrated to real-life experiences. Emphasize that the major part of the unit's value will come from its interdisciplinary approach. Decide with the students how a final title will be selected—perhaps by brainstorming possibilities and then voting on them. The agreed upon title should be one that makes academic sense and that has meaning to the students.

DEVELOPING SCOPE AND SEQUENCE FOR CONTENT AND INSTRUCTION

Once the theme has been selected and named, develop a schedule for the unit to assign dates to certain topics and identify activities in a logical sequence. This sequence could incorporate any or a combination of the following arrangements.

Primary Focus on One Content Area

Sometimes when selecting a theme, you may find that it is specifically related to one discipline, such as history. Consider the following examples:

- Civilization, cultural diffusion, and innovation (e.g., the evolution of major civilizations)
- Human interaction with the environment (e.g., people's choices made available by geography)
- Values, beliefs, political ideas, and institutions (e.g., the evolution of democratic societies)
- Conflict and cooperation (e.g., causes of conflicts and war, and approaches to peace)
- Comparative history of major developments (e.g., revolutionary, reactionary, and reform periods across time and place)
- Social and political interactions (e.g., changes in class, ethnic, gender, and racial relations and patterns)

Although one discipline (e.g., history/social studies) may be the primary focus in the unit's sequence of activities, a multitude of other areas may be included in the activities as well. Consider, for example, an ITU whose theme is "children and their families in America's colonies." The sequence of activities might include several related to history/social studies, such as the colonists' connections to the rest of the world, their activities in their daily lives, their economic status, and their beliefs and manners. Each of the activities, or study areas, could comprise a certain time period, and students would learn within an historical context as they explore art, biographies of famous people, drama, music, and literature, as well as how the politics of the time affected children and their families.

Equal Focus on Two Content Areas

Consider that both history/social studies and English/language arts play equal roles of importance in the unit's sequence of activities. You might draw upon children's literature to establish connections to make the time period and the theme, "children and their families in America's colonies," come alive for the students. This arrangement emphasizes English literature to provide the background needed to bring the lives of the people of that time to the attention of the students.

Equal Focus on Three (or More) Content Areas

When three or more disciplines such as history/social studies, English/language arts, and science play equal roles of importance, the goal is to integrate the areas just as they are integrated in our lives. For a unit whose theme is "children and their families in America's colonies," you can engage the students not only in the activities mentioned in the previous two arrangements, but also in science activities. You might assist the students in locating the colony of Jamestown on a map. You might ask them to research climatic conditions at that time, the wildlife that was prevalent in that region, and in consideration of their findings, you might ask them where they would locate the colony if they were the first settlers. Perhaps you would like to design a problem-solving inquiry similar to the one illustrated in Figure 2.10.

If working solo, you may find it valuable to give a copy of the sequence of your activities to a teaching colleague. If working as a member of a team, then you and members of the team will need to exchange ideas. Ask for a colleague's suggestions about the activities and the sequence you have identified. If most of the remarks are positive, you will know that the sequence you planned appears workable from another's point of view. If difficulties arise, you may want to consider modifications in the activities themselves or in the sequence in which they are offered.

Developing Focus Questions

Following the selection of a theme title, in collaboration with members of your teaching team and your students, you will develop focus questions to guide the study. Consider the following examples:

- How did African Americans begin their journey to freedom?
- What happened during Columbus's journeys?
- Why can some constructions be called grand constructions?
- What are the reasons people celebrate liberty? How do they celebrate?

Planning and Selecting Learning Activities for the Unit

When planning and selecting learning activities for meaningful understanding, it is important to select activities that are as direct as possible. You will want

FIGURE 2.10   Locating a Colony: A Problem-Solving Inquiry

Presentation of the Problem. In groups of three or four, students receive the following information:

Background. You (your group is considered as one person) are 1 of 120 passengers on the ship, *The Prince Charles.* You left England 12 weeks ago. You have experienced many hardships, including a stormy passage, limited rations, sickness, cold and damp weather, and hot foul air below deck. Ten of your fellow immigrants to the New World, including three children, have died and were buried at sea. You are now anchored at an uncertain place, off the coast of the New World, which your captain believes to be somewhere north of the Virginia Grants. Seas are so rough and food is so scarce that you and your fellow passengers have decided to settle here. A landing party has returned with a map they made of the area. As one of the elders, you must decide at once where the settlement is to be located. The tradespeople want to settle along the river, which is deep, even though this seems to be the season of low water levels. Within 10 months, you and others expect deep water ships from England with more colonists and merchants. Those within your group who are farmers say they must have fertile, workable land. The officer in charge of the landing party reported seeing a group of armed natives that fled when approached. He feels the settlement must be located so that it can be defended from the natives and from the sea.

Directions.

Step One. You (your group) are to select a site on the attached map which you feel is best suited for a colony. Your site must satisfy the different factions aboard the ship. Several possible sites are already marked on the map (letters A–G). You may select one of these locations or use them as reference points to show the location of your colony. When your group has selected its site, list and explain the reasons for your choice. When each group has arrived at its tentative decision, these decisions will be shared with the whole class.

Step Two. After each group has made its presentation and argument, a class debate is held about where the colony should be located.

Notes to teacher: For the debate we suggest you have a large map drawn on the writing board or on an overhead transparency, where each group's mark can be made for all to see and discuss. After each group has presented its argument for its location and against the others, we suggest that you then mark on the large map, the two, three or more hypothetical locations (assuming that, as a class, there yet is no single favorite location). Then take a straw vote of the students, allowing each to vote on his or her own, independently rather than as members of a group. At this time, you can end the activity by saying that if the majority of students favor one location, then that is the solution to the problem—the colony is located at the site that the majority of class members indicate. No sooner will that statement be made by you than someone will ask, "Are we correct?" or "What is the right answer?" They will ask such questions because, as students in school, they are used to solving problems that have right answers (Level I inquiry teaching). In real-world problems, however, there are no "right" answers, although some answers may seem better than others. It is the process of problem solving that is important. You want your students to develop confidence in their ability to solve problems and also understand the tentativeness of "answers" to real-life problems.

(*Source:* J. Devine and D. Devine, by permission)

students involved in direct hands-on experiences to encourage the full use of their learning modalities— auditory, visual, tactile, and kinesthetic—which often results in the most effective and longest lasting learning. Figure 2.11 illustrates types of learning experiences, ranging from the most concrete (direct) at the bottom of the ladder, where students are likely to be using all their sensory input channels and their learning is integrated, to the most abstract (least direct) at the top of the ladder, where learners are using only one or two sensory input channels.

Planning the Details

Team members work together to schedule dates, coordinate topics, and identify activities in a logical

FIGURE 2.11   The Learning Experiences Ladder

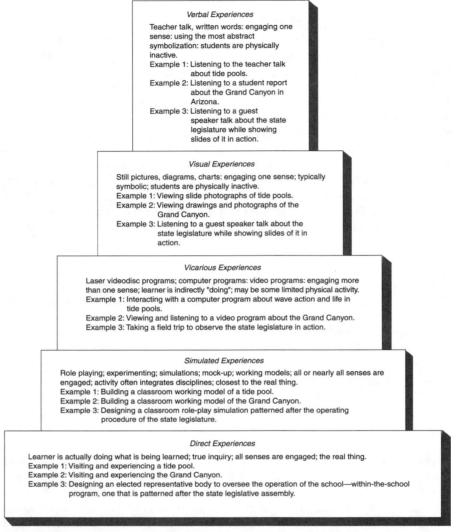

Verbal Experiences

Teacher talk, written words: engaging one sense: using the most abstract symbolization: students are physically inactive.

Example 1: Listening to the teacher talk about tide pools.

Example 2: Listening to a student report about the Grand Canyon in Arizona.

Example 3: Listening to a guest speaker talk about the state legislature while showing slides of it in action.

Visual Experiences

Still pictures, diagrams, charts: engaging one sense; typically symbolic; students are physically inactive.

Example 1: Viewing slide photographs of tide pools.

Example 2: Viewing drawings and photographs of the Grand Canyon.

Example 3: Listening to a guest speaker talk about the state legislature while showing slides of it in action.

Vicarious Experiences

Laser videodisc programs; computer programs: video programs: engaging more than one sense; learner is indirectly "doing"; may be some limited physical activity.

Example 1: Interacting with a computer program about wave action and life in tide pools.

Example 2: Viewing and listening to a video program about the Grand Canyon.

Example 3: Taking a field trip to observe the state legislature in action.

Simulated Experiences

Role playing; experimenting; simulations; mock-up; working models; all or nearly all senses are engaged; activity often integrates disciplines; closest to the real thing.

Example 1: Building a classroom working model of a tide pool.

Example 2: Building a classroom working model of the Grand Canyon.

Example 3: Designing a classroom role-play simulation patterned after the operating procedure of the state legislature.

Direct Experiences

Learner is actually doing what is being learned; true inquiry; all senses are engaged; the real thing.

Example 1: Visiting and experiencing a tide pool.

Example 2: Visiting and experiencing the Grand Canyon.

Example 3: Designing an elected representative body to oversee the operation of the school—within-the-school program, one that is patterned after the state legislative assembly.

(Source: Earlier versions of this concept are found in C. F. Hoban, Sr., et al., *Visualizing the Curriculum* (New York: Dryden, 1937), p. 39; J. S. Bruner, *Toward a Theory of Instruction* (Cambridge: Harvard University Press, 1966), p. 49; E. Dale, *Audio-Visual Methods in Teaching* (New York: Holt, Rinehart & Winston, 1969), p. 108; and E. C. Kim and R. D. Kellough, *A Resource Guide for Secondary School Teaching, 2nd edition* (Englewood Cliffs, NJ: Merrill/Prentice Hall, 1978), p. 136).

sequence. With the school calendar in mind, a time line or schedule for the ITU is agreed upon. Establish and write important dates on the calendar, including deadlines for having certain material prepared and the beginning and closing dates of the unit study. Indicate dates that will be important to the students, such as when reports are due and when the final culminating activity will be held.

This time line, called Time Line A, should contain a record of all dates by which any assigned work must be done by a team member, that is, any work that must be completed for the development of the ITU. The team can then turn its attention to a second time line, Time Line B, which should contain all dates important to both the students and the teachers. For example, Time Line B can indicate when the ITU begins (and in which periods), various due dates during the unit, and when the ITU ends.

Now explore the scope and sequence of an ITU by doing Exercises 2.3 and 2.4, found on pages 59 through 61.

THE COMMUNITY AS A RICH RESOURCE

In your community are many people who will be willing to serve as resources and there are many places that you and the students can visit (we discuss these options later in this section). You will want to identify and select those persons and places that will contribute to the students' understanding of the theme-related topics.

Student Choices

A class meeting is sometimes beneficial in focusing students' attention on decisions to be made about the use of community resources. Figure 2.12 shows a sample web that can be used as a discussion focus, suitable for an overhead transparency (Planning Master 2.2). With that web as a model, students can write their own headings, questions, responses, and responsibilities on a blank transparency.

People

As witnessed by the West Salem Middle School experience (Chapter 1), people from the community can make a significant contribution to a thematic unit of instruction. When invited with care, a community resource person can be asked to spend time with the students for an instructional purpose related to the unit. A discussion with the students and a quick survey of the yellow pages in your telephone directory can provide a wealth of information about the people who could serve as resources.

Bringing outside speakers into your classroom can be a valuable educational experience for students, but not always. In essence, guest speakers are on a spectrum of four types, two of whom should be avoided as guest speakers. (1) Ideally, a speaker is both informative and inspiring. (2) A speaker might be inspiring but with nothing substantive to offer, and except for the diversion he or she may offer from the usual rigors of classroom

FIGURE 2.12   Planning a Field Trip

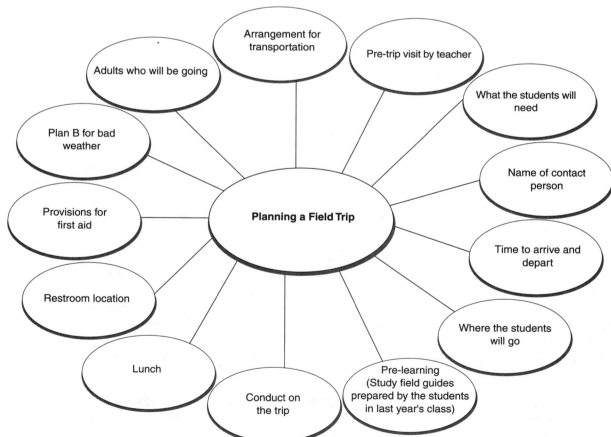

work, this speaker makes the experience a waste of valuable instructional time. (3) A speaker might be informative but boring to students. (4) At the worst end of this spectrum is the speaker who is both boring and uninformative. Therefore, as with any other instructional experience, the bottom line is to make the experience most effective, which takes careful planning on your part. To make the experience most beneficial for student learning, consider the following guidelines:

- If at all possible, meet and talk with the guest speaker in advance to inform the speaker about your students and your expectations for the presentation, and to gauge the speaker's amount of motivation and worthwhile information. If you believe the speaker might be informative but boring, then perhaps you can help structure the presentation in some way to make the presentation a bit more inspiring. For instance, stop the speaker every few minutes and involve the students in questioning and discussion of points made. Be sure that this plan has been discussed with and agreed to by the speaker.
- Prepare your students in advance with key points of information that you expect the students to obtain.

- Prepare students with questions to ask the speaker, things the students want to find out, and information you want them to inquire about during the presentation.
- Follow up the presentation with a class-generated thank-you letter to the guest speaker, and perhaps further questions that developed during class discussions subsequent to the speaker's presentation.

Places

When you plan a class excursion to a place off the school campus, make sure the trip coincides with the ITU and anticipate any problems that might arise during the outing. For all fieldtrips, you will want to have a clear purpose, keeping the safety of the students foremost in mind and creating good public relations between the students and the citizens in the community. Possible locations for off-campus excursions and resource persons are shown in Figure 2.13.

Field Trips

Off-campus excursions are often vital components to successful interdisciplinary thematic instruction.

FIGURE 2.13   Community Resources for Speakers and Field Trips

airport	farm/factory	newspaper plant
apiary	fire department	observatory
aquarium	fish hatchery	oil refinery
archeological site	flea market	park/nature area
art gallery	foreign embassy	poetry reading meeting
assembly plant	forest/forest preserve	post office/delivery company
bakery	freeway under construction	police station
bird and wildlife sanctuary	gas company	recycling center
book publisher	geological site	retail store
book store	health department/hospital	sanitation department
broadcasting/tv station	highway construction site	sawmill/lumber company
building constructed/razed	highway patrol station	shopping mall
canal lock	historical sites/monuments	shoreline (stream, lake, ocean)
cemetery	industrial/computer plant	telecommunication center
data information business	legislative session	town meeting
chemical plant	levee and water reservoir	utility company
city/county planning commission	library and archive	universities and colleges
courthouse	Native American reservation	warehouse
dairy	mass transit authority	water reservoir/treatment plant
dam and flood plain	military installation	wetlands/wildlife park
dock and harbor	mine	weather bureau/storm center
doctor's office/clinic	museum	zoo

These children are taking advantage of a superb community resource, the zoo.

To prepare for and implement a successful field trip, consider three important stages of planning—before, during, and after—and critical decisions concerning each stage.

Before a Field Trip. Today's schools often have very limited funds for the transportation and liability costs for field trips. In some cases, there are no field trip funds at all. At times, parent-teacher groups and civic organizations help by providing financial resources so that students get valuable first-hand experiences that field trips so often can offer. When planning a field trip, follow these guidelines:

- When the field trip is your idea (and not the students) discuss the idea with your principal, teaching team, or department or division chair, especially when transportation will be needed, before mentioning the idea to your students. There is no cause served by getting students excited about a trip before you know if it is feasible.

- Once you have obtained the necessary, but tentative, approval from school officials, take the trip yourself, if possible. A previsit allows you to determine how to make the field trip most productive and what arrangements will be necessary. For this previsit, you might want to consider taking a couple of your students along (who have permission) for their ideas and help. If a previsit is not possible, you still will need to arrange for travel directions, arrival and departure times, parking, briefing by the host if there is one, storage of students' personal items such as coats and lunches, provisions for eating, use of restrooms, and fees, if any.

- If there are fees, you need to talk with your administration about who will pay the fees. If the trip is worth taking, the school should cover the costs. If that is not possible, perhaps students can plan a fund-raising activity or obtain financial assistance from some other source, such as the parent-teacher organization or the special parent club that supports your school/department in particular. If this does not work, you might consider an alternative experience that does not involve costs.

- Arrange for official permission from the school administration. This usually requires a form for requesting, planning, and reporting field trips.

- After permission has been obtained, you can discuss the field trip with your students and arrange for permission from their parents or guardians. You need to realize that although parents or guardians sign official permission forms allowing their children to participate in the trip, these only show that the parents or guardians are aware of what will take place and that they give their permission for the activity. Although the permission form should include a statement that the parent or guardian absolves the teacher and the school from liability should an accident occur, it does not lessen the teacher's and school's responsibilities should there be negligence by a teacher, driver, or chaperone.

- Arrange for students to be excused from their other classes while on the field trip. Using an information form prepared and signed by you and perhaps by the principal, the students should then assume responsibility for notifying their other teachers of the planned absence from classes and assure them that they will make up whatever work is missed. In addition, you will need to make arrangement for your own teaching duties to be covered. In some schools, teachers co-operate by taking over the classes of those who will be gone. In other schools, substitute teachers are hired. Occasionally, teachers have to hire their own substitutes.

- Arrange for whatever transportation is needed. Your principal, or the principal's designee, will help with the details. In many schools, this detail is done by someone else. In any case, the use of private automobiles is ill-advised, because you and the school could be liable for the acts of the drivers.
- Arrange for the collection of money that is needed for fees. If there are out-of-pocket costs to be paid by students, this information needs to be included on the permission form. No students should ever be excluded from the field trip because of a lack of money. This can be a tricky issue, so try to antici-pate problems; hopefully the school or some or-ganization can pay for the trip so that students pay nothing and you avoid potential problems.
- Plan details for student safety and monitoring of their safety from departure to return. Included should be a first-aid kit and a system of student control, such as a buddy system where students must remain paired throughout the trip. The pairs sometimes are given numbers that are recorded and kept by the teacher and the chaperones, and then checked at departure times, periodically during the trip, and again upon return.
- Use adult chaperones. As a very general rule, there should be one adult chaperone for every 10 students. Some districts have a policy regarding this issue.
- Plan the complete route and schedule, including any scheduled stops. If transportation is being provided, you will need to discuss the plans with the provider.
- Establish and discuss rules of behavior with your students to the extent you believe necessary. In-cluded in this might be details of the trip, its pur-pose, directions, what they should wear and bring, academic expectations of them (consider, for instance, giving each student a study guide), and follow-up activities. Also included should be information about what to do if anything should go awry, for example, if a student is late for the de-parture or return, loses a personal possession along the way, gets lost, is injured, becomes sick, or misbehaves. For the latter, never send a misbe-having student back to school alone. While on a field trip, all students should be under the direct supervision of an adult at all times. Involve the adult chaperones in the previsit discussion. All this information should be included on the parental permission form.
- If a field trip is to promote some kind of learning, as is probably the case, then the learning expecta-tions need to be clearly defined and the students given an explanation of how and where they may encounter the learning experience. This should not be left to chance.
- Before the field trip, students can be preassessed with such questions as "What do we know about _____?" and "What do we want to find out about _____?" and "How can we find out?" Then an ap-propriate guide can be prepared for the students to use during the field trip.
- Plan the follow-up activities. As with any other lesson plan, the field trip lesson is complete only after a proper introduction and a well-planned closure.

During a Field Trip. If your field trip has been care-fully planned according to the preceding guidelines, then it should be a valuable and safe experience for all. While at the trip location, you and your adult chaperones should monitor student behavior and learning just as you do in the classroom. While on the trip, your students may take notes and follow a prepared study guide. You may want to take recorders and cameras so the experience can be re-lived and shared in class upon return.

After a Field Trip. All sorts of follow-up activities can be planned as an educational wrap-up to this valuable and exciting firsthand experience. For in-stance, a bulletin board committee can plan and pre-pare an attractive display summarizing the trip. Stu-dents can write about their experiences in their journals or as papers. Small groups can give oral re-ports to the class about what they did and learned. Their reports can then serve as springboards for fur-ther class discussion. Finally, for future planning, all who were involved should contribute to an assess-ment of the experience.

SHARING MATERIALS BEFORE AND DURING UNIT IMPLEMENTATION

When working independently, you may find it of value to give a copy of your unit to a colleague for comments and suggestions about the unit, including any suggestions about print and nonprint materials and other resources. Your unit cannot function with-out materials, and so you must plan for the resources that are needed, including media equipment, references, reading materials, and community resources. If most of your colleague's remarks are positive, you will know that the unit you planned appears workable from another's point of view. If there are difficulties, you may want to consider more modifications in the ITU.

When working as a team, it is useful for each member to provide other team members with two copies of his or her draft unit. Each member then reviews the draft copies of other members, particu-

larly examining a member's attention to the organization of the materials—media equipment and materials, reference books, reading sources, resource people, and other community resources. Each member then returns one of the two copies to each of the other members, with comments and suggestions, keeping the other copy to plan complementary lessons. Depending on the remarks and feedback from other team members, a member can have confidence in his or her plan or make modifications as needed.

SUMMARY

You have been provided with an overview of how to initiate an ITU, including selecting a theme to study and planning the scope and sequence of the unit. You can use guiding questions to isolate concept words and then use the concept words to write generalizations that represent knowledge related to the thematic study. As in the previous chapter, sugges-

tions in this guide are guidelines, not universals and absolutes for developing an ITU. There are perhaps as many successful variations on these guidelines as there are successful implementations of interdisciplinary thematic units. For more reading about some of those successful ventures, see "For Further Reading".

QUESTIONS AND ACTIVITIES FOR DISCUSSION

1. Explain the value of organizing instruction into units. For a specific grade level, identify and describe criteria for selecting a topic for a unit of study. Describe the types of activities that could be used in the introductory phase of a unit and in the culminating phase.

2. The use of community resources can add a great deal to your students' background knowledge and frame of reference for learning. In addition to the suggestions presented in this chapter, what other useful suggestions for community involvement in an ITU do you have to share?

3. In addition to the documents discussed in this chapter, what additional resources have you found that enhance a teacher's development of an ITU? For example, what useful websites have you discovered that you can tell others about?

4. What evidence can you discover that indicates that Goals 2000 is being reached? In what ways can an ITU help a teacher reach part of Goals 2000?

5. Share any evidence you can discover that indicates that the national standards for the various content areas have made an impact on curriculum documents being produced by teachers from schools in your local geographical area.

6. Share with others in your class whether you believe there is any difference, or should be, in what is a "theme," a "topic," and a "theme title" regarding an ITU.

7. Share with others your opinion as to whether it is easier or more difficult to prepare an ITU solo rather than collaboratively as a member of an interdisciplinary team.

8. Discuss with your classmates the significance of the learning experiences ladder as related to using integrated instruction.

9. Do you have concerns about using interdisciplinary thematic instruction and not being able to cover all the content you believe you should be covering? Think back to your own schooling. What do you really remember? Most likely you remember projects, yours and other students' presentations, the lengthy research you did, and your extra effort for the artwork to accompany your presentation. Maybe you remember a compliment by a teacher or a pat on the back by peers. Most likely you do not remember the massive amount of content that was covered. Discuss your feelings about this with your classmates. Share common experiences and concerns.

INDIVIDUAL NOTES

EXERCISE 2.1

Beginning an ITU: An Exercise in Collaboration

Instructions.   The purpose of this exercise is to collaboratively work with a partner or partners to gain insight into selecting a theme for an ITU. First divide your class into partnerships representing elementary, middle, or high school interests, and then have two or more partnerships work together. Each group is to decide the grade level for which their ITU will be suitable.

1. If desired, simulate a cooperative group structure, assigning the following roles to members in each group of partnerships. (If this is not desired, move on to step 2.)

   Facilitator. The person responsible for seeing that every member in the group gets the assistance that he or she needs.

   Checker. The person responsible for seeing that every member finishes his or her work for the day.

   Reporter. The person responsible for discussing what the group members learned during the final debriefing session held each day after group work.

2. The task is to select a theme for study just as the students in your classroom could self-select their lines of inquiry. Theme:

   What sources will you consult *before* you finally select a theme?

	Yes	No
a. National curriculum standards for particular subjects	_____	_____
b. State Curriculum Frameworks	_____	_____
c. Local curriculum guides and documents	_____	_____
d. Student textbooks and teacher's guide for adopted textbooks	_____	_____
e. Students' interests and questions	_____	_____
f. Resources on the Internet	_____	_____
g. Professional literature	_____	_____
h. Other	_____	_____

3. Working individually, brainstorm as many word and phrase associations about the theme as possible. Write your theme in the center of the space provided and group your associations around the theme (i.e., construct a visual web). Then share your ideas with others in your group.

4. Join a small group or the total group and contribute the word and phrase associations from step 3 to the common sharing of ideas. Have a volunteer write everyone's ideas in the form of a visual web, and then replicate the web in the space provided. Take notes on any discussion about it. Keep the web for the reference as you continue your study of ITUs.

5. Ask any questions you have related to any of the words and phrases on the web. Assist the group members as they classify all members' questions into categories. Draw lines to connect any related categories and then label the categories with the headings of your choice (thereby making the visual web a concept web). Sketch the categories and their labels in the space provided.

EXERCISE 2.2

Beginning an ITU: Investigating Specific Questions and Identifying Selected Resources

Instructions.   The purpose of this exercise is to develop your skills in investigating specific questions and in selecting resources related to an interdisciplinary thematic unit. For this exercise, use the theme and questions your group developed in Exercise 2.1.

1. From Exercise 2.1, select three (or more) questions about the group's theme that you would like to investigate.

   a.

   b.

   c.

   d.

2. Now focus on the interdisciplinary aspect of the unit by writing questions about the theme from the perspective of people from various disciplines. You might begin with the disciplines that are closely related to your theme. Ask yourself, "What would an anthropologist want to know about this theme? an artist? a biologist? an historian? a mathematician? a sociologist?" Writing these questions will help you determine how many subject areas you will incorporate in your thematic unit—a great many or just a few? Consult with others in your class if necessary. For each of the disciplines, an example is given related to an ITU you will examine in Chapter 5, called Migrations: Newcomers in North America. Use the examples to spur your own thinking.

   Anthropologist (Example: How have anthropologists helped us learn about the topic? How can we discover a relationship about the people's behavior and their beliefs?)

   Artist (Example: How can we show what we know about the topic through art, music, dance, etc.? What contributions did art, music, and dance make in the lives of early explorers and settlers?)

   Historian (Example: What contributions did history make in the lives of explorers and early settlers? How have historians helped us learn about the topic? How has the acceptance or rejection of the idea of colonies changed through time?)

   Mathematician (Example: In what ways did early explorers and settlers use mathematics? In what ways can we express what we know about the topic through mathematics? How have mathematicians helped us learn about this topic?)

   Sociologist (Example: What groups in society operate to bring us information about the topic? How have sociologists contributed to the topic?)

   Other

3. Reread your questions and underline words that represent concepts to be learned. What generalizations (big ideas) related to the theme can be written related to this thematic study?

4. Select one or more of the generalizations from step 3. Then look at the student textbooks, the teacher manuals, and the curriculum guidelines for your grade to see if your generalizations can be taught through the topic identified in any of these resources. What did you discover?

5. For each question that you selected for further study (step 1), identify the resources you could/would consult to investigate the question further. The resources can range from using the community as a laboratory to reading printed material. Make a list of the resources.

EXERCISE 2.3

Making Some Early Decisions: More about Scope and Sequence

Instructions. The purpose of this exercise is to begin planning the scope and sequence plan of your interdisciplinary thematic unit. In your ITU plan, you want to incorporate the major concepts and generalizations that are in the curriculum guide for your grade level, plus the ones you identified in Exercise 2.2. You also need to make various decisions about grouping, unit length, unit structure, and disciplines to be included.

1. *Individual work and group work.* You might plan to have all types of grouping in your thematic unit. For example, you could begin each elementary day or period with a theme and then have students work with partners or in small groups. As an alternative, you could invite students to participate in a whole-group study of the theme and ask students to request—and thus "reserve"—one area of related study for their individual inquiries. Decisions about individual work and group work:

2. *Length of study.* Your theme study can be of varying lengths. You may develop an ITU for a 2-week grading period or a 6-week grading period. You may plan four separate thematic units during the entire year, or you may plan another time length of your choice. Decisions about length of study:

3. *Concentrated structure and/or expanded structure.* You may decide on an expanded structure in which the students have common experiences in whole-group situations, and then select separate areas of study to explore as individual inquiries or small-group inquiries. Conversely, you could decide on a concentrated structure in which the students learn mainly in whole-group situations with some partnership and small-group work. In the concentrated structure, the students realize the ITU has a beginning and an end. Decisions about structure:

4. *Disciplines to include.* You may decide to include many subject areas or only a few. Decisions about disciplines:

EXERCISE 2.4

Developing the Scope and Sequence of Initial Weekly Plans for an ITU

Instructions.   The purpose of this exercise is to develop the scope and sequence of an interdisciplinary thematic unit of study. Work with a partner or small group as you plan.

1. Select one of your generalizations related to your theme (Exercise 2.2, step 3) and write it in the appropriate space that follows. Review the students' texts to determine the extent of any material related to the thematic study. Write the page numbers or chapter numbers from the texts for future reference. If different generalizations are to be the foci of the other remaining weeks, also review the texts for the material related to those generalizations.

Theme:

First Week

Generalization/overall question to focus on (underline words that reflect concepts):

                    Science   Social Sciences   Expressive Arts   Math

Pages/chapters:

Ways teacher gives input:

Ways students give input:

Second Week

Generalization/overall question to focus on (underline words that reflect concepts):

                    Science   Social Sciences   Expressive Arts   Math

Pages/chapters:

Ways teacher gives input:

Ways students give input:

Third Week

(Note: If your ITU is planned for longer than 3 weeks, make additional blank copies of this format.)

Generalization/overall question to focus on (underline words that reflect concepts):

                    Science   Social Sciences   Expressive Arts   Math

Pages/chapters:

Ways teacher gives input:

Ways students give input:

2. What plans do you have for your students to take an active part in the development of the thematic unit? (Examples: developing the final title of the theme; developing a question map; reserving a particular question for individual inquiry; suggesting resources and references to search for information; naming community and identifying Internet resources; hands-on activities; small-group work; and whole-group instructional conversations)

CHAPTER NOTES

1. Contact National Council of Teachers of Mathematics (NCTM), 1906 Association Drive, Reston, VA 22091.
2. National Research Council, *National Science Education Standards* (Washington, DC: National Academy of Sciences, 1996), p. 52. Adapted by permission of the National Academy of Sciences.
3. National Research Council, p. 113. Adapted by permission of the National Academy of Sciences.

FOR FURTHER READING

Association for Supervision and Curriculum Development. (1996). *Curriculum Materials Directory.* Alexandria, VA.

Betts, F. (1996, May). Only the best: Hot links to good resources. *Educational Leadership, 53*(8), 38–39.

Danielson, C. (1996). *Enhancing professional practice: A framework for teaching.* Alexandria, VA: Association for Supervision and Curriculum Development.

Dever, M. T., & Jared, E. J. (1996, March). Remember to include art and crafts in your integrated curriculum. *Young Children, 51*(3), 69–73.

Harris, D., & Carr, J. (1996). *How to use standards in the classroom.* Alexandria, VA: Association for Supervision and Curriculum Development.

Kendall, J. S., & Marzano, R. J. (1996). *Content knowledge: A compendium of standards and benchmarks for K–12 education.* Alexandria, VA: Association for Supervision and Curriculum Development.

Knapp, C. E. (1996). *Just beyond the classroom: Community adventures for interdisciplinary learning.* Charleston, WV: ERIC Clearinghouse on Rural Education and Small Schools.

Marzano, R. J., & Kendall, J. S. (1996). *A comprehensive guide to designing standards-based districts, schools, and classrooms.* Alexandria, VA: Association for Supervision and Curriculum Development.

Post, T. R. et al. (1997). *Interdisciplinary approaches to curriculum: Themes for teaching.* Upper Saddle River, NJ: Merrill/Prentice Hall.

Shaw, D. G., & Dybdahl, C. S. (1996). *Integrating science and language arts: A sourcebook for K–6 teachers.* Boston: Allyn & Bacon.

Sunal, C. S., & Sunal, D. W. (1996, March/April). Interdisciplinary social studies and science lessons with a Native American theme. *Social Studies, 87*(2), 72–88.

SELECTED INTERNET ADDRESSES

Internet Public Library, Teen Division (www.cyberteens.com/ctmain.html)
Has sections related to issues, conflicts, drugs, gangs, and violence.

Straight Talk about School (www.balancenet.org)
Encourages teens to stay in school and consider careers and college attendance. Sponsored by National Association of Secondary School Principals.

Virtually React (www.react.com)
Has updated educational material weekly and the users can share thoughts and ideas.

CHAPTER 3

Developing Objectives and Learning Activities

*Something deeply hidden had to be behind things.
I can still remember—or at least believe I can remember—that this
experience (seeing a compass needle always turn north) made a
deep and lasting impression upon me.*

—Albert Einstein

INTERDISCIPLINARY THEMATIC UNIT FOR PRIMARY STUDENTS: EXTINCTIONS—LEARNING FROM DINOSAURS

After determining a theme, teachers plan instruction around a sequence of activities that focus on the theme. Common to many elementary school teachers, and to some middle school teachers, is the theme of "extinctions" that centers around the topic of dinosaurs.[1] Whatever its selected title might be in a given situation, a thematic unit on dinosaurs can encompass any number of multidisciplinary activities related to the topic. Following are some examples.

- *History.* Students develop a graphic time line showing the long time frame that dinosaurs were dominant on this earth; they visit a museum that features dinosaur exhibits.
- *Mathematics.* Students categorize the types of dinosaurs and create graphs illustrating the variety and proportional sizes of dinosaurs.
- *Reading, writing, and art.* Students create and write illustrated stories about a favorite dinosaur.

- *Science.* Students speculate on both why the dinosaurs were so successful and how the events led to their rather quick disappearance.

In her self-contained second-grade classroom, Kristie Darras (Elk Grove, California), guided her students in a thematic unit centered around dinosaurs. Learning activities integrated science and math, drawing and crafts, music and reading, and publishing original books to support the study. Connecting reading to music, the students listened to a song about each dinosaur being studied. Students read sentence strips with the words of the song. They added sound effects, sang the song several times, and added a rhythmic beat with their fingers and hands. Additionally, students prepared their own dinosaur-shape books, wrote original pages, and created illustrations. To survey favorite dinosaurs, graphing was introduced. The students built their own graph in the classroom by drawing a favorite dinosaur and contributing it to a large graph. Students used individual copies of the graph to record what was added to the large graph and marked *X*s with their pencils in the appropriate places. When the class graph was finished, the students read it with guidance from the teacher and talked about the information they had gathered.

The culminating event took place at the school's spring open house. The students' assignment for open house was to bring one adult and explain to that person what they had been learning at school. Confidently, the students told their visitors about dinosaurs and proudly displayed their dinosaur books, dinosaur mobiles, dinosaur body shapes made from felt, and dinosaur clay models.

This guide was developed specifically to assist you in designing a unit for an integrated curriculum. In developing an ITU, you need to write an overview of the scope and sequence of the thematic study, as in Chapter 2. You also need to plan the objectives and specific learning activities that will be the heart of the unit. As discussed in Chapter 2, you can use the questions generated by the theme as foci and then locate resources that might be useful in exploring those questions. Information from such resources can be recorded by the students in various ways—in charts, graphs, notes in learning logs, and so on.

In this chapter, you will learn how to prepare the objectives and learning activities for an ITU, which is the next step in developing your own ITU.

AIMS, GOALS, AND OBJECTIVES: A CLARIFICATION

Once you have identified your theme and some of its related topics and subtopics, you need to identify specific performance expectations—what students will be expected to do as a result of the learning experiences of the ITU. These performance expectations are stated as specific instructional objectives, known also as performance, behavioral, or terminal objectives. (The term *terminal objective* is sometimes used to distinguish between instructional objectives that are intermediate and those that are final, or "terminal" to an area of learning.) Instructional objectives are statements describing what the student will be able to do upon completion of the instructional experience.

As a teacher, you frequently will encounter the compound structure that reads "goals and objectives," as you likely found in the curriculum documents that you reviewed for Chapter 2. To distinguish the difference between goals and objectives, consider your intent.

Goals are ideas that you intend to reach—ideals that you would like to have accomplished. Goals may be stated as teacher goals, as student goals, or collaboratively as team goals. Ideally in all three, the goal is the same. If, for example, the goal is to improve students' reading skills, it could be stated as follows: "To help students develop their reading skills" (teacher or team goal), or "To improve my reading skills" (student goal).

Educational goals are general statements of intent and are prepared during the preactive phase of decision making and ITU planning (see Chapter 1). (Note: Although some writers use the phrase "general goals and objectives," it is incorrect usage. Goals are general; objectives are specific.) Goals are useful when planned cooperatively with students and/or when shared with students as advance mental organizers for the purpose of establishing a mind-set toward some learning to be done. The students then know what to expect and will begin to prepare mentally to learn it. From the goals, specific objectives are prepared and written in performance (behavioral) terms. The value of stating learning objectives in terms of performance (i.e., what the student will be able to do) and in providing advance organizers is well documented by research.[2] Objectives are *not* intentions. They are actual behaviors that teachers intend to cause students to display. In short, objectives are what students do.

The most general educational objectives are often called aims; the general objectives of schools and curricula are called goals; the objectives of units and lessons are called instructional objectives. Instructional objectives are quite specific. Although some authors distinguish between instructional objectives (referring to objectives that are not behavior specific) and behavioral or performance objectives (referring to objectives that are behavior specific), the terms are used here interchangeably, as if they are synonymous, to emphasize the importance of writing instructional objectives in terms that are measurable.

INSTRUCTIONAL OBJECTIVES AND THEIR RELATIONSHIP TO ALIGNED CURRICULUM AND AUTHENTIC ASSESSMENT

As implied in the previous section, goals guide the instructional methods; objectives drive student performance. Assessment of student achievement in learning should be an assessment of this performance. When the assessment procedure matches the instructional objectives, the assessment is referred to as aligned or **authentic** (discussed further in Chapter 4). When objectives, instruction, and assessment match the stated goals, we have what is referred to as an *aligned curriculum.*

Goals are general statements, usually incomplete sentences often beginning with the infinitive *to,* which identify what the teacher intends students to learn. Objectives, stated in performance (behavioral) terms, are specific actions and should be written as complete sentences that include the verb *will* to indicate what is expected of each student as a result of the instructional experience.

Although instructional goals may not always be quantifiable (i.e., readily measurable), instructional objectives should be measurable. Furthermore, those objectives then become the essence of what is measured for in instruments designed to assess student learning. Consider the examples shown in Figure 3.1.

GOAL INDICATORS AND RESULTS-DRIVEN EDUCATION

One purpose for writing objectives in performance terms is to be able to assess with precision whether the instruction has resulted in the desired learning. In many school districts, the educational goals are established as competencies (i.e., the desired results) that the students are expected to achieve. These goals are then divided into specific performance objectives, sometimes referred to as goal indicators. Instruction is designed to teach toward those objectives. When students perform the competencies called for by these objectives, their education is considered successful. This instruction is known variously as results-driven, criterion-referenced, competency-based, performance-based, or outcome-based education. Expecting students to achieve one set of competencies before moving on to the next set is called mastery learning. The success of the school, teacher performance, and student achievement may each be assessed according to these criteria.

FIGURE 3.1 Examples of Goals and Objectives

Goals

1. To acquire knowledge about the geologic history of the Earth
2. To develop an appreciation for music
3. To develop enjoyment for reading

Objectives

1. On an Earth's geologic time line map, the student will identify the time that the dinosaurs were the dominant creatures on the Earth.
2. The student will identify ten different musical instruments by listening to a tape recording of the Boston Pops Symphony Orchestra and identify which instrument is being played at specified times as determined by the teacher.
3. Within a 2-month period, the student will read two books, three short stories, and five newspaper articles at home and will maintain a daily written journal log of these activities.

Overt and Covert Behavior

Assessment of student learning is not difficult to accomplish when the desired performance outcome is **overt behavior,** that is, when it can be observed directly. Each of the sample objectives shown in Figure 3.1 is an example of an objective that is overt. Assessment is more difficult to accomplish when the desired performance outcome is **covert behavior,** that is, when it is not directly observable. Although certainly no less important, behaviors that call for appreciation, discovery, or understanding, for example, are not directly observable because they occur within a person, and so are covert behaviors. Since covert behavior cannot be observed directly, the only way to tell whether the objective has been achieved is to observe behavior that may be indicative of that achievement. The objective, then, is written in overt language, and evaluators can only assume or trust that the observed behavior is, in fact, reasonably close to being indicative of the expected learning outcome.

Furthermore, when assessing whether an objective has been achieved—whether learning has occurred—the assessment device must be consistent with the desired learning outcome; otherwise the assessment is not aligned—it is invalid. As stated, when the measuring device and the learning objective are compatible, we say that the assessment is authentic. For instance, a person's competency to teach specific skills in physical education to middle school students is best measured (i.e., with highest reliability) by directly observing the teacher doing exactly that—teaching specific skills in physical education to middle school children. Using a standardized paper-and-pencil test of multiple-choice items to determine a person's ability to teach specific physical education skills to middle school children is not authentic assessment.

Balance of Behaviorism and Constructivism

Whereas behaviorists (behaviorism) assume a definition of learning that deals only with changes in observable (overt) behavior, constructivists (constructivism or cognitivism) hold that learning entails the construction or reshaping of mental schemata and that mental processes mediate learning and so are concerned with both overt and covert behaviors.[3] Does this mean that you must be one or the other, a behaviorist or a constructivist? Probably not, but for now the point is that when writing instructional objectives, you should write most or all of your basic expectations (minimal competency expectations) in overt terms (the topic of the next section). On the other hand, you cannot be expected to either foresee all learning that occurs, especially when using integrated thematic instruction, or translate all that is learned into behavioral terms, most certainly not before it occurs.

Any effort to write all learning objectives in behavioral terms is, in effect, neglecting the individual learner who deserves concern; such an approach does not allow for diversity among learners. Learning that is most meaningful to children is not so neatly or easily predicted or isolated. Rather than teaching one objective at a time, you should primarily direct your teaching toward the simultaneous learning of multiple objectives, understandings, and appreciations. When you assess for learning, however, assessment is clearer when objectives are assessed one at a time.

PREPARING INSTRUCTIONAL OBJECTIVES

When preparing instructional objectives, you must ask yourself, "How is the student to demonstrate that the objective has been reached?" or "What student performance will indicate that the objective has been achieved." The objective must include an action that demonstrates whether the objective has been achieved. Inherited from behaviorism, this portion of the objective is sometimes called the terminal behavior or the **anticipated measurable performance**.

Four Key Components to Writing Objectives

When written in behavioral terms, an instructional objective has four key components: audience, behavior, conditions, and degree of expected performance. To aid your understanding and remembering, you can refer to these as the ABCDs of writing performance objectives.

The audience is the student for whom the objective is intended. To address this aspect, sometimes teachers begin their objectives with the phrase, "The student will be able to," or, to personalize the objective, "You will be able to" (Note: To conserve space, in examples that follow we eliminate use of "be able to," and write simply, "The student will" For greater brevity, writers of objectives sometimes use the abbreviation, TSWBAT for "The student will be able to)."

The expected behavior should be written with verbs that are measurable, that is, with action verbs, to allow direct observation that an objective has been reached. As discussed, some verbs are vague,

FIGURE 3.2   Verbs to Avoid when Writing Overt Objectives

appreciate	familiarize	learn
believe	grasp	like
comprehend	indicate	realize
enjoy	know	understand

ambiguous, and not clearly measurable. When writing objectives, you should avoid verbs that are not clearly measurable—verbs that are covert, such as *appreciate, comprehend,* and *understand* (see Figure 3.2). For the three examples given in Figure 3.1, for objectives 1 and 2 the behaviors (action or overt verbs) are "will identify," and, for objective 3, the behaviors are "will read and maintain."

Now do Exercise 3.1 on page 85 to assess and further understand how to select verbs for objectives.

The third ingredient, conditions, includes the setting in which the behavior will be demonstrated by the student and observed by the teacher. For the three sample objectives (Figure 3.1) the conditions are "on a map," "by listening to a tape recording of the Boston Pops Symphony Orchestra," "specified times as determined by the teacher," and "at home within a 2-month period."

Lastly, the degree (or level) of expected performance is not always included in objectives written by teachers. When mastery learning is expected (achievement of 85% to 100%), the level of expected performance is usually omitted (because it is understood). In teaching for mastery learning, the performance-level expectation is 100%. In reality, however, the performance level will most likely be between 85% and 95%, particularly when working with a cohort of students rather than with an individual student. The 5% to 15% difference allows for human error, as can occur when using written and oral communication.

Now do Exercise 3.2 on pages 87 through 88 to reinforce your comprehension and recognition of the components of a behavioral objective.

Performance level is used to assess student achievement, and sometimes to evaluate the effectiveness of the instruction. When given, student grades might be based on performance levels, and evaluation of teacher effectiveness might be based on the level of student performance.

Now do Exercise 3.3 on page 89 to try your skill at recognizing objectives that are measurable.

THE DOMAINS OF LEARNING AND THE DEVELOPMENTAL NEEDS OF STUDENTS

Educators attempt to design learning experiences to meet the five areas of developmental needs of the total child: intellectual, physical, emotional/psychological, social, and moral/ethical. As a teacher, you must include objectives that address learning within each of these categories of needs, not all necessarily in one daily lesson, but certainly all within a single ITU.

Classifying Instructional Objectives

When planning instructional objectives, it is useful to consider the three domains of learning objectives: **cognitive domain**—involves mental operations from the lowest level of the simple recall of information to complex, high-level evaluative processes; **affective domain**—involves feelings, attitudes, and values and ranges from the lower levels of acquisition to the highest level of internalization and action; and **psychomotor domain**—originally dealt with gross to fine motor control, but as used in this guide, ranges from the simple manipulation of materials to the communication of ideas, and finally to the highest level of creative performance. Whereas the intellectual needs are primarily within the cognitive domain and the physical needs are within the psychomotor domain, the other three areas of developmental needs (emotional/psychological, social, and moral/ethical) are mostly within the affective domain.

Too frequently, teachers focus on the cognitive domain while only assuming that the psychomotor and affective domains will take care of themselves. Many experts argue that teachers should do just the opposite; that when the affective domain is directly considered, the psychomotor and cognitive domains naturally develop. In our opinion (we have no strong research basis for this opinion), the use of integrated thematic instruction not only allows but encourages this situation to happen, so as the affective domain is considered, the psychomotor and cognitive domains develop.

As we shall emphasize later in this chapter, the preceding information is not to imply the imposition of an inflexible, linear learning hierarchy. It is intended, however, to imply that there are levels of learning, but recent research about learning indicates that students can be engaged in higher-order thinking about a topic right from the start, as opposed to being guided from the lowest to highest levels of operation within each domain.[4] That is the reason why so many teachers today structure their thematic units around key ideas and central questions designed to encourage student inquiry and self-directed learning. It is the basis for curriculum integration, problem-based learning, and project-centered teaching. Regardless of the name given to the method of helping students to interlink and correlate ideas across content areas, the intent is to facilitate the union of their experiences with knowledge. Learning is complex and not so neatly compartmentalized as this text may seem to imply.

The three domains are discussed next to guide your understanding of each of the five areas of needs. Notice the illustrative verbs within each hierarchy. These verbs help you fashion objectives when developing your ITUs and lessons. Be aware, however, that considerable overlap may occur among the levels at which some action verbs may be appropriately used. For example, the verb *identifies* is appropriate in each of the following objectives at different levels (identified in parentheses) within the cognitive domain:

The student will identify the correct definition of the term *osmosis.* (knowledge)

The student will identify examples of the principle of osmosis. (comprehension)

The student will identify the osmotic effect when a cell is immersed into a hypotonic solution. (application)

The student will identify the osmotic effect on pressure when the cell is placed in a hypotonic solution. (analysis)

Cognitive Domain

In a widely accepted taxonomy of objectives, Bloom and his associates arranged cognitive objectives into classifications according to the complexity of the skills and abilities they embodied.[5] The result was a ladder ranging from the simplest to the most complex intellectual processes. (Theoretically within each domain, prerequisite to a student's ability to function at one particular level of the hierarchy, is the ability to function at the preceding level or levels. In other words, when a student is functioning at the third level of the cognitive domain, that student is automatically also functioning at the first and second levels. Rather than an orderly progression from simple to complex mental operations as illustrated by Bloom's taxonomy, other researchers prefer an organization of cognitive abilities that ranges from simple information storage and retrieval, through a higher level of discrimination and concept attainment, to the highest cognitive ability to recognize and solve problems.[6]

The six major categories (or levels) in Bloom's taxonomy of cognitive objectives are (1) knowledge (recognizing and recalling information), (2) compre-

hension (understanding the meaning of information), (3) application (using information), (4) analysis (dissecting information into its component parts to comprehend their relationships), (5) synthesis (putting components together to generate new ideas), and (6) evaluation (judging the worth of an idea, notion, theory, thesis, proposition, information, or opinion). In this taxonomy, the top four categories or levels—application, analysis, synthesis, and evaluation—represent what are called higher-order thinking skills, as are the higher categories of the affective and psychomotor domains.[7] Although space does not allow elaboration here, Bloom's taxonomy includes various subcategories within each of these six major categories. For reasons implied in the previous section, it is our opinion that it is less important that an objective be absolutely classified than it is to be cognizant of hierarchies of thinking and doing and to understand the importance of attending to student intellectual behavior from lower to higher levels of operation in all three domains. Discussion of each of Bloom's six categories follows.

Knowledge.   The basic element in Bloom's taxonomy concerns the acquisition of knowledge—the ability to recognize and recall information. Although this is the lowest of the six categories, the information to be learned may not itself be of a low level. In fact, it may be of an extremely high level. Bloom includes here knowledge of principles, generalizations, theories, structures, and methodologies and knowledge of facts and ways of dealing with facts.

Action verbs appropriate for this category include *choose, complete, define, describe, identify, indicate, list, locate, match, name, outline, recall, recognize, select,* and *state.*

Following are two example objectives at the knowledge level. Note especially the verb (in italics) used in each example.

- From memory, the student *will recall* the letters in the English alphabet that are vowels.
- The student *will name* the positions of players on a soccer team. (Note: for additional sample objectives at various levels within each of the three domains, see the objectives of the sample lesson plan in Figure 5.3).

The remaining five categories of Bloom's taxonomy of the cognitive domain deal with the use of knowledge. They encompass the educational objectives aimed at developing cognitive skills and abilities, including comprehension, application, analysis, synthesis, and evaluation of knowledge.

Comprehension.   Comprehension includes the ability to translate, explain, or interpret knowledge and to

FIGURE 3.3   Examples of Verbs for Bloom's Categories

1. Knowledge Action Verbs

choose	complete	define	describe	identify	indicate
list	locate	match	name	outline	recall
recognize	select	state			

2. Comprehension Action Verbs

change	classify	convert	defend	estimate	expand
explain	generalize	infer	interpret	paraphrase	predict
recognize	summarize	translate			

3. Application Action Verbs

apply	calculate	demonstrate	develop	discover	modify
operate	participate	perform	plan	predict	relate
show	use				

4. Analysis Action Verbs

analyze	break down	categorize	compare	contrast	debate
deduce	diagram	differentiate	discriminate	identify	illustrate
infer	outline	relate	separate	subdivide	

5. Synthesis Action Verbs

arrange	categorize	combine	compile	constitute	create
design	develop	devise	document	explain	formulate
generate	modify	organize	originate	plan	produce
rearrange	reconstruct	revise	rewrite	summarize	synthesize
tell	transmit	write			

6. Evaluation Action Verbs

appraise	argue	assess	compare	conclude	consider
contrast	criticize	decide	discriminate	evaluate	explain
interpret	judge	justify	rank	rate	relate
standardize	support	validate			

extrapolate from it to address new situations. Action verbs appropriate for this category include *change, complete, define,* and other terms listed in Figure 3.3. Following are examples of objectives in this category:

- From a sentence, the student *will recognize* the letters that are vowels in the English alphabet.
- The student *will recognize* the positions of players on a soccer team.

Application.   Once learners understand information, they should be able to apply it. Action verbs in this category of operation include *apply, compute, demonstrate,* and others included in Figure 3.3. Following are examples of objectives in this category:

- The student *will use* in a sentence a word that contains at least two vowels.
- The student *will relate* how the positions of players on a soccer team depend upon each other.

Analysis.   This category includes objectives that require learners to use the skills of analysis. Action verbs suitable for this category include *analyze, break down, categorize,* and other terms in Figure 3.3. Following are examples of objectives in this category:

- From a list of words, the student *will differentiate* between those words that contain single vowel sounds from those that do not.

- Using a writing board, the student *will illustrate* the different positions of players on a soccer team.

Synthesis.   The category of synthesis includes objectives that involve such skills as designing a plan, proposing a set of operations, and deriving a series of abstract relations. Action verbs appropriate for synthesis include *arrange, categorize, combine,* and others listed in Figure 3.3. Following are examples of objectives in this category:

- From a list of words, the student *will rearrange* them into several lists according to the vowel sounds contained in each.
- Using the writing board, the student *will illustrate* an offensive plan that uses the different positions of players on a soccer team.

Evaluation.   The highest category of Bloom's cognitive taxonomy, evaluation, includes offering opinions and making value judgments. Action verbs appropriate for this category include *appraise, argue, assess,* and the other related verbs listed in Figure 3.3. Following are examples of objectives in this category:

- The student *will listen to and evaluate* other students' identifications of vowels from words in sentences written on the board.
- The student *will interpret* the reasons for an opposing team's offensive use of the different positions of players on a soccer team.

Affective Domain

Krathwohl, Bloom, and Masia developed a useful taxonomy of the affective domain.[8] Following are the major levels or categories, from least internalized to most internalized: (1) *receiving* (i.e., being aware of the affective stimulus and beginning to have favorable feelings toward it); (2) *responding* (i.e., taking an interest in the stimulus and viewing it favorably); (3) *valuing* (i.e., showing a tentative belief in the value of the affective stimulus and becoming committed to it); (4) *organizing* (i.e., placing values into a system of dominant and supporting values); and (5) *internalizing* (i.e., demonstrating consistent beliefs and behavior that have become a way of life). Although one category considerably overlaps another within the affective domain, these categories give a basis by which to judge the quality of objectives and the nature of learning within this area. A discussion of each of the five categories follows.

Receiving.   At the receiving level, which is the least internalized, the learner exhibits willingness to give attention to particular phenomena or stimuli, and the teacher is able to arouse, sustain, and direct that attention. Action verbs appropriate for this category include *ask, choose, describe,* and others found in Figure 3.4.

Responding.   At the responding level, learners respond to the stimulus they have received. They may do so because of some external pressure, because they find the stimulus interesting, or because responding gives them satisfaction. Action verbs appropriate for this category include *answer, applaud, approve,* and others in Figure 3.4. Following are examples of objectives at this level:

- The student *discusses* what others have said.
- The student *cooperates* with others during group activities.

Valuing.   Objectives at the valuing level deal with the learner's beliefs, attitudes, and appreciations. The simplest objectives concern the acceptance of beliefs and values; the higher ones involve learning to prefer certain values and finally becoming committed to them. Action verbs appropriate for this level include *argue, assist, complete,* and others found in Figure 3.4. Following are examples of objectives in this category:

- The student *supports* a position on biological evolution.
- The student *argues* a position on pro-choice for women.

Organizing.   This fourth level in the affective domain concerns the building of a personal value system. Here the learner is conceptualizing and arranging values into a system that recognizes their relative importance. Action verbs appropriate for this level include *adhere, arrange, balance,* and others found in Figure 3.4. Following are examples of objectives in this category:

- The student *integrates* his or her values into a personal work ethic.
- The student *defends* the important values of a particular subculture.

Internalizing.   The last and highest category within the affective domain, internalizing is the level at which the learner's behaviors have become consistent with his or her beliefs. Action verbs appropriate for this level include *act, complete, display,* and others in Figure 3.4. Following are examples of objectives in this category:

- The student *practices* accurate verbal and nonverbal communication.
- The student *performs* independently.

FIGURE 3.4   Examples of Verbs for the Affective Domain

1. Receiving Verbs

ask	choose	describe	differentiate	distinguish	hold
identify	locate	name	point to	recall	recognize
reply	select	use			

2. Responding Verbs

answer	applaud	approve	assist	command	comply
discuss	greet	help	label	perform	play
practice	present	read	recite	report	select
spend (leisure time in)		tell	write		

3. Valuing Verbs

argue	complete	describe	explain	follow	form
initiate	invite	join	justify	propose	protest
read	report	select	share	study	support
work					

4. Organizing Verbs

adhere	alter	arrange	balance	combine	compare
defend	identify	integrate	modify	order	organize
prepare	relate	synthesize			

5. Internalizing Verbs

act	complete	display	influence	listen	modify
perform	practice	propose	qualify	question	revise
serve	solve	verify			

Psychomotor Domain

Whereas identification and classification within the cognitive and affective domains are generally agreed upon, less agreement exists on the classification within the psychomotor domain. Originally, the goal of this domain was simply to develop and categorize proficiency in skills, particularly those dealing with gross and fine muscle control. The classification of the domain presented here follows this lead, but includes at its highest level the most creative and inventive behaviors, thus coordinating skills and knowledge from all three domains. Consequently, the objectives are in a hierarchy ranging from simple gross locomotor control to the most creative and complex control, requiring originality and fine locomotor control, for example, from simply turning on a computer to designing a software program. Harrow offers the following taxonomy of the psychomotor domain: (1) moving, (2) manipulating, (3) communicating, and (4) creating.[9] A discussion of each of the four categories follows.

Moving.   The moving level involves gross motor coordination. Action verbs appropriate for this level include *adjust, carry, clean, grasp, jump, locate, obtain,* and *walk.* Sample objectives for this category include the following:

- The student *will correctly grasp* the putter.
- The student *will carry* the microscope to the desk correctly.

Manipulating.   The manipulating level refers to fine motor coordination. Action verbs suitable for this level include *assemble, build, calibrate, connect, play, thread,* and *turn.* Sample objectives for this category include the following:

- The student *will play* the C-scale on the clarinet.
- The student *will turn* the fine adjustment until the microscope is in focus.

Communicating.   The communicating level involves the communication of ideas and feelings. Action verbs appropriate for this level include *analyze, ask, describe, draw, explain,* and *write.* Sample objectives for this category include the following:

- The student *will draw* what he or she observes on a slide through the microscope.
- The student *will describe* his or her feelings about the cloning of humans.

Creating. The highest level of this domain and all domains, creating represents the student's coordination of thinking, learning, and behaving in all three domains. Action verbs appropriate for this level include *create, design,* and *invent.* Sample objectives for this category include the following:

- The student *will create, choreograph, and perform* a dance pattern.
- The student *will invent and build* a kite pattern.

Now do Exercise 3.4 on page 91 to assess your recognition of performance objectives according to which domain they belong. If needed, turn to Planning Masters 3.1, 3.2, and 3.3 for more objectives to classify with the whole group. Then do Exercise 3.5 on page 93 to begin practice writing your own objectives for use in your ITU.

CHARACTER EDUCATION

Related especially to the affective domain, although not exclusive of the cognitive and psychomotor domains, and also related to integrated curriculum, is the development of students' values. Instruction in regard to honesty, kindness, respect, and responsibility involves what is sometimes called **character education.** Wynne and Ryan state that "transmitting character, academics, and discipline—essentially, 'traditional' moral values—to pupils is a vital educational responsibility."[10] Thus, if one agrees with that interpretation, then the teaching of moral values is the transmission of character, academics, and discipline and clearly implies learning that transcends the three domains of learning presented in this chapter. Whether defined as ethics, citizenship, moral values, or personal development, character education has long been part of public education in this country.[11] Today, stimulated by a perceived need to reduce student antisocial behaviors (such as drug abuse and violence) and to produce more dignified, respectful, and responsible citizens with a primary focus on the affective domain, many schools are developing integrated thematic instruction in character education and in conflict resolution, with the ultimate goal of developing in students values that lead to responsible community and national citizenship and moral action. Specific instructional strategies include (1) sensi-

tizing students to value issues through role play and creative drama; (2) having students take opposing points of view in discussions; (3) promoting higher-order thinking about value issues through inquiry; and (4) action-oriented community-based service projects, inviting parents and community members to assist in the projects, highlighting examples of class and individual cooperation in serving the school and community, and making student service projects visible in the school and community.[12]

USING THE TAXONOMIES

Theoretically, the taxonomies are so constructed that students achieve each lower level before they move to the higher levels. Because categories and behaviors overlap, however, this theory does not always hold in practice. "Thoughts and feelings are inextricably interconnected—we 'think' with our feelings and 'feel' with our thoughts."[13]

The taxonomies are important in that they emphasize the various levels to which instruction must aspire. For student learning to be worthwhile, you must formulate and teach objectives from both the higher levels and the lower levels of the taxonomies. Student thinking and behaving must be moved from the lowest to the highest levels of thinking and behavior. In the end, it is perhaps the highest level of the psychomotor domain (creating) to which we aspire.

In using the taxonomies, remember that the point is to formulate the best objectives for the job to be done. In schools that use results-driven education models, those models describe levels of mastery standards (**rubrics**) for each outcome. The taxonomies provide the mechanism for ensuring that you do not spend a disproportionate amount of time on facts and other low-level learning that is relatively trivial, and can be of tremendous help when teachers are expected to correlate learning activities to one or more of the school or district's outcome standards (see Figure 3.5).

Preparing objectives is essential to the preparation of good items for the assessment of student learning. Clearly communicating your performance expectations to students, and then specifically assessing student learning against those expectations, makes the teaching most efficient and effective and makes the assessment of the learning closer to being authentic. However, you will not always write performance objectives for everything taught, or be able to accurately measure what students have learned. Learning that is meaningful to students is not as easily compartmentalized as the taxonomies of educational objectives would imply.

FIGURE 3.5   Sample School District Expected Learning Outcome Standards

Results-driven education helps produce people who have high self-esteem, are lifelong learners and effective communicators, and are

1. **Problem solvers who**
   - are able to solve problems in their academic and personal lives
   - demonstrate higher-level analytical thinking skills when they evaluate or make decisions
   - are able to set personal and career goals
   - can use knowledge, not simply display it
   - are innovative thinkers

2. **Self-directed learners who**
   - are independent workers
   - can read, comprehend, and interact with text
   - have self-respect with an accurate view of themselves and their abilities

3. **Quality producers who**
   - can communicate effectively in a variety of situations (oral, aesthetic/artistic, nonverbal)
   - are able to use their knowledge to create intelligent, artistic products that reflect originality
   - have high standards

4. **Workers who**
   - are able to work independently and collaboratively
   - show respect for others and their points of view
   - have own values and moral conduct
   - have an appreciation of different cultures

5. **Community contributors who**
   - have an awareness of civic, individual, national, and international responsibilities
   - have an understanding of basic health issues
   - have an appreciation of diversity

OBSERVING FOR CONNECTED (MEANINGFUL) LEARNING: LOGS, PORTFOLIOS, AND JOURNALS

As discussed, in regard to learning that is most important and most meaningful to students, the domains are inextricably interconnected. Consequently, when assessing for student learning, both during instruction (formative assessment) and at the conclusion of the instruction (summative assessment), you must look for these connections.

Ways of looking for connected learning include (1) maintaining a teacher's (or team's) log with daily or nearly daily entries about the progress of each student, and (2) asking the students to maintain individual learning portfolios that document their thinking, work, and learning experiences.

Dated and chronologically organized items that students place in their portfolios can include the following:

-awards	-notes and communications
-brainstorming records	-photos of bulletin board contributions
-records of peer coaching	-sketches of charts, posters, displays and models made by the students
-visual maps	-record of debate contributions
-learning contract(s)	-record of demonstrations/ presentations
-peer evaluations	-mnemonics created by student
-reading record	-contributions to class/team
-records of service	-test and grade records work

Depending on the age and maturity level of the students, another way is to have the students keep a response journal in which they reflect and respond to their learning, using the following five categories:[14]

1. *"I never knew that."* In this category, student responses are primary to factual information, to their new knowledge, and to the bits and pieces of raw information often expected to be memorized regardless of its value to students. However, because this knowledge is fragmented and merely scratches the surface of meaningful learning, it must not be the end of all student learning. Learning that is truly meaningful goes beyond the "I never knew that" category, and students should be encouraged to expand upon the bits and pieces, connect them to something previously known when possible, and write about how the facts make sense related to what they are learning as individuals.

2. *"I never thought of that."* Here, student responses reveal an additional way of perceiving. Their responses may include elements of "not knowing," but also higher-level thinking as a result of their reflection on that knowledge.

3. *"I never felt that."* In this category, student responses are connected to the affective response, eliciting more of an emotional than a cognitive statement. Learning that is truly meaningful is much more than intellectual understanding—it includes a "felt" meaning.[15]

4. *"I never appreciated that."* Responses in this category reflect a sense of recognition that one's own life can be enriched by what others have created or done, or that something already known can be valued from an additional perspective.

5. *"I never realized that."* In this category, student responses indicate an awareness of overall patterns and dynamic ways in which behavior is holistic, establishing meaningful and potentially useful connection among knowledge, values, and purposes.

The topics of portfolios and student journals are discussed further in Chapter 4.

LEARNING THAT IS NOT IMMEDIATELY OBSERVABLE

Unlike behaviorists, constructivists do not limit the definition of learning to that which is observable behavior, nor should you. Bits and pieces of new information are stored in short-term memory, where the new information is "rehearsed" until ready to be stored in long-term memory. If the information is not rehearsed, it eventually fades from short-term memory. If it is rehearsed and made meaningful through connections with other stored knowledge, then this new knowledge is transferred to and stored in long-term memory, either by building existing schemata or by forming new schemata. As a teacher, your responsibility is to provide learning experiences that will result in the creation of new schemata and to modify existing schemata.

To be an effective teacher, your challenge is to use performance-based criteria simultaneously with a teaching style and learning experiences that encourage the development of intrinsic sources of student motivation. Such sources allow, provide, and encourage coincidental learning—learning that goes beyond what might be considered predictable, immediately measurable, and representative of minimal expectations. Interdisciplinary thematic instruction can provide an important educational vehicle for accomplishing this task. Also related to this challenge is selecting appropriate learning activities, which is the topic of the second half of this chapter.

REFINEMENT OF GOALS AND OBJECTIVES: ANOTHER SHARING OF MATERIALS

As a raison d'être for your ITU, you should write its educational goals, especially those linked to pertinent school, district, and state documents, to give you an overview and help you identify the topic of the unit and what the students are to learn as recommended/mandated/suggested by the documents. An overview of the unit can be extended to indicate what you hope the students will learn—your teacher goals. You can include what understanding the students will develop, what skills will be fostered, and what attitudes and appreciations will be addressed during the unit.

After writing the raison d'être/overview, it is an appropriate time for you to complete your goals and polish your objectives for the ITU that you want to initiate. If you are working as a member of a teaching team, each team member should give every other team member a copy of goals and objectives written independently. Then each member can refine the ITU from that member's point of view as he or she reads and reviews the objectives and goals of the other team members. This process should help the team avoid any confusion in the students' minds when the unit is presented. It should also help eliminate any unnecessary overlap of process or content.

SELECTING AND DEVELOPING LEARNING ACTIVITIES

Activities that engage the students in learning constitute the heart and spirit of the ITU. Some activities start a unit into motion; they begin the unit-initiating momentum. Some learning activities comprise the heart of the unit (ongoing activities), and some activities bring the unit to a natural closure (culminating activities). Although nearly limitless, the list in Figure 3.6 gives you many options from which you can choose activities for any of these three categories. Some may overlap in regard to category or naturally fit one category better than another.

The Common Thread

Central to the selection and development of learning activities for interdisciplinary thematic instruction is a common thread of four tightly interwoven components: (1) instruction that is centered around a large, meaningful idea (theme) rather than on factitious subject areas; (2) decision making and responsibility for learning that is shared by the students and the teacher; (3) selected learning activities that actively engage all students in their learning, which means they are physically active (hands-on learning) and mentally active (minds-on learning); and (4) reflection and sharing about what is being done and what is being learned.

Initiating Activities

An ITU can be initiated in countless ways. You must decide which ways are appropriate for your educational goals and objectives, for your own group of students and their interests, abilities, and skills, and for the time that can be devoted to the duration of the unit. You might start with a current event, a community problem, an artifact, a book, or something interesting found on the Internet. Consider some of the following approaches to initiating a unit. (Note: the terms in bold type were used to initiate the studies in the examples that follow.)

display	**learning center**	**inquiry**
current event	painting	**role play**
problem-focus	**questions**	social actions
replica	people/places in community	outdoor adventure

At Marquette Middle School (Madison, Wisconsin), for example, students initially were asked to list questions about themselves and their world. They were then asked to identify a number of themes suggested by their questions. From their list of possibilities students then selected one theme, "Living in the Future." They next began listing activities they might use to find possible answers to their questions related to their selected theme.[16]

Sometimes teachers introduce the unit with a focus on some problem or current event, such as a video showing a prom night automobile accident (refer to the "Inspector" example discussed in Chapter 1).

FIGURE 3.6   Examples of Instructional Strategies

Assignment	Group work	Problem solving
Autotutorial	Guest speaker	Project
Brainstorming	Homework	Questioning
Coaching	Individualized instruction	Review and practice
Collaborative learning	Inquiry	Role play
Cooperative learning	Interactive media	Self-instructional module
Debate	Journal writing	Script writing
Demonstration	Laboratory investigation	Simulation
Diorama	Laser videodisk	Study guide
Discovery	Lecture	Symposium
Drama	Library/resource center	Telecommunication
Drill	Metacognition	Term paper
Expository	Mock-up	Textbook
Field trip	Multimedia	Think-pair-share
Game	Panel discussion	Tutorial

Often, to help students see the connections between various content areas, the ITU activities are designed to allow students to assume roles of real-world professionals. An initiating activity for elementary students could be centered around introducing them to points of view from various disciplines. Such an introduction does not have to be deadly dull. For instance, you and the students might begin a particular study by reading books related to an underlying guiding question (idea/problem/topic/theme), a process that perhaps lasts 2 or 3 days. Then the students might plan an ITU or review a proposed plan, individually reserving "ownership" of some inquiries. Over the next few days, you and the students might approach the unit from the point of view of a particular discipline, perhaps moving on to a different discipline approximately every few days.

Suppose the perspective of an archeologist is needed for an ITU. As the teacher, you could first solicit and introduce questions an archeologist would ask and discuss, and then demonstrate how an archeologist would organize and share information about the topic. To help students understand an archeologist's perspective, you could briefly and succinctly introduce knowledge and skills unique to that discipline. For example, you might choose to do this by using excerpts from the book, *You Can Be a Woman Egyptologist,* by Betsy M. Bryan and Judith L. Cohen (New York: Cascade Press, 1993). In this work, an Egyptologist explains how she became interested in the profession, what work she does, and what discoveries she has made. This book is suitable for reading aloud.

If the perspective of a paleontologist is needed for an ITU, you might consider using excerpts from the novel, *My Daniel,* by Pam Conrad (New York: Harper & Row, 1989). In this story, 80-year-old Julia Creath Summerwaite takes her grandchildren to New York's Museum of Natural History to see the dinosaur exhibit. She also tells them about her brother, Daniel, a paleontologist, his passion for fossils, and how he engaged in fierce competition with other paleontologists for treasures in Nebraska.

On subsequent days, you could encourage students to see things from the vantage point of various other disciplines—economics, anthropology, history, and so on. Through this process, you get the students involved in thinking about what can be explored and what inquiries can be made from the perspective of various disciplines. Once the students are introduced to some of the knowledge and skills of different disciplines, they can use what they have learned as they make their own interdisciplinary inquiries through an ITU.

One effective way to introduce students to the perspective of a discipline is to encourage them to assume the role of a professional in that discipline as they examine some topic or content. Figure 3.7 might give you some ideas about how to help students assume such roles (see also Planning Master 3.4).

Some teachers use outdoor adventures to stimulate interest in a particular unit of interdisciplinary thematic instruction.[17] Possibilities include the following:

- fast-food fact finding
- local pollution problem
- nature in the city
- reading a cemetery "story"
- urban predator-prey relationships

- people, places, and things at the shopping center
- one city block
- starting a homestead

As another example, while detailing the collaboration between two teachers of different grade levels, one teacher writes of her experience using the theme of "discoveries on the outside and the inside" to integrate the disciplines within her self-contained fifth-grade classroom, while immersing her students in colonial life and using reading, writing, simulations, and debates to bring life to the era. To collaborate, the sixth-grade teacher and her students in language arts stepped into the lives of colonial characters unlike themselves to explore the differences in culture, race, and social class.

Ongoing Activities

Once the ITU has been initiated, the students become occupied with a variety of ongoing activities such as those listed in Figure 3.6. In working with students in selecting and planning the ongoing learning activities, you will want to keep in mind the concept represented by the learning experiences ladder (Figure 2.11) and your predetermined goals and objectives.

If there are specific curriculum requirements from the state, district, or school that must be addressed in the ITU, you can reference the requirements by activity in the scope-and-sequence plan. If desired, you may also reference which sections of the state framework, district curriculum document(s), and local school documents are being addressed through each activity. Your reference notes may look like the following:

Activities in Scope-and-Sequence Plan	*State, District, and School Documents as References*
1. Activity A	1. Reference(s) for A

FIGURE 3.7 Assuming Roles as a Way to Introduce Students to Various Disciplines

Anthropology

Taking the role of an anthropologist. The students can ask, "How will our experience(s) in our own culture help us understand the way other people live?" or "How might ethnocentric views and limited experiences hinder our understandings of other cultures?" When the students take this role, they show that they are getting involved in direct observation as the primary way to gather data. They focus on a relationship between people's behaviors and their beliefs. While taking the anthropologist's role, students see each culture as one variety of human behavior among the many possibilities and can inquire, "What direct observations can we make to see a relationship about the behavior of people and their beliefs?"

Economics

Taking the role of an economist. The students can ask, "How is work in the economy done by people to develop and bring information to us?" In this role, the students can show that they are interested in the resolution of problems, such as unemployment, that exist in our society. In this role, they can also inquire, "What economic problem(s) can be identified?" and "What resolutions of the problem(s) can be suggested?"

Expressive Arts

Taking the role of an artist. The students can ask, "How can we show what we know about the subject through the visual and performing arts, such as art, music, dance, and sculpture?" Taking this role, the students can demonstrate they are interested in art and artists and the messages they send through visual representations.

Geography

Taking the role of a geographer. The students can ask, "How has geography influenced the topic and what we know about the topic?" The students show that they are interested in the natural features of an area. In this role, they can also inquire, "What features—land, water—can be described?" and "What distribution of living things, that is, plant and animal life, is featured?"

History

Taking the role of an historian. The students can ask, "How has this topic changed over time?" and "How have ways we receive information about the topic changed over time?" In this role, the students can demonstrate that they are interested in a record of facts about a person, place, or event, including ancestry, environment, and past experiences. They can also inquire, "How have past events been explained?"

Mathematics

Taking the role of a mathematician. The students can ask, "How can we express what we know about the topic through mathematics?" and "How can mathematics help us learn more about this topic?" In this role, the students can demonstrate that they are interested in a record of relations about known quantities related to the theme/topic.

Political Science

Taking the role of a political scientist. The students can ask, "How have people organized themselves to provide information about the topic?" In this role, they expand their knowledge about government and politics.

Science

Taking the role of a scientist. The students can ask, "What scientists operate to bring us information about the topic?" and "How can science help us learn more about this?" In this role, they can expand their understanding of science through observation and classification of facts.

Sociology

Taking the role of a sociologist. The students can ask, "What groups in society operate to bring us information about the topic?" and "In what ways in the community can we participate to resolve a real problem related to the topic?" In this role, they can show ways they are committed to understanding aspects of sociology that can give a sense of the relationship between humans and society and a sense of how the world is or is not predictable.

Other Disciplines

Disciplines selected by the students and teacher.

Olé! This culminating activity provides students with a fun and interesting way to end a unit on Mexico.

As an example of ongoing learning activities, a third-grade teacher used a learning center to initiate an ITU centered around the theme of changes and the topic of chromatography (the separation of mixtures, often into various colored layers). While working at the center, students tested the colors of water-soluble ink markers, making predictions about the separations of their colors. For example, they tested the ink of a green marker (blue and yellow), the ink of an orange marker (red and yellow), the ink of a purple marker (red and blue), and the ink of other markers selected by the students. They recorded their predictions and results on data sheets with headings similar to the following:

Ink I Used	What I Predicted	What I Observed
1. green		
2. orange		
3. purple		
4. other		

Using long strips of paper towels, the students folded the top of each strip so that it hung from the rim of a drinking glass, while the other end almost touched the inside bottom. Once the strips were folded to the correct length, the students marked a band of color about 2 inches up from the bottom of the strip. After placing a marked strip in the glass, students would add about 1 inch of water, 0.5 inch or more below the color band and enough to cover about 0.25 inch of the bottom of the paper. They then observed what happened as the water moved up the strip (by capillary action) and into, through, and above the colored band, recording the results of their observations on their data sheets.

Following are examples of how the teacher and students connected this activity to other disciplines.

- *Art.* The student put colors on coffee filters and re-did their chromatography experiment. They then cut different shapes from the filters to mount on a class mural to demonstrate what colors the different inks separated into during their experiments. Insect and other animal shapes were cut from the filters, and the teacher suggested that the students glue those shapes to paper. Drawings were added that camouflaged the creatures, showing the effectiveness or lack of effectiveness some of the colors might have in protecting living things from danger.
- *Ecology.* The camouflage activity (from art) was used to initiate further study about rain forest habitats and the camouflage used by living creatures there.
- *History.* The students researched individuals in history who had in some way or another been protected by camouflage, such as the "mossbackers" of Civil War days who hid in the southern swamps to avoid conscription.
- *Language arts.* The students were presented with a fictional situation in which spots of a foreign material were found on a piece of clothing, and then the students created a mystery/detective story about it.
- *Literature.* Literature was introduced that was related to the ITU. *Hide and Snake* by Keith Baker (New York: Harcourt, 1991) was presented so the students could see how a snake hid near familiar objects in a game of hide and seek. A nature hunt was reviewed using *How to Hide a Butterfly and Other Insects* by Ruth Heller (New York: Grossett &

Dunlap, 1985). The teacher also showed illustrations from the book on an opaque projector and asked students to locate camouflaged bees, butterflies, inchworms, and other hidden creatures.

Throughout the unit of study, a classroom rack of books related to color was located near the learning center. Among the many titles, it displayed the following: *Color Dance* by Ann Jonas (New York: Greenwillow, 1989), in which dancers demonstrate what happens when red and yellow (and other colors) are mixed; Arnold Lobel's *The Great Blueness and Other Predicaments* (New York: Harper & Row, 1968), a story set in a colorful world that describes a wizard and his paint pots who explores why the red mice that once lived with blue trees, yellow ice, and black cheese have disappeared; and *Mouse Paint* by Ellen Stoll (New York: Harcourt, Brace, Jovanovich, 1989), in which color concepts are introduced through the actions of three mice. The mice cavort in and out of red, yellow, and blue paint, making paint puddles and thus discovering the colors of green, orange, and purple.

At various times during the study, different color experiments and activities were available at the learning center, such as placing celery in food dye to observe the movement of molecules (also caused by capillary action), learning the technique of marbleizing paper, and using litmus paper to determine if a substance is acidic or basic.

Students designed and constructed three pairs of eyeglasses with ear frames, using heavy art paper. The lenses (color filters) were made from red, yellow, and blue cellophane. Students observed items through the different color filters and made predictions about what would happen to the color of the items when viewed through the different filters. They tested their predictions and recorded their results on a journal page with the following headings:

Colored Item I Selected	What I Predicted	What I Observed
1.	1.	1.
2.	2.	2.
3.	3.	3.

At the beginning of the chromatography unit, the teacher captured the students' attention with the development of a question map, a useful way to initiate an ITU. To have the experience of recording questions on a question map, just as you would do in your own classroom, do Exercise 3.6 on page 95. After you complete Exercise 3.6, do Exercise 3.7 on pages 97 to 98 to identify investigations that could prove useful in inquiring about the questions. After Exercise 3.7 is complete, do Exercise 3.8 on pages 99 through 104, where you are asked to write a specific teaching plan.

Culminating Activities

An ITU is brought to closure with a culminating activity. Such an activity often includes sharing the product of the students' study. You could accept the students' suggestions for a culminating activity if it engages them in summarizing what they have learned with others. A culminating activity that brings closure to a unit can give the students an opportunity for synthesis (by assembling, constructing, creating, inventing, producing, or incorporating a product) and even an opportunity to present that synthesis to an audience, such as by establishing an Internet website or sharing their product on an existing school website. See, for example, the web page of Artis Elementary School (Ypsilanti, Michigan) at <http://www.microstore.com/ardis/index.html> or that of Goodby High School (Tallahassee, Florida) and other elementary, middle, and high schools at <http://www.seri.fsu.edu/~dennisl/cms.html>.

With a culminating activity, you can provide opportunity for the students to move from recording information to reporting on their learning. Examples of culminating activities are endless:

- At North Middle School (O'Fallon, Missouri), four interdisciplinary core teachers taught an interdisciplinary thematic study about immigrants. It culminated when the students as immigrants became naturalized citizens by completing a required assignment. The assignment included a group presentation, a spreadsheet and graph, a fairy tale from the home country, and a natural resource map. Activities leading up to this finale included the students assuming an identity and receiving an official document that contained visas for the unit. The students also went through processing and naturalization as "immigrants," encountering the problems and prejudices faced daily by many real immigrants.
- At the end of an interdisciplinary thematic unit taught by an interdisciplinary core team of teachers (mathematics, science, social studies, and reading), seventh graders developed an earthquake safety guide.
- Another activity can schedule the students to take field trips to study something related to the theme and then synthesize their learning after the trip in a way that culminates the study. On field trips, students can be given notepads similar to the ones reporters use and asked to take notes and make sketches of what they learn. They can discuss what questions they have on the ride to the site. They can discuss what they liked and did not like on the ride back to the school. They can videotape both discussions and replay them in the classroom. After

Working independently, this teacher takes the time to plan the activities of the unit in a logical sequence.

the trip, the students individually choose something interesting that they saw on the trip and then build a scale model of it. The teacher and students might devote a full afternoon or more to working with rulers, yardsticks, cardboard, clay, and other materials to create their models. The students could then invite other classes to examine the scale models and listen to student reports about why an object caught their interest. Students might also present an art show of drawings about the unit's theme, with a narration that informs others about their study.

- As still another culminating activity, you can ask students to report on individual projects—the aspect each student formerly reserved for individual study.

Culminating activities are opportunities for students to proudly demonstrate and share their learning in different and individual ways. Now gain additional insight into how to bring an ITU to closure by doing Exercise 3.9 on pages 105 through 107.

SUMMARY

As a result of studying this chapter, you have prepared objectives, selected resources, and planned learning activities for a minimum time frame. Through a review of the learning activities, you were engaged in identifying intellectual processes, disciplines, subject areas, and learning styles and needs of the students. You have learned about closing the ITU with a final activity that allows the students to proudly share what they have learned and to creatively display what their skills have produced during the unit. You have learned that you can choose from a variety of beginnings and activities for a unit and choose specific areas of the curriculum to include in the study. You also participated in a simulation with others in the activity of developing a question map to initiate a unit, and used the questions to identify concept words for the unit. In essence, you have started to develop an ITU. In Chapter 4 you will learn more about the assessment component of interdisciplinary thematic instruction.

QUESTIONS AND ACTIVITIES FOR DISCUSSION

1. In small groups, discuss the complex and challenging tasks of collaborative learning, cooperative learning, negotiated curriculum, risk-taking, group-initiated learning, and visuals as teaching and learning processes that can be a part of an ITU approach. Each member of the group can be responsible for presenting information about one of the approaches. Discuss the uses of each approach, and if time allows, any abuses you know about from personal experience.

2. Explore research articles, professional journals, and the Internet to find additional examples of ITUs, especially for their initiating and culminating activities. Share what you find with your classmates.

3. From your experiences and personal observations, clearly identify one specific example of educational practice that seems contradictory to exemplary practice or theory as presented in this chapter. Present your explanation for the discrepancy.

4. Do you have concerns about selecting activities for an ITU? Recall your own schooling and what you remember about the activities in which you were involved. With your classmates, share your experiences and the pluses and minuses related to them.

5. Do you have other questions generated by the content of this and the previous two chapters? If so, list them and discuss with your colleagues ways to find answers.

INDIVIDUAL NOTES

EXERCISE 3.1

Recognizing Verbs that Are Acceptable for Overt Objectives— a Self-Check Exercise

Instructions.:   The purpose of this exercise is to check your recognition of verbs that are suitable for use in overt objectives. From the following list of verbs, circle those that should not be used in overt objectives—those that describe covert behaviors that are directly observable and measurable. Check your answers against the answer key that follows. Discuss any problems that you have with this exercise with your classmates and instructor.

1. apply	11. design	21. know
2. appreciate	12. diagram	22. learn
3. believe	13. enjoy	23. name
4. combine	14. explain	24. outline
5. comprehend	15. familiarize	25. predict
6. compute	16. grasp	26. realize
7. create	17. identify	27. select
8. define	18. illustrate	28. solve
9. demonstrate	19. indicate	29. state
10. describe	20. infer	30. understand

Answer key

The following verbs should be circled: 2, 3, 5, 13, 15, 16, 19, 21, 22, 26, 30. If you missed more than a couple, then you need to review the preceding sections and discuss your errors with your classmates and instructor.

EXERCISE 3.2

Recognizing the Parts of Criterion-Referenced Behavioral Objectives

Instructions. The purpose of this exercise is to practice your skill in recognizing the four components of a behavioral objective that establishes criteria—standards and preset guidelines for student behaviors. In the following two objectives, identify the parts of each objective by underlining once the *audience,* twice the *behavior,* three times the *conditions,* and four times the *performance level* (the degree or standard of performance).

Check your answers against the answer key that follows, and discuss any problems that you have with your classmates and instructor.

1. Given a metropolitan transit bus schedule, at the end of the lesson the students will be able to read the schedule well enough to determine at what time buses are scheduled to leave randomly selected locations, with at least 90% accuracy.
2. Given five rectangular figures, you will correctly compute the area in square centimeters of at least four figures, by measuring the length and width with a ruler and computing the product using an appropriate calculation method.

Answer key

	objective 1	*objective 2*
audience (underlined once)	The student	You
behavior (underlined twice)	will be able to read the schedule	will compute
conditions (underlined three times)	given a metropolitan transit bus schedule	given five rectangular figures
performance level (degree) (underlined four times)	well enough to determine (and) with at least 90% accuracy	correctly compute the area in square centimeters for at least four figures (80% accuracy)

NOTES

EXERCISE 3.3

Recognizing Objectives That Are Measurable

Instructions. The purpose of this exercise is to assess your ability to recognize objectives that are measurable. Place an X before each of the following that is an overt, student-centered behavioral objective, a learning objective that is clearly measurable. Although the terms *audience*, *conditions*, or *performance levels* may be absent, ask yourself, "As stated, is this a student-centered and measurable objective?" If so, place an X in the blank. A self-checking answer key follows. After checking your answers, discuss any problems you have with the exercise with your classmates and instructor.

_____ 1. To develop an appreciation for literature

_____ 2. To identify those celestial bodies that are known planets

_____ 3. To provide meaningful experiences for the students

_____ 4. To recognize antonym pairs

_____ 5. To boot up a selected program on the computer

_____ 6. To analyze and compare patterns of data or specific quartile maps

_____ 7. To develop skills in inquiry

_____ 8. To identify which of the four causes is most relevant to the major events leading up to America's Civil War

_____ 9. To use maps and graphs to identify the major areas of world petroleum production and consumption

_____ 10. To know the causes for the diminishing atmospheric ozone concentration

Answer key

You should have marked items 2, 4, 5, 6, 8, and 9.

Items 1, 3, 7, and 10 are inadequate because of their ambiguity. Item 3 is not even a student learning objective—it is a teacher goal. "The phrases to develop" and "to know" can have too many interpretations. Although the conditions are not given, items 2, 4, 5, 6, 8, and 9 are clearly measurable. The teacher would have no difficulty recognizing when a learner has reached those objectives.

NOTES

EXERCISE 3.4

A Self-Check on Assessing Recognition of Cognitive, Affective, and Psychomotor Objectives

Instructions.   The purpose of this exercise is to recognize objectives and classify them as being in the cognitive, affective, or psychomotor domain. In the blank space, write the appropriate letter according to the domain: (C) cognitive, (P) psychomotor, and (A) affective. Check your responses at the end of this exercise.

_____ 1.   The student will jump rope until he or she can jump it 10 subsequent times without missing.

_____ 2.   The student can identify and spell the capitals of all 50 states.

_____ 3.   The student can summarize the origin of the Peace Corps in the United States.

_____ 4.   The student will demonstrate an interest in using the microscope by volunteering to work with it during free time.

_____ 5.   The student will volunteer to help keep the classroom tidy.

_____ 6.   The student will be able to identify respective poets, after reading and discussing several poems.

_____ 7.   The child will translate a Spanish poem into English.

_____ 8.   The student will accurately predict the results of combining genes from the available gene pool.

_____ 9.   The student will voluntarily read additional material about ancient Greek civilization.

_____ 10.   The student will practice the ring toss until achieving a minimum of 7 in 10 attempts.

How did you do with this exercise? If you scored 100%, then go on to Exercise 3.5. If you missed any, talk them over with your classmates.

See answer key on following page

Answer key to Exercise 3.4

    (A) 4, 5, 9
    (P) 1, 10
    (C) 2, 3, 6, 7, 8

EXERCISE 3.5

Preparing My Objectives for an ITU

Instructions.   The purpose of this exercise is to give you an opportunity to write your own instructional objectives. To begin, select a grade level and content topic you will likely teach. Write nine specific instructional objectives for the topic, and include both performance and conditions.

_____

(grade level)

_____

(content topic)

Cognitive knowledge

Cognitive comprehension

Cognitive application

Cognitive analysis

Cognitive synthesis

Cognitive evaluation

Psychomotor

Affective (low level)

Affective (high level)

When you have completed this exercise, exchange papers with a member of your group. Discuss the objectives that were written and make any changes that are needed.

EXERCISE 3.6

Initiating an ITU with a Question Map

Instructions. The purpose of this exercise is to work with a partner or partners and write questions related to a theme you identified in Chapter 2. With your partners taking the role of students, have them participate in a discussion concerning "what we want to know" about the theme. Write their questions on a question map located on the writing board. Show the partners how you can group their related questions (main questions and subquestions). Ask them to think of headings for the different categories of related questions. Use the following format for recording the input.

1. Theme:

2. Main question:

3. Related subquestions:

   a.

   b.

   c.

Copy the question map from the board to this page so you can use it as a reference.

EXERCISE 3.7

Connecting Questions and Activities for an ITU

Instructions.   The purpose of this exercise is to work to connect the questions related to your theme and to ongoing learning activities in specific detail. Learning activities can be planned around some central questions (and subquestions) about the theme. The investigative activities needed to inquire about the questions can provide various opportunities for you to respond to the learning styles and needs of your students.

   With your partners, return to the "what we want to know" question map that originated from Exercise 3.6. Use the information to design some learning activities for the unit. (Figure 1.3 shows some examples of questions and related activities).

List of learning activities related to the questions and subquestions:

1.

2.

3.

4.

5.

6.

EXERCISE 3.8

Combining Objectives, Resources, and Learning Activities for a Teaching Plan

Instructions.   The purpose of this exercise is to write a specific teaching plan for a minimum of 1 day, incorporating what you have done to prepare goals, write objectives, select resources, and select and plan learning activities. You may want to reference the learning activities to state frameworks, district documents, and local school curriculum. Ask a peer to read and react to your teaching plan. Does your plan convey what you intended to say? What new questions came to mind as you wrote the plan and as it was reviewed by others?

Teaching Plan

Interdisciplinary unit theme:

Main focus question:

Related subquestions:

Objectives:
(What will the students learn?)

(What thinking skills such as observing, communicating, comparing, categorizing, inferring, and applying will the students develop?)

(What attitudes will be fostered?)

Resources (media, display visuals, artifacts, computer and software):

Specifics of Learning Activity/Activities

Preassessment of Student Learning (How will you determine what students know or think they know about the subject at the start of the unit?)

Example 1. Consider introducing the strategy of think-pair-share, during which the topic/question is written on the board and the students are asked in pairs to think about the topic, discuss it between themselves, and then together share with the whole class what they know or think they already know about the topic while the teacher writes the major thoughts on the board, perhaps in the form of a concept web.

Example 2. Consider using the KWL reading comprehension strategy, with the teacher directing the discussion. Label three columns on the board or overhead projector. The left-hand column contains what students already *know* or think they know about the topic; the middle column contains a list of what the students *want* to learn about the topic; the right-hand column is left blank and filled in at the end or during the study with what is and has been *learned* about the topic.

Formative Evaluation (techniques used to assess student learning in progress to ensure that they are on the right track)

Check discipline areas used   *Provide a brief description of how areas were used*

_____ 1.   Sciences

_____ 2.   Social sciences/history

_____ 3.   Mathematics

_____ 4.   Reading and language

_____ 5.   Poetry and prose

_____ 6.   Music and dance

_____ 7.   Painting and sculpture

_____ 8.   Health and physical education

_____ 9.   Other

Feedback

1. What was the reaction of your peer to your teaching plan?

2. In your opinion, does your plan effectively convey what you originally envisioned?

3. Does it need more detail or revision?

4. Do your selected learning activities appropriately address the varied learning styles of your students?

5. What new questions came to mind as you wrote the plan and as it was reviewed?

EXERCISE 3.9

Planning Culminating Activities

Instructions. The purpose of this exercise is to develop a closure for the unit (even though you realize that inquiry can be lifelong and has no official closure). In this exercise, you must determine what will affect the length of your unit—the interest of your students in the topic, the resources that are available or unavailable, the school holidays, the academic calendar for your school year, and any competing events such as picture day, assemblies, athletic events, and field trips.

1. Which of the following would you incorporate into the culmination of a unit? Explain why.

   a. Creating new problems related to the topic and demonstrating a way to resolve them

   b. Designing a chart, map, time line, classroom museum of exhibits, an interdisciplinary thematic fair, and a classroom "main street" with booths (learning centers) and reporting on the data the design represents

   c. Preparing an oral and written presentation on an aspect of the topic; using such creative ways to present data as sketches, sculpture works, cartoons, popular songs, a comic strip format, costume props, a story board, puppets, flannel board figures, rhymes, limericks, and other forms of poetry

d. Creating and producing a drama

e. Writing and publishing a newsletter or brochure on the topic

f. Writing and publishing a book

g. Creating a class or student cohort web page regarding the unit

h. Presenting data with one or more of the following:

advertisements	fables and myths	poetry
art works	fairy tales and folktales	puppet shows
albums and books	family trees	scrapbooks
book jackets	filmstrips and slides	scripts for skits
bulletin boards	greeting cards	songs and instruments
card and board games	illustrations for stories	stencils
collages	maps and murals	tape recordings
costumes	pantomimes	video recordings

i. Other

2. What activity/activities could you plan that would permit your students to synthesize what they have learned in the unit and then report the synthesis to a selected audience?

3. From the activities suggested in question 2, evaluate each suggestion and narrow the choices to two options by considering various needs in your classroom (i.e., diversity and learning value of the activity). Record the two choices here.

INDIVIDUAL NOTES

CHAPTER NOTES

1. P. L. Roberts, *A Green Dinosaur Day: A Guide for Developing Thematic Units in Literature-Based Instruction, K–6* (Needham Heights, MA: Allyn & Bacon, 1993); Courtesy of Kristie Darras of the Elk Grove Unified School District, Elk Grove, CA.
2. T. L. Good and J. E. Brophy, *Looking in Classrooms* (7th ed), New York: Longman, 1997), p. 240.
3. See J. A. Zahorik, *Constructivist Teaching* (Bloomington, IN: Fastback 390, Phi Delta Educational Foundation, 1995).
4. T. L. Good and J. E. Brophy, *Looking in Classrooms* (New York: Longman, 1997), p. 399.
5. B. S. Bloom (ed.), *Taxonomy of Educational Objectives, Book I, Cognitive Domain* (White Plains, NY: Longman, 1984).
6. See R. M. Gagné, L. J. Briggs, and W. W. Wager, *Principles of Instructional Design* (4th ed.), (New York: Holt, Rinehart and Winston, 1994).
7. Compare Bloom's higher-order thinking skills with R. H. Ennis's "A Taxonomy of Critical Thinking Dispositions and Abilities," and Qellmalz's "Developing Reasoning Skills," both in J. B. Barron and R. J. Sternberg (eds.), *Teaching Thinking Skills: Theory and Practice* (New York: W. H. Freeman, 1987), and with Marzano's "complex thinking strategies" in R. J. Marzano, *A Different Kind of Classroom: Teaching with Dimension of Learning* (Alexandria, VA: Association for Supervision and Curriculum Development, 1992).
8. D. R. Kratwohl, B. S. Bloom, and B. B. Masia, *Taxonomy of Educational Goals, Handbook 2, Affective Domain* (New York: David McKay, 1964).
9. A. J. Harrow, *Taxonomy of the Psychomotor Domain* (New York: Longman, 1977). A similar taxonomy for the psychomotor domain is that of E. J. Simpson, *The Classification of Educational Objectives in the Psychomotor Domain. The Psychomotor Domain: Volume 3* (Washington, DC: Gryphon House, 1972).
10. E. A. Wynne and K. Ryan, *Reclaiming Our Schools: A Handbook on Teaching Character, Academics, and Discipline* (Upper Saddle River, NJ: Prentice Hall, 1993), p. 3; see also P. L. Roberts, *Family Values in Fiction for Grades K–3* (Lanham, MD: Scarecrow Press, 1999).
11. K. Burrett and R. Rusnak, *Integrated Character Education* (Bloomington, IN: Fastback 351, Phi Delta Kappa Educational Foundation, 1993), p. 10.
12. See, for example, the articles in the theme issues "Youth and Caring," *Phi Delta Kappan*, 76(9), (May, 1995), and "Education for a Democratic Society," *Educational Leadership*, 54 (5), (February, 1997).
13. G. Caine and R. N. Caine, "The Critical Need for a Mental Model of Meaningful Learning," *California Catalyst*, (Fall, 1992), p. 19.
14. Adapted from S. Fersh, *Integrating the Trans- National/Cultural Dimension* (Bloomington, IN: Fastback 361, Phi Delta Kappa Educational Foundation, 1993), pp. 23–24.
15. G. Caine and R. N. Caine, p. 19.
16. J. Beane, *Integrated Curriculum in the Middle School* (Urbana, IL: ERIC Clearinghouse on Elementary and Early Childhood Education, 1992).
17. See, for example, C. E. Knapp, *Just Beyond the Classroom: Community Adventures for Interdisciplinary Learning* (Charleston, WV: ERIC Clearinghouse on Rural Education and Small Schools, 1996).

FOR FURTHER READING

Kellough, R. D. (1997). *A resource guide for teaching: K–12* (2nd ed.). Upper Saddle River, NJ: Merrill/Prentice Hall.

Kellough, R. D., & Kellough, N. G. (1999). *Secondary school teaching: A guide to methods and resources.* Upper Saddle River, NJ: Merrill/Prentice Hall.

Kellough, R. D., & Roberts, P. L. (1998). *A resource guide for elementary school teaching: Planning for competence* (4th ed.). Upper Saddle River, NJ: Merrill/Prentice Hall.

McTighe, J. (1996, December/January). What happens between assessments? *Educational Leadership*, 54(4), 6–12.

Novick, R. (1996). *Developmentally appropriate and culturally responsive education: Theory in practice.* Portland, OR: Northwest Regional Educational Laboratory.

Roberts, P. L. (1997). *Literature-based history activities for children, grades 1–3.* Boston: Allyn & Bacon.

Roberts, P. L. (1997). *Literature-based history activities for children, grades 4–8.* Boston: Allyn & Bacon.

Roberts, P. L. (1997). *Taking humor seriously in children's literature.* Boston: Allyn & Bacon.

Schmoker, M. (1997). Setting goals in turbulent times. In A. Hargreaves (Ed.), *Rethinking educational change with heart and mind* (pp. 128–148). Alexandria, VA: ASCD Yearbook, Association for Supervision and Curriculum Development.

Sternberg, R. J., & Williams, W. M. (1996). *How to develop student creativity.* Alexandria, VA: Association for Supervision and Curriculum Development.

SELECTED INTERNET ADDRESSES

Compaq Teacher Grants
(http://www.compaq.com.education)
Compaq Computer Corporation and associates have
grants for teacher development related to helping
teachers use technology.
CIA World Factbook
(http://www.odci.gov/cia/publications/nsolo/) A
good source of data on governments, economics, and
geography.

National Education Association (http://www.nea.org/)
Offers classroom techniques from the NEA CD-ROM
called "It's All About Kids," which teachers,
especially first-year teachers, can use.

CHAPTER 4

Assessment of Student Learning

If you have a problem, come to me with it. You will never disturb me, since I can interrupt my work at a moment and resume it immediately.

—Albert Einstein

INTERDISCIPLINARY THEMATIC UNIT: AFRICAN-AMERICANS' JOURNEY TO FREEDOM[1]

Addressing multicultural education through an interdisciplinary thematic study of African American history, teachers Janet Hickman and Rudine Sims Bishop linked historical issues related to the theme with various disciplines such as music, science, and sociology. Expressive language and other skills were taught with the unit content. Approaching African American history through a variety of activities related to several disciplines, students had choices to involve themselves in one or more activities that included the following:

- *Communications and social studies.* A student assumed the role of an historical figure, presented relevant material, and held a news conference. The other class members acted as reporters who then composed newspaper articles from their notes.

- *History.* Students compared a chapter in a book, such as *Now Is Your Time: The African American Struggle for Freedom* by Walter Dean Myers (New York: HarperCollins, 1991), with material about the same time period in a standard history text.

- *Language arts.* Students collected the works of African American illustrators, authors, and poets and interviewed relatives and neighbors who collect stories of holidays and such family traditions as celebrating Kwanzaa.
- *Music.* Students sang and listened to spirituals and developed accompaniment for various songs.
- *Science.* Students used biographies and other reference materials to write nominations for the students' African American hall of fame, which included scientists, inventors, entrepreneurs, and others. Photos of candidates were displayed in the room; arguments were presented for them, and the students voted for their favorite 10 candidates.
- *Sociology.* Students compared recent stories of African American families (and communities) with similar stories written in the past, noting differences in society and attitudes.

By now, you probably understand that students' personal inquiries are central to learning by interdisciplinary thematic instruction. How is that learning assessed? That is the topic of this chapter, but before we begin, let us review some of the important aspects of assessment.

PURPOSES OF ASSESSMENT

Assessment of achievement in student learning is designed to serve in the following ways.

1. *To assist in student learning.* This purpose is usually the first one considered when speaking of assessment, and it is the principal topic of this chapter. For you, a classroom teacher using interdisciplinary thematic instruction, it and the next purpose are (or should be) the most important purposes.

2. *To identify students' strengths and weaknesses.* Identification and assessment of students' strengths and weaknesses are necessary for two reasons: to structure and restructure the learning activities and to restructure the curriculum. Concerning the first reason, data on student strengths and weaknesses in conceptual and procedural understandings, for example, are important in planning activities appropriate for both skill development and intellectual development. This identification results in diagnostic assessment (known also as preassessment). As for the second reason, data on student strengths and weaknesses in conceptual and procedural understandings are useful for making appropriate modifications both during the process of the ITU in particular and to the curriculum in general.

3. *To assess the effectiveness of a particular instructional strategy.* It is important for you to know how well a particular strategy helped accomplish a particular goal or objective. Competent teachers continually reflect on and evaluate their strategy choices, using several sources: student achievement as measured by assessment instruments, their own intuition, informal feedback given by the students, and sometimes informal feedback given by colleagues, such as members of a teaching team or mentor teachers.

4. *To assess and improve the effectiveness of curriculum programs.* Components of the curriculum are continually assessed by committees of teachers and administrators. The assessment is done while students are learning (formative assessment) and afterward (summative assessment). For example, some schools that have restructured their programs, such as changing from a traditional to a nontraditional schedule (Chapter 1) and from traditional instructional methods to integrated learning, have or are comparing student achievement data to determine the effectiveness in learning that has resulted either directly or indirectly from the changes.

5. *To assess and improve teaching effectiveness.* To improve student learning, teachers are periodically evaluated on the basis of (1) their commitment to working with students at a particular level, (2) their ability to cope with students at a particular age or grade level, and (3) their ability to show mastery of appropriate instructional techniques and their willingness to risk trying new techniques.

6. *To provide data that assist in decision making about a student's future.* Assessment of student achievement is important in guiding decision making about course and program placement, promotion, school transfer, class standing, eligibility for honors and scholarships, and career planning.

7. *To communicate with and involve parents and guardians in their children's learning.* Parents, communities, and school boards all share in an accountability for the effectiveness of the children's

learning. Today's schools are reaching out and engaging parents, guardians, and the community in their children's education. All teachers play an important role in the process of communicating with, reaching out to, and involving parents.

PRINCIPLES THAT GUIDE AN ASSESSMENT PROGRAM

Because the welfare and, indeed, the future of so many people depend on the outcomes of assessment, it is impossible to overemphasize its importance. For a learning endeavor to be successful, the learner must have answers to basic questions: Where am I going? Where am I now? How do I get where I am going? How will I know when I get there? Am I on the right track for getting there? These questions are integral to a good program of assessment. Of course, in the process of teaching and learning, the answers may be ever changing, and the teacher and students continue to assess and adjust plans as appropriate and necessary.

Based on these questions are the following eight principles that guide an assessment program and that are reflected in the discussions in this chapter.

1. Teachers need to know how well they are doing.
2. Students need to know how well they are doing.
3. Assessment is a reciprocal process, and includes assessment of teacher performance and student achievement.
4. The program of assessment should aid teaching effectiveness and contribute to the intellectual and psychological growth of children.
5. Evidence and input data for knowing how well the teacher and students are doing should come from a variety of sources and types of data-collecting devices.
6. Assessment is an ongoing process. The selection and implementation of plans and activities require continual monitoring and assessment to check progress and change or adopt strategies to promote desired behavior.
7. Reflection and self-assessment are important components of any successful assessment program. Reflection and self-assessment are important if students are to develop the skills necessary for them to assume increasingly greater ownership of their own learning.
8. A teacher's responsibility is to facilitate student learning and to assess student progress in that learning, and for that, the teacher is, or should be, held accountable.

TERMS USED IN ASSESSMENT: A CLARIFICATION

When discussing the assessment component of teaching and learning, it is easy to be confused by the terminology. The following clarification of terms is offered to aid your reading and comprehension.

Assessment and Evaluation

Although some authors distinguish between the terms **assessment** (the process of finding out what the students are learning; a relatively neutral process) and **evaluation** (making sense of what was found; a subjective process), for the purposes of this guide, we do not. We consider the difference too slight and thus consider the terms to be synonymous.

Measurement and Evaluation

Measurement refers to quantifiable data about specific behaviors. Tests and the statistical procedures used to analyze the results are examples. Measurement is a descriptive and objective process, relatively free from human value judgments.

Assessment includes objective data from measurement, but also other types of information, some of which are more subjective such as information from anecdotal records and teacher observations and ratings of student performance. In addition to the use of objective data (data from measurement), assessment also includes arriving at value judgments made on the basis of subjective information.

Consider the following example. A teacher may share the information that Penny Brown received a score in the 90th percentile on the eighth-grade statewide achievement test in reading (a statement of measurement) but may add that "according to my assessment of her work in my language arts class, she has not been an outstanding student" (a statement of assessment).

Validity and Reliability

The degree to which a measuring instrument actually measures that which it is intended to measure is the instrument's **validity.** For example, when we ask if an assessment instrument has validity, key questions concerning that instrument are as follows: Does the instrument adequately sample the intended content? Does it measure the cognitive, affective, and psychomotor knowledge and skills that are important to the unit of content being tested? Does it sample all the instructional objectives of that unit?

The accuracy with which a technique consistently measures a procedure is its **reliability.** If, for example, you know that you weigh 114 pounds, and a scale consistently records 114 pounds when you stand on it, then that scale has reliability. However, if the same scale consistently records 100 pounds when you stand on it, we can still say the scale has reliability. By this example, then, it should be clear that an instrument could be reliable (it produces similar results when used repeatedly) although not necessarily valid. In this second instance, the scale is not measuring what it is supposed to measure, so although it is reliable, it is invalid. Although a technique might be reliable but not valid, a technique must have reliability before it can have validity. The greater the number of test items or situations on a particular objective, the higher the reliability. The higher the reliability, the more consistency there will be in students' scores measuring their understanding of that particular objective.

ASSESSMENT OF STUDENT ACHIEVEMENT: A THREE-STEP PROCESS

As discussed in Chapter 3, assessing student achievement is a three-step process. These three steps are (1) diagnostic assessment (sometimes called pre-assessment)—the assessment of the student's knowledge and skills before the new instruction; (2) formative assessment—the assessment of learning during the instruction; and (3) summative assessment—the assessment of learning after the instruction, ultimately represented by the student's final term, semester, or year's achievement grade.

Grades shown on chapter tests, progress reports, and deficiency notices, are examples of formative evaluation reports. However, an end-of-chapter test or a unit test is summative when the test represents the absolute end of the student's learning of material for that instructional unit.

AVENUES FOR ASSESSING STUDENT LEARNING

The three general avenues for assessing a student's achievement in learning are (1) what the student says—for example, the quantity and quality of a student's contributions to class discussion, (2) what the student does—for example, a student's performance (e.g., the quality of a student's participation in the culminating activities of the ITU), and (3) what the

student writes or draws—for example, as shown by items in the student's portfolio (e.g., assignments, project work, and written tests). These avenues of assessment will be discussed in more detail later in this section.

Although your own situation and personal philosophy will dictate the levels of importance and weight you give to each avenue of assessment, you should have a strong rationale if you value and weigh the three avenues for assessment differently than one-third each.

Authentic Assessment

When assessing for student achievement, it is important that you use procedures that are compatible with the instructional objectives. As mentioned in earlier chapters, this measurement is referred to as **authentic assessment.** Other terms used for authentic assessment are *accurate, active, aligned, alternative,* and *direct.* Although performance assessment is sometimes used, this term refers to the type of student response being assessed, whereas authentic assessment refers to the assessment situation. Although not all performance assessments are authentic, those that are authentic are most assuredly performance assessments.

In English/language arts, for example, it may seem fairly easy to develop a criterion-referenced test, administer it, and grade it, but tests often measure language skills rather than language use. It is extremely difficult to measure students' communicative competence with a test. Tests do not measure listening and talking very well, and a test on punctuation marks, for instance, does not indicate the students' ability to use punctuation marks correctly in their own writing. Instead, tests typically evaluate students' ability to add punctuation marks to a set of sentences created by someone else or to proofread and spot punctuation errors in someone else's writing. An alternative and far better approach is to examine how students use punctuation marks in their own writing.[2] An authentic assessment of punctuation, then, would be an assessment of a performance item that involves students in writing and punctuating their own writing. For the authentic assessment of the student's understanding of that which the student has been learning, you would use a performance-based assessment procedure.

In another example, "if students have been actively involved in classifying objects using multiple characteristics, it sends them a confusing message if they are then required to take a paper-and-pencil test that asks them to 'define classification' or recite a memorized list of characteristics of good classifications schemes."[3] An authentic assessment technique would be a performance item that actually involves the students in classifying objects. In other words, to obtain an accurate assessment of a student's learning, the teacher uses a performance-based assessment procedure—a procedure that requires students to produce rather than select a response.

Advantages and Limitations.   Advantages of using authentic assessment include (1) the direct—performance-based, results-driven, criterion-referenced, or outcome-based—measurement of what students should know and can do, and (2) an emphasis on higher-order thinking. Conversely, limitations of using authentic assessment include a difficulty in making results consistent and usable, problems with validity, reliability, and comparability, and a higher cost to the schools in both time and money.

Assessing What a Student Says and Does

When evaluating what a student says, you should (1) listen to the student's oral reports, questions, responses, and interactions with others, and (2) observe the student's attentiveness, involvement in class activities, creativeness, and responses to challenges. Notice that we say you should listen and observe. While listening to what the student is saying, you should also be observing the student's nonverbal behaviors. For this observation, you can use checklists and rating scales, behavioral-growth record forms, observations with scoring rubrics of the student's performance in learning activities (you will see sample checklists and sample scoring rubrics later in this chapter), and periodic conferences with the student.[4]

Figure 4.1 illustrates a sample generic form for recording and evaluating teacher observations of a student's verbal and nonverbal behaviors. With modern technology, such as is afforded, for instance, by the software program *Learner Profile*, you can record observations electronically anywhere and at any time.[5]

With each technique used, you must proceed from your awareness of anticipated learning outcomes (the instructional objectives) and assess a student's progress toward meeting those objectives. This process is called *criterion-referenced assessment*.

Debriefings for Specific Experiences.   A debriefing for specific experience is a "what we learned" type of discussion with the purpose of assessing a single event or happening, such as a field trip or visit to the classroom participating in the culmination of an ITU. In a class meeting, the students usually summarize the information and activities they thought were important and any new learning they acquired. You will have the students record their remarks on a chart, the writing board, or an overhead transparency, perhaps using the KWL format discussed in Chapter 3. If a class meeting was held before the specific experience, in which students discussed what they wanted to learn through the experience, then the debriefing should focus on comparing what students anticipated learning with what they actually learned.

Guidelines for Assessing What a Student Says and Does.   Regardless of the grade level you teach, guidelines and steps to follow when assessing a student's verbal and nonverbal behaviors in the classroom are as follows:

- List the desirable behaviors for a specific activity; check the list against the specific instructional objectives.
- Maintain an anecdotal record book or folder and keep a separate section in it for your records of each student.
- Record your observations as quickly as possible following your observation. Audio or video recordings, and of course computer software programs, can help you maintain records and check the accuracy of your memory. If using these devices is not always possible, you should spend time during school, immediately after school, or later that evening recording your observations while they are still fresh in your memory.
- Record your professional judgment about the student's progress toward the desired behavior, but consider it carefully before transferring it to a permanent record.
- Write reminders to yourself such as "Check validity of observation by further testing" or "Discuss observations with student's parent/guardian/mentor (adult representative from the community)" or "Discuss observations with the student or with other teachers on the teaching team."

Assessing What a Student Writes or Draws

When assessing what a student writes or draws, you can use worksheets, written homework and papers, student journal writing, student writing projects, student portfolios, and tests (all discussed next). In many schools, portfolios, worksheets, and homework assignments are the tools primarily used for the formative evaluation of each student's achievement. Tests, too, should be a part of this evaluation, but tests are also used for summative evaluation at the end of a unit and for diagnostic purposes.

Student Journal.   A **journal** (sometimes called a **learning log**) usually takes the form of a spiral

FIGURE 4.1   Sample of a Form for Evaluating and Recording Student Verbal and Nonverbal Behaviors

Student _____   Course _____   School _____

Observer _____   Date _____   Period _____

_____

Objective   Desired behavior   What student did, said, wrote

Teacher's/observer's comments:

notebook that contains a student's writings. In general, journal entries indicate that which is being learned in the ITU. (See also discussion of student journals in Chapter 3). A journal might include personal writing about the student's interests and experiences, in which case it is sometimes called a *life-writing journal,* or a student's personal reactions to material related to the ITU, in which case it is sometimes called a **thinkbook.** A journal might also contain entries written by the student every afternoon before leaving school about what he or she learned that day, in which case, it is sometimes called a **cooperative teacher-student log.**

You can communicate in writing with each student through any type of journal. It is crucial, however, for you to write comments for each student when the approach taken is the cooperative teacher-student log. In this type of log, the student writes about what

he or she thinks has been accomplished for the day, what was personally interesting during the day's study, and what he or she wants to read, write, or study next. Schedule time to read the logs often and make meaningful written responses back to students.

If you want to include the cooperative teacher-student log as part of the ITU, you may want to read the logs as part of the overall assessment of the unit and recognize the students for the effort that they put into their journal entries with some type of awards and bonuses. In addition, the students can reread their journals at the end of the ITU, creating an end-of-the-unit review of what they have learned after rereading their entries. The students might number the journal pages, write titles for the different entries on different pages, create a table of contents page, decorate a cover and a title page, develop a glossary or index, and write a self-evaluation as a summary on the last page of the journal to establish a closure for the ITU.

Writing Folder. A writing folder is usually a three-ring binder containing a number of cardboard pockets, labeled to show the different styles of writing the student accomplishes. For example, the pockets may be labeled "First Drafts" for all the beginning writing a student does, "Current Writing" for the ongoing pages, and "Finished Drafts" for the final products. A fourth pocket might be labeled "Writing Ideas" for a list of topics for future writing and a fifth pocket might be labeled "Personal" for a student's reflections on any matters related to the unit. If appropriate, you can ask the students to begin a list of the independently "published" classroom books that each has developed through the unit. Inside the back cover, you can place a checklist of writing skills to indicate what each student has accomplished and maintained through the unit of study.

Peer Conference Group. A peer conference group normally consists of five or six students who meet to assess the reports written by the group members related to the ITU. Each student takes a turn telling the others what they need in the way of help, feedback, and ideas. The students hand their papers to their peers on the left and silently read the papers they receive. Each member writes his or her suggestions for improvement on duplicated response sheets, using such phrases as "Can you explain . . . ?" "Can you tell more about . . . ?" "I like . . ." and "I thought this was interesting because . . ." The response sheets are given to the appropriate authors of the reports so each student gets feedback from all the other group members.

Teacher-Student Conferences and Conference Log. A teacher-student conference is an arranged 10- to 15-minute meeting that you have with an individual student during the school day. The purpose is to help guide the student to self-assess his or her own educational progress, with a focus on the student's self-direction in learning. During the conference, one or two elements from the student's educational materials may be reviewed, including the log, various recordings, a writing folder, and the daily journal. The atmosphere should remain friendly and helpful (i.e., nonjudgmental), and the student can be encouraged to do most of the talking—focusing on any difficulties the student is having, discussing his or her feelings about the assignments, and telling about any problems in the school environment that may be threatening or interrupting the student's learning progress.

A conference log is a notebook in which you write notes about each student's conference. It also contains a time schedule of meetings with the individual students. Using a sheet with the student's name and conference date on it, you can record what was discussed and what elements from the student's educational materials were reviewed. For instance, if a portion of the student's writing was discussed, you could make notes about the student's work and, if mentioned by the student, what the next writing project would concern. Notes might also be made in the conference log about the student's invented spelling (if any) and about the teacher's suggestions related to grammar and structure for the student's final revision.

Guidelines for Assessing Student Writing. When assessing what a student writes, use the following guidelines.

- Correlate student writing assignments and test items with specific instructional objectives (i.e., objectives should be criterion referenced).
- Read nearly everything a student writes, except, of course, for personal writing in a student journal (see the following guideline).
- Provide positive written or verbal comments about the student's work.
- Think before writing a comment on a student's paper by asking yourself how you think the student (or parent or guardian) will interpret and react to the comment and if that is a correct interpretation or reaction to your intended meaning.
- Encourage students to write about their experiences in and out of school and especially about their experiences related to what is being learned. Provide a nonthreatening and free environment for this activity. Engage them in writing, in thinking about their thinking, and in recording their creative thoughts. Provide students practice in expressing themselves in written form and in connecting their learning.
- Avoid writing evaluative comments or grades in student journals. These types of comments and evaluations might discourage creative and spontaneous expression. When responding to a student's journal writing, Gibbs and Earley[6] suggest that the following "don'ts" may be more important than any "dos." Do not correct spelling or grammar. Do not probe. Resist the temptation to ask for more than the student chooses to share. Do not respond with value judgments. Simple empathic statements such as "I understand your point of view" and "Thanks for sharing your thoughts" can be used to avoid making value judgments. Do not require students to share their

entries with you or their peers. Suggest that certain pages that students do not want you to read be folded shut and marked "Personal."

- Do not grade student journals. Talk individually with students about their journals to seek clarification about their expressions. Each student's journal will be useful to you in understanding a student's thought processes and writing skills (part of diagnostic evaluation). For grading purposes, you can simply record the extent to which the student is maintaining a journal and, perhaps, a judgment about the quantity of writing in it, but no judgment should be made about the quality (see Figure 4.2).

- Do not grade student portfolios or compare them in any way with those of other students. Review the portfolios and discuss with students individually the progress in their learning as shown by the materials in their portfolios. The purpose of the portfolios is for student self-assessment and to show progress in learning. For this to happen, the students should keep in their portfolios all or major samples of papers related to a particular study. (Student journals and portfolios are discussed again later in this chapter.)

Assessment for Affective and Psychomotor Domain Learning.   Whereas evaluation of cognitive domain objectives lends itself to traditional written tests of achievement, the evaluation of affective and psychomotor domains requires the use of performance checklists where student behaviors can be observed in action. However, as in earlier discussion and for cognitive learning as well, educators today are encouraging the use of alternative assessment procedures (i.e., alternatives to traditional paper-and-pencil testing). As also mentioned in preceding chapters, in regard to learning that is most important and has the most meaning to students, the domains are inextricably interconnected. Learning that is meaningful to students is not as easily compartmentalized as the taxonomies of educational objectives (Chapter 3) would imply. Alternative assessment strategies include the use of group projects, portfolios, skits, papers, oral presentations, and performance tests.

In schools where you work in groups or teams of teachers who remain with the same cohort of students for more than a year, you will probably have the opportunity to observe the positive changes in your students' values and attitudes.[7] Unfortunately, if you work in an educational situation where you only see a student for a given school semester or year, then you may never see the effects you have had on a student.

COOPERATIVE GROUP LEARNING AND ASSESSMENT

Group learning, including cooperative group learning, is an integral part of learning by ITUs. The purpose of a cooperative learning group is for the group to learn, which means that individuals within the group must learn. Group achievement in learning, then, depends on the learning of individuals within the group. Rather than competing for rewards for achievement, members of the group cooperate by helping each other to learn so the group reward will be good. It is well documented in research studies that when small groups of students of mixed backgrounds, skills, and capabilities work together toward a common goal, they increase their liking and respect for one another. As a result, each student's self-esteem and academic achievement also increase.

When recognizing the achievement of a cooperative learning group, both group and individual achievement are rewarded. Remembering that the emphasis must be on peer support rather than peer pressure, you must be cautious about giving group grades.[8] Some teachers give bonus points to all members of a group to add to their individual scores when everyone in the group has reached preset criteria. In establishing preset standards, they can be different for individuals within a group, depending on each member's ability and past performance. It is important that each member of a group feel rewarded and successful. Some teachers also give subjective grades to individual students on their role performances within the group (see Figure 4.2). For determination of students' report card grades, individual student achievement can be measured later through individual results on tests and other sources of data. The final grade can be based on those results and the student's performance in the group.

STUDENT INVOLVEMENT IN ASSESSMENT

The students' continuous self-assessment should be planned as an important component of your unit. If the students are to progress in their understanding of their own thinking (metacognition) and in their intellectual development, then they must receive instruction and guidance in how to become more responsible for their own learning. During the empowerment process, they learn to think better of themselves and of their individual capabilities. To achieve this self-understanding

FIGURE 4.2 Sample Scoring Rubric for Assessing Individual Students in Cooperative Learning Project Work

	9–10	8	7	1–6
Goals	Consistently and actively helps identify group goals; works effectively to meet goals.	Consistently communicates commitment to group goals; carries out assigned roles.	Sporadically communicates commitment to group goals; carries out assigned role.	Rarely, if ever, works toward group goals or may work against them.
Interpersonal Skills	Cooperates with group members by encouraging, compromising, and/or taking a leadership role without dominating; shows sensitivity to feelings and knowledge of others.	Cooperates with group members by encouraging, compromising, and/or taking a leadership role.	Participates with group, but has own agenda; may not be willing to compromise or to make significant contributions.	May discourage others, harass group members, or encourage off-task behavior. Makes significant changes to others' work without their knowledge or permission.
Quality Producer	Contributes significant information, ideas, time, and/or talent to produce a quality product.	Contributes information, ideas, time, and/or talent to produce a quality product.	Contributes some ideas, though not significant; may be more supportive than contributive; shows willingness to complete assignment but has no desire to go beyond average expectations.	Does little or no work toward the completion of group product; shows little or no interest in contributing to the task; produces work which fails to meet minimum standards for quality.
Participation	Attends daily; consistently and actively utilizes class time by working on the task.	Attends consistently; sends in work to group if absent; utilizes class time by working on the task.	Attends sporadically; absences/tardies may hinder group involvement; may send work when absent; utilizes some time; may be off-task by talking to others, interrupting other groups, or watching others do the majority of the work.	Frequent absences or tardies hinder group involvement; fails to send in work when absent; wastes class time by talking, doing other work, or avoiding tasks; group has asked that member be reproved by teacher or removed from the group.
Commitment	Consistently contributes time out of class to produce a quality product; attends all group meetings as evidenced by the group meeting log.	Contributes time out of class to produce a quality product; attends a majority of group meetings as evidenced by the group meeting log.	Willing to work toward completion of task during class time; attends some of the group meetings but may arrive late or leave early; may keep inconsistent meeting log.	Rarely, if ever, attends group meetings outside of class or may attend and hinder progress of the group; fails to keep meeting log.

(Courtesy of Susan Abbott and Pam Benedetti, Elk Grove School District, Elk Grove, CA.) Explanation for use: Possible score = 50. Scorer marks a relevant square in each of the six categories (horizontal rows) and student's score for that category is the small number in the top right corner within that square.

and improved self-esteem requires the experiences afforded by successes, with guidance in self-understanding and self-assessment.

To meet these goals, you can provide opportunities for students to think about what they are learning, how they are learning it, and how far they have progressed. One way to do this task is to engage the students in maintaining portfolios of their own work and in using rating scales or checklists periodically to self-assess their progress.

Using Portfolios

Student portfolios fall into three general categories, and the purpose in a given situation may transcend some combination of or all three categories. The categories are (1) the **selected works portfolio** in which students maintain samples of their work after a teacher prompt, (2) the **longitudinal portfolio** in which student work samples are oriented toward outcome-driven goals and represent work from the beginning to the end of a specified period (such as the start to finish of an ITU or a semester or term) to exemplify achievement toward the goals, and (3) the **career portfolio** in which samples of student work will document the student's readiness to move forward in his or her educational careers, such as moving from one school grade level to another, or from high school to a work situation, or on to postsecondary education.

Student portfolios should be well organized chronologically and, depending on the grade level, contain some of the following: anecdotal records which are useful for recording spontaneous events; checklists or inventories which are useful for recording development of skills; rating scales; the students' responses to questions; assignment record sheets; class worksheets; records of homework; project binders that include a project record and successive drafts of the students' work; forms for student self-evaluation and reflection on the work done; and other class materials thought important by the students and teacher.[9] If appropriate for your students, send their writing portfolios home periodically with a "response paper" for the parent or guardian. If any writing needs further work, add the words "work in progress" so an adult will understand why errors are still found in the writing. Ask the adult in the home to look through the portfolio with the student and complete your enclosed response paper. The response paper asks for feedback about the student's writing. Here are some examples for feedback questions.

- What is your favorite piece of writing in the portfolio? Why?

- Where do you see that your child is doing well in the enclosed work?
- Where have you seen improvement in your child's writing in the enclosed work?
- What were some of the surprises (if any) that you found in the portfolio?

Request that both the student and the adult sign the paper before it is returned to you. To engage the adult or guardian in the home further, you may develop a student portfolio in thirds, which means the adult in the home selects from the student's work sent home to insert as one-third of the portfolio; the student selects material for another third; and you select the remaining one-third of the material.

Although portfolio assessment as an alternative to traditional methods of evaluating student progress has gained momentum in recent years, setting standards has been very difficult. Research on the use of portfolios for assessment indicate that validity and reliability of teacher evaluation are often quite low. Before using portfolios as an alternative to traditional testing, you will want to consider and clearly understand the reasons for doing it, carefully decide on portfolio content, establish rubrics or expectation standards, anticipate grading problems, and consider parent and guardian reactions.

While emphasizing the criteria for assessment, rating scales and checklists provide students with means of expressing their feelings and give you as the teacher still another source of input data for use in assessment. To provide students with reinforcement and guidance to improve their learning and development, you can meet with individual students to discuss their self-assessments. Such conferences can provide your students with understandable and achievable short-term goals and help them develop and maintain an adequate self-esteem.[10]

Although almost any instrument used for assessing student work can be used for student self-assessment, in some cases it might be better to construct specific instruments with the student's understanding of the instrument in mind. Student self-assessment and self-reflection should be done on a regular and continuing basis so comparisons can be made periodically by the student. You will need to help students learn how to analyze these comparisons, because they should provide a student with information previously not recognized about his or her own progress and growth.

Using Checklists

One item maintained by students in their portfolios is a series of checklists. Items on the checklist will

FIGURE 4.3   Sample Checklist: Assessing a Student's Oral Report

Oral Report Assessment Checklist			
Did the student . . .	**Yes**	**No**	**Comments**
1. Speak so that everyone could hear?			
2. Finish sentences?			
3. Seem comfortable in front of the group?			
4. Give a good introduction?			
5. Seem well informed about the topic?			
6. Explain ideas clearly?			
7. Stay on the topic?			
8. Give a good conclusion?			
9. Use effective visuals to make the presentation interesting?			
10. Give good answers to questions from the audience?			

vary depending on your purpose, subject, and grade level (see sample forms in Figures 4.3 and 4.4). Checklist items can be used easily by a student to compare with previous self-assessments. Open-ended questions such as those found in the checklist in Figure 4.5 allow the student to provide additional information and to do some expressive writing. After a student has demonstrated each of the skills satisfactorily, a check is made next to the student's name, either by you independently or in conference with your student.

Guidelines for Using Portfolios for Assessment.
Following is a summary of guidelines for using student portfolios in the assessment of learning:

- Contents of the portfolio should reflect instructional aims and objectives.
- Students should date everything that goes into their portfolio.
- Contents for the portfolio should be determined and announced clearly (perhaps post a schedule in the classroom) when, how, and by what criteria portfolios will be reviewed by you.
- Students should be given the responsibility for the maintenance of their portfolios and keep them in the classroom.
- Content in the portfolio should not be graded or compared in any way with those of other students as mentioned earlier in this chapter. Its purpose is for student self-assessment and for showing

progress in learning. For this process to happen or be successful, students should keep in their portfolios all papers or major sample papers related to an ITU or course. For grading, you can simply record the extent to which the portfolio was maintained and use a checklist to show which required materials are in the portfolio.

MAINTAINING RECORDS OF STUDENT ACHIEVEMENT

You must maintain well-organized and complete records of student achievement, perhaps in a written record book or on an electronic record book (i.e., a computer software program, either commercially developed or one you develop perhaps by using a computer software program spreadsheet). At the very least, the record book should include attendance records and all records of scores on tests, homework, projects, and other assignments. At the high-tech end of record keeping, a record-keeping and learner profile system is available that uses a computer and the Apple Newton™ or a bar code scanner, to help you plan, customize assessment criteria, observe and collect data anywhere without interrupting the learning process, make reports, and assist in student self-assessment.

Daily interactions and events occur in the classroom that may provide informative data about a

FIGURE 4.4   Sample Form: Student Self-Assessment of Writing

Student Self-Assessment Form

Student _____   Date _____

Teacher _____   Number _____

Draft Title of Paper: _____

Answer the following questions about the draft of your own paper after all group members have shared their papers by reading them aloud to others in the group.

	Yes	No
1. In my introduction, I put forth my thesis.	_____	_____
2. In the beginning, I orient the reader by providing relevant background information and sources.	_____	_____
3. I support my interpretive claims by providing (circle those that apply): textual evidence, specific quotations, personal experience, related readings.	_____	_____
4. I explain how my examples support my claim by using words such as *shows, demonstrates, proves,* and *illustrates.*	_____	_____
5. My supporting evidence provides the bulk of my composition.	_____	_____
6. I take a strong, consistent stance and maintain it.	_____	_____
7. I convince my readers that my interpretation is valid.	_____	_____

8. What I like best about my paper is:

_____

_____

_____

_____

9. A part where I need more information is:

_____

_____

_____

_____

10. Other revisions I might make are:

_____

_____

_____

_____

Source: Adapted from unpublished material by Pam Benedetti. Using Portfolios to Strengthen Student Assessment in English/Language Arts (Grades 6–12), Copyright 1991 by Pam Benedetti, p. 29)

student's intellectual, emotional, and physical development. Maintaining a dated record of your observations of these interactions and events can provide important information that might otherwise be forgotten. At the end of a unit, and again at the conclusion of a grading term, you will want to review your records. During the course of the school year, your anecdotal records (and those of other members of your teaching team) will provide important information about the intellectual, psychological, and physical development of each child and ideas for attention to be given to individual students, as well as changes that you and your team may want to make in future use of the ITU or another one.

GRADING AND MARKING STUDENT ACHIEVEMENT

If conditions were ideal (which they are not), and if you and your teaching colleagues did your jobs perfectly well (which many of us do not), then all students would receive top marks (the ultimate in mastery or quality learning), and there would be less of a need here to talk about grading and marking. Master learning implies that some end point of learning is attainable, but that end point probably does not exist. In any case, because conditions for teaching are never ideal and we as teachers are mere humans, although limited by the nature and scope of this guide, let us continue to discuss this topic of grading, because it is undoubtedly of special interest to you, to your students, to their parents or guardians, and to school counselors, administrators and school boards, potential employers, providers of scholarships, and college admissions officers.

As educators, we frequently use the term *achievement*, but what is meant by this term? Achievement means accomplishment, but is it accomplishment of the instructional objectives against preset standards, or is it simple accomplishment? Most teachers probably would choose the former, during which you as the teacher subjectively establish a standard that must be met for a student to receive a certain grade for an assignment, project, test, quarter, semester, or course. Achievement, then, is decided by degrees of accomplishment.

Preset standards are usually expressed in percentages (degrees of accomplishment) needed for marks or ABC grades. On one hand, if no student achieves the standard required for an A grade, for example, then no student receives an A. On the other

hand, if all students meet the preset standard for the A grade, then all receive As. As mentioned, determining student grades on the basis of preset standards is referred to as *criterion-referenced grading*.

Criterion-Referenced versus Norm-Referenced Grading

Whereas criterion-referenced (or competency-based) grading is that based on preset standards, norm-referenced grading measures the relative accomplishment of individuals in the group (e.g., one classroom of chemistry students) or in a larger group (e.g., all students enrolled in the same chemistry course) by comparing and ranking students, and is commonly known as "grading on a curve." Because it encourages competition and discourages cooperative learning, *norm-referenced grading is not recommended* for the determination of student grades. After all, each student is an individual and should not be converted to a statistic on a frequency distribution curve. Grades for student achievement should be tied to performance levels and determined on the basis of each student's achievement toward preset standards.[11]

In criterion-referenced grading, your aim is to communicate information about an individual student's progress in knowledge and work skills in comparison with that student's previous attainment or in the pursuit of an absolute, such as content mastery. Criterion-referenced grading is featured in continuous-progress curricula, competency-based curricula, and other programs that focus on individualized education.

Criterion-referenced grading is based on the level at which each student meets the specified objectives (standards) for the unit, grade level, or course. The objectives must be clearly stated to represent important student learning outcomes. This approach implies that effective teaching and learning result in high grades (As) or marks for most students. In fact, when a mastery concept is used, the student must accomplish the objectives before being allowed to proceed to the next learning task. In this approach, the comparison is between what Sally the student could do yesterday and what she can do today and how well these performances compare with the preset standard.

Most schools use some sort of combination of both norm-referenced and criterion-referenced data usage. Sometimes both kinds of information are useful. For example, a report card for Sally in the eighth grade might indicate how Sally is meeting certain criteria, such as an A grade for addition of fractions. Another entry might show that this mastery is expected, however, in the sixth grade. Both criterion- and norm-referenced data may be communicated to Sally's parents or guardians and to Sally herself. Appropriate procedures include the following:

- a criterion-referenced approach to show the extent to which the student can accomplish the task, and if so, to what degree;
- a norm-referenced approach to show how well a student performs compared with the larger group to which the student belongs. The latter, for instance, is important data for college admissions officers and for committees that offer academic scholarships.

Determining Grades

Once entered onto school transcripts, grades have a significant impact on the students' future. When determining achievement grades for student performance, you must make several important and professional decisions. These decisions relate to your school's policy about giving marks such as E, S, and I or pass/no pass or about using percentages of accomplishment and letter grades for courses taught in middle schools and high schools.[12] Consider what decisions you will make related to the guidelines discussed in the paragraphs that follow. Guidelines for Determining Grades

- *Explain your marking and grading policies.* At the start of the school term, clearly discuss your policies for grading first to yourself, then to your students and to their parents or guardians at back-to-school night or through a written explanation that you send home, or use both methods to contact the student's home. Share examples of scoring and grading rubrics with students and parents.
- *Be as objective as possible.* When converting your interpretation of a student's accomplishments to a letter grade, be objective. For the selection of criteria for ABC grades, select a percentage standard such as 92% for an A, 85% for a B, 75% for a C, and 65% for a D. Cutoff percentages used are your decision, although the district or school may have established guidelines that you are expected to follow.
- *Use a point system and preset standards.* For the determination of the students' final grades, we recommend a point system, where things that students write, say, and do are given points and then the possible point total determines the grade. (We remind you to not give points for the writing in journals or portfolios except when the student writes something in his or her journal or portfolio).

Related to grade determination, if 92% is the cutoff for an A and 500 points are possible, then any student with 460 points or more (500 × 92) has achieved an A. Likewise, for a test or any other assignment, if the value is 100 points, the cutoff for an A is 92 (100 × 92). With a point system and preset standards, you and the students at any time during the grading period always know the current points possible and can easily calculate a student's current grade standing. Then, as far as a current letter grade is concerned, students always know where they stand in their work related to their grade level, unit of study, or course.

- *Develop your policy for grading.* Build your grading policy around degrees of accomplishment rather than failure, and around the idea that students proceed from one accomplishment to the next.
- *Clarify your terms for students and parents/guardians.* Remember that assessment and grading are not synonymous. Recall that assessment implies the collection of information from a variety of sources, including measurement techniques and subjective observations. These data then become the basis for arriving at a final grade, which in effect is a final value judgment. Grades are one aspect of evaluation and are intended to communicate educational progress to students and to their parents or guardians. To be valid as an indicator of that progress, you must use a variety of sources of data for the determination of a student's final grade.

TESTING FOR ACHIEVEMENT

One source of information used for determining grades is data obtained from testing for student achievement. In this section about testing, we first consider briefly the difference between standardized and nonstandardized tests, then the purposes and frequency of testing, test construction, and administering tests.

Standardized and Nonstandardized Tests

Standardized tests are those that have been constructed and published by commercial testing bureaus and are used by states and districts to determine and compare student achievement, principally in the core subjects of reading, science, social studies, and math. Standardized norm-referenced tests are best for diagnostic purposes and should not be used for determining student grades. Space in this book does not allow our consideration of standardized achievement testing so our focus will be on nonstandardized tests that are designed by you or by your teaching team for your own unique group of students.

Considering commercial materials, you realize that textbook publishers' tests, test item pools, and standardized tests are available from a variety of sources because schools, teachers, and students are different. Considering teacher-designed materials, you realize that you will be designing (or collaboratively participating in the designing) and preparation of tests for your own purposes for your distinct cohort of students.

Purposes for Testing

Competent planning, preparing, administering, and scoring of tests is an important professional skill for you to develop. The paragraphs that follow provide guidelines that will be of reference to you as a student teacher, and again during your initial years as an employed teacher.

Tests can be designed for several purposes, and a variety of tests and alternate test items will keep your testing program interesting, useful, and reliable. Related to your college or university days when you were a student, you are probably most experienced with tests that measure for achievement, but as the teacher you will use tests for other reasons as well. Tests are also used to assess and aid in curriculum development; to help determine teaching effectiveness; to help your students develop positive attitudes, appreciations, and values; to help your students increase their understanding and retention of facts, principles, skills, and concepts; to motivate students; to provide diagnostic information for planning for individualization of instruction; to provide review and drill to enhance teaching and learning; and to serve as informational data for the students and their parents/guardians.

Frequency of Testing

Assessment for student learning should be continual—it should be ongoing every minute of every class day. To clarify this concept, Brookhart points out that assessment means how you gather evidence of your students' achievement in the context of your classroom instruction, and that what you should know about assessment can be organized into words represented by the three P's—pervasive, pivotal, and primary. Assessment is pervasive because you are always doing it; it is pivotal because it provides data for your decisions that affect the students; and it is primary because it is central and important to your teaching.[13]

For grading or marking purposes, it is difficult to generalize about how often to formally test for student achievement, but we believe that testing should be cumulative and frequent. Cumulative indicates that the items for each assessment should measure for the student's understanding of previously learned materials and for the current unit of study. Frequent means as often as once a week. Advantages of assessment that are cumulative include the review, reinforcement, and articulation of old material with the most recent material. The advantages of frequent assessment include a reduction in student anxiety over tests and an increase in the validity of the final summative assessment.

Test Construction

After determining the reasons for which you are designing and administering a test, you need to identify the specific instructional objectives the test is being designed to measure. (As emphasized in Chapter 3, your written instructional objectives are specific so that you can write assessment items to measure against those objectives, which involves criterion-referenced assessment.) So we suggest that the first step in test construction is to identify the purpose(s) for the test. The second step is to identify the objectives to be measured, and the third step is to prepare the test items. The best time to prepare draft items is after you have prepared your instructional objectives—while the objectives are fresh in your mind, which means before the lessons are taught. After teaching a lesson, you will then want to rework your first draft of the test items related to that lesson to modify any draft items as a result of the instruction that occurred.

Administering Tests

The actual administration of a test involves several factors. Some of these are as follows:

Reduce test anxiety. For many children, test taking can be a time of high anxiety. Students demonstrate test anxiety in various ways. Just before and during testing some students are quiet and thoughtful, others are noisy and disruptive. To more accurately measure student achievement you will want to take steps to reduce their anxiety. To control or reduce student anxieties, consider the following discussion as guidelines for administering tests.

Keep to a familiar routine. Because children respond best to familiar routine, plan your formative assessment program so tests are given at regular intervals and administered at the same time and in the same way—perhaps a time during Friday afternoon can be set aside for a spelling test on words related to the unit of study. Additionally, in some middle level and high schools, days of the week are assigned to departments for administering major tests. For example, Tuesdays might be assigned for language arts and mathematics testing while Wednesday is the day for social studies and science testing.

Keep tests short. Avoid tests that are too long and time consuming. Perhaps you have known a teacher who had an unreasonable expectation of his or her students and their attention spans during testing. That teacher should have used frequent testing with frequent sampling of student knowledge—it is preferred over infrequent and long tests that attempt to cover everything.

Attend to the physical comforts in the test situation. Try to arrange the classroom so it is well ventilated, has comfortable temperature, and room to move around desks and seats. If spacing is a problem, then consider group testing or using alternate forms of the test, during which students who are seated adjacent to one another receive different forms of the same test (for example, multiple-choice answer alternatives are arranged in different order).

Clearly explain to students what they are to do. Before distributing the test, explain to the students what they are to do when they are finished (work on another task, quietly write in their journals, work on their portfolios, or begin a homework or reading assignment). This task—an anchor task—was explained on the first day of school and rehearsed repeatedly with the students. The students know that they are to work on this task when they have extra class time, because not all students will finish at the same time and it is unreasonable to expect most students to sit quietly after finishing a test. Students occupy this quiet time with an anchor task.

Test quickly and efficiently. When ready, begin the test promptly. Hand out the tests quickly. Once testing has begun, avoid interrupting the students. Important announcements or other information can be written on the board, or if unrelated to the test, held until all students are finished with the test. Stay in the room and visually monitor the students. If the test is not going to take an entire class period (and most should not) and it is a major test, then give it at the beginning of the period, if possible, unless you are planning a test review just prior to it (although that seems rather late to conduct a meaningful review).

PREPARING ASSESSMENT ITEMS

Preparing and writing good assessment items is yet another professional skill to develop. Proficiency in test development takes study, time, practice, and reflection. As a professional educator, you should take time to study different types of assessment items that can be used and how best to write them, and then practice writing them. As discussed, when preparing assessment items, ensure that they match and sufficiently cover the instructional objectives. In addition, you should prepare each item carefully enough to be reasonably confident that each item will be understood by the student in the manner that you anticipate. With the diversity of students in today's classrooms, this factor is quite important. Finally, after administering a test, take time to analyze the results and reflect on the value of each item before using the item again.

Classification of Assessment Items

Assessment items can be classified as verbal (oral or written words), visual (pictures and diagrams), and manipulative or performance (handling of materials and equipments and performing). For upper grades, written verbal items are those that have traditionally been most frequently used in testing. However, visual items and visual tests are useful, for instance, when working with students who lack fluency with the written word or when testing students who have limited or no proficiency in the English language.

Performance items and tests are useful when measuring for psychomotor skill development. Common examples are performance testing of a student's ability to carry a microscope or hold a jumping rope in place (gross motor skill) or to focus a microscope or to jump rope (fine motor skill). Performance testing also can and should be part of a wider testing program that includes testing for higher-level thinking skills and conceptual knowledge, for example, when a student or small group of students assume the problem of creating from discarded materials a habitat for an imaginary animal and then display, write about, and orally present their product to the rest of the class.

Performance testing/assessment has received a rekindled interest from educators as a means of assessing learning that is close to measuring the real thing—that which is authentic. An example of performance assessment is the student teaching experience in a program for teacher preparation. In this experience, performance assessment is used to assess the teacher candidate's ability to teach (to perform). It seems axiomatic that assessment of student teaching is a more authentic assessment of a candidate's ability to teach than a written (paper-and-pencil test) or verbal (oral test) form of assessment. Although less direct and perhaps less reliable than a checklist observation and analysis of a teacher candidate actually teaching, an observation of a candidate's analysis of a videotaped episode of another teacher's performance would be another way of more authentically assessing a candidate's ability to teach than a strictly paper-and-pencil response item test.

PERFORMANCE TESTING: EXPENSIVE AND TIME INTENSIVE

As you might conclude from our preceding discussion, performance testing is usually more expensive and time consuming than verbal testing, which in turn is more time demanding and expensive than written testing. However, a good program of assessment will use alternate forms of assessment and not rely solely on one form (such as written) and one type of written item (such as multiple choice). You also should avoid using one form of assessment when assessing student learning during and at the conclusion of an ITU of instruction.

The type of test and items that you use depend on your purpose and objectives. Carefully consider the alternatives within that framework. To provide validity checks and to account for the individual differences of students, a good assessment program should include items from all three types, which is what writers of articles in professional journals are referring to when they talk about "alternative assessment." They are encouraging the use of multiple assessment items, as opposed to the traditional heavy reliance on objective items such as multiple-choice questions.

GENERAL GUIDELINES FOR PREPARING FOR ASSESSMENT

As you plan the assessment component of your ITU of instruction, consider the following seven general guidelines: (1) include several kinds of items and assessment instruments (see the types that follow); (2) ensure that content coverage is complete (i.e., that all objectives are being measured); (3) ensure that each item is reliable—that it measures the intended objective (one way to check item reliability is to have more than one item measuring the same objective); (4) ensure that each item is clear and unambiguous to all students; (5) plan each item to be difficult enough for the poorly prepared student but easy enough for the student who is well prepared; (6) maintain a bank of items with each item coded according to its matching instructional objective and to its domain of learning (cognitive, affective, or

psychomotor) and whether it requires recall of information, processing of information, or the application of information; and (7) consider using a ready-made test item bank available on computer disks that accompany many programs or textbooks. If you use them, be certain that the items match your instructional objectives and that they are well written. Just because they were published does not mean that the items are well written.

Every test that you administer to your students should represent your best professional effort—clean and without spelling and grammatical errors. A test that has been quickly and poorly prepared can cause you more grief than you can imagine. A test that is obviously hurriedly prepared and sprinkled with spelling and grammatical errors will be frowned upon by discerning parents/guardians and, if you are a teacher candidate, will certainly bring about an admonishment from your cooperating teacher and your university supervisor.

ATTAINING CONTENT VALIDITY

To ensure that your test measures the appropriate objectives, you can construct a table of specifications. A two-way grid indicates behavior in one dimension and content in another (see Figures 4.5 and 4.6). In the grid in Figure 4.5, behavior relates to the cognitive, affective, and psychomotor domains. In this figure, the cognitive domain is divided according to Bloom's taxonomy (see Chapter 3), into the six categories of knowledge or simple recall, comprehension, application, analysis, synthesis (often involving an original product in oral or written form), and evaluation. The specifications table of Figure 4.6 does not specify levels within the affective and psychomotor domains.

To use a table of specifications. you can examine objectives for the unit and decide what emphasis should be given to the behavior and to the content. For instance, if vocabulary development is a concern for this sixth-grade study of "civilizations: ancient Greece," then probably 20% of the test on vocabulary would be appropriate, but 50% would be unsuitable. This planning enables you to design a test to fit the situation rather than have a haphazard test that does not correspond to the objectives either in content or behavior emphasis. Consider the following example: You realize that recall questions are easy to write and note that tests often fail to go beyond this level even though the objectives state that the student will analyze and evaluate. The sample table of specifications for an ITU on "civilizations: ancient Greece" indicates a distribution of questions

FIGURE 4.5   Table of Specifications I

CONTENT	BEHAVIORS								TOTAL
Social Studies Grade 6	Cognitive						**Affective**	**Psychomotor**	
Ancient Greece	**Knowledge**	**Comprehension**	**Application**	**Analysis**	**Synthesis**	**Evaluation**			
I. Vocabulary development		2 (1, 2)	1 (2)						3
II. Concepts		2 (3, 4)	2 (4)						4
III. Applications	1 (5)	1	1 (5)	1 (5)	1 (5)	1 (5)			6
IV. Problem solving		1 (6)		1 (6)					2
TOTAL	**1**	**6**	**4**	**2**	**1**	**1**			**15**

FIGURE 4.6   Table of Specifications II

CONTENT	BEHAVIORS							TOTAL
	Cognitive			Affective		Psychomotor		
	Input	**Processing**	**Application**	**Low**	**High**	**Low**	**High**	
I.								
II.								
III.								
IV.								
TOTAL								

on a test. Since this test is to be an objective test and it is considered unnecessary to test for affective and psychomotor behaviors on this test, this table of specifications calls for no test items in these areas. If these categories are included in the unit objectives, other assessment devices can be used to test learning in these domains. As the teacher, you could also show the objectives tested, as indicated in parentheses in Figure 4.5. Then a later check on inclusion of all objectives is easy to perform.

Preferred by some teachers is the alternative table shown in Figure 4.6. Rather than differentiating among all six of Bloom's cognitive levels, this table separates cognitive objectives into three levels: those that require simple low-level recall of knowledge, those that require information processing, and those that require application of the new knowledge. In addition, the affective and psychomotor domains are each divided into low- and high-level behaviors.

TYPES OF ASSESSMENT ITEMS: DESCRIPTIONS, EXAMPLES, AND GUIDELINES FOR PREPARING AND USING

In this section, we present descriptions of assessment items, some advantages and limitations, and several guidelines for preparing and using various types of items. When reading about the advantages and limitations of each, you will notice that only some types are appropriate for use in direct or performance assessment. The guidelines that follow also include special suggestions for using the item with mainstreamed students.

Arrangement Type

Description. Terms, sentences, or real objects (realia) are to be arranged in a specified order.

Example. Arrange the following list of events on a time line in order of their occurrence: The *Mayflower* anchored in the harbor. The crew and passengers of the *Mayflower* assembled for a meeting to determine their self-government. The pilgrims on the *Mayflower* signed the Mayflower Compact to establish a government of just and equal laws and promised to obey such laws.

Advantages. This type of item tests for knowledge of sequence and order and is good for review and for starting discussions and for performance assessment.

Limitations. Scoring can be difficult, so be cautious and meticulous when using this type for grading purposes.

Guidelines for use. To enhance reliability, you may need to add instructions to the students to include the rationale for their arrangement, making it a combined arrangement and short explanation type of assessment and allowing space for explanations on an answer sheet. This type is useful for small, heterogeneous group assessment to allow students to share and learn from their combined thinking and reasoning.

Completion Type

Description. This type is sometimes called a fill-in item during which an incomplete sentence is presented and the student is to complete it by filling in the blank space(s) or is to complete an incomplete drawing.

Example. To test their hypotheses, social scientists conduct _____ .

Advantages. This type of item requires less time than a complete answer or drawing, which might be required in an essay type item. This type is easy to devise, take, and score.

Limitations. Take care with the instructions so students do not misinterpret the expectation, and be flexible in accepting the response. Your answer key may have "experiments" as the correct answer for the item in the above mentioned example, but a student might answer with "investigations" or "tests" or some other response that is equally valid.

Guidelines for use. This type is useful for small, heterogeneous group assessment to allow students to share and learn from their group thinking and reasoning and to measure conceptual knowledge. You can make the item a combined drawing-completion and short explanation type and engage the students in including their rationales for their thinking behind the completions. Allow additional space for the explanations or for the responses of students with motor control difficulties. For sentence completion, use one blank per item and keep the blanks equal in length.

Correction Type

Description. This type is similar to the completion type with the following variation: patterns, complete sentences, or paragraphs are given with underlined or italicized words that are to be changed to make the sentences/paragraphs correct.

Example. After the settlement of Jamestown, Virginia, in 1607, Plymouth Colony was the second English *sand castle* in North America. The *sand castle* was established on the rocky shore of Cape Cod Bay in 1620. The colonists called their new *castle* Plymouth after the English *castle* Plymouth from which they had set sail on the *Mayflower* to North America.

Advantages. This type of item is very useful for introducing procedures, patterns such as the Fibonacci number series (1, 1, 2, 3, 5, 8, . . .), words with multiple meanings, or information. Writing this type can be fun for the teacher for the purpose of preassessment of student knowledge or for a review. Students may enjoy this type especially when used only occasionally, for the tension relief afforded by the incorrect absurdities.

Limitations. As with the completion type, the correction type tends to measure for low-level recall and rote memory except in cases when a student is unfamiliar with the patterns or information; the item then becomes a relatively high-level question. The underlined incorrect items also could be so humorous that they might cause more classroom disturbance than you want.

Guidelines for use. Use occasionally for diversion and discussion. When possible, write items that measure for higher-level cognition or consider making it a combined correction and short explanation type. Allow space for student explanations.

Essay Type

Description. This type is used when a question or problem is presented and the student is asked to compose a response in the form of sustained prose, using the student's own words, phrases, and ideas within the limits of the question or problem.

Example. Related to the pilgrims' Mayflower Compact, what contributions about self-government would you have made to the Compact if you had been a pilgrim on the *Mayflower* in 1620? Justify your contributions.

Advantages. This type of item measures conceptual knowledge and higher mental processes such as the ability to synthesize material and to express ideas in clear and precise written language. It is especially useful in integrated thematic teaching. It provides practice in written expression and can be used in performance assessment such as in predicting how long a plant will live after seeing that it is growing in certain conditions of soil, light, and temperature.

Limitations. An essay item requires a good deal of time to read and to score. It can provide an unreliable sampling of achievement and is vulnerable to teacher subjectivity and unreliable scoring. Further, an essay item tends to punish the student who writes slowly and laboriously, who has limited proficiency in the written language but who may have achieved as well as a student who writes faster and is more proficient in the language. An essay item tends to favor students who have fluency with words but whose achievement many not necessarily be better. In addition, do not assume that all students understand all the verbs unless you have given instruction in the meaning of key directive verbs.

Guidelines for use. When preparing an essay-only test, prepare many questions that require a relatively short prose response (similar to the short explanation type). Short response questions are preferable to a smaller number of questions that require long prose responses. Briefer answers tend to be more precise and the use of many items provides a more reliable sampling of student achievement. When you prepare short prose response questions, be sure to avoid using words verbatim from the student textbook. Also consider the following hints.

1. Allow students adequate test time for a full response.

2. Consider having the students answer the same questions as opposed to them selecting essay items from a list. This continuity will give you different qualities of achievement than the student responses that you can compare.

3. Prepare the essay items, make a tentative scoring key, and decide the key ideas you expect the students to identify. Decide the number of points that will be allotted to each item.

4. Inform the students about the relative test value for each item. Point values, if different for each item, can be listed in the margin of the test next to each item.

5. Have the students write their names on the backs of the papers or use a number code rather than having students put their names on the front of essay papers. This practice will keep you unaware of whose paper you are reading and will nullify the "halo effect" that can occur when you know whose paper you are correcting.

6. Read all student papers for one essay item response at a time in one sitting, and while doing that, make notes to yourself; then repeat and while reading that item again, score each student's paper for that item. Repeat the process for the next essay item, but change the order of the pile of papers so you are not reading them in the same order. While scoring the essay responses, keep in mind the nature of the objective being measured, which may include the qualities of handwriting, grammar, spelling, punctuation, and neatness.

7. Mark the papers with positive and constructive comments and show students how they could have explained or responded better. Remember to be patient, tolerant, positive, and prescriptive, understanding that while having some understanding of a concept, some students will not yet be facile with written expression.

8. Give instruction and practice to students in responding to key directive verbs that will be used before using this type of test item (see Figure 4.7).

Grouping

Description. Several items are presented and the student is to select and group those that are related in some way.

Example. Separate the following words into two groups; those that are related to Plymouth Colony, place in group A and those that are not, place in group B. Words: pilgrims, sand castle, compact, jet, self-government, automobile, *Mayflower,* 1620.

Advantages. This type tests knowledge of grouping and can be used to measure conceptual knowledge and

FIGURE 4.7   Meaning of Key Directive Verbs for Essay Item Responses

Compare asks for an analysis of similarity and difference but with a greater emphasis on similarities or likenesses

Contrast asks more for differences than for similarities

Criticize asks for the good and bad of an idea or situation

Define means to express clearly and concisely the meaning of a term as from a dictionary or in the student's own words

Diagram means to put quantities or numerical values into the form of a chart, graph, or drawing

Discuss means to explain or argue, presenting various sides of events, ideas, or situations

Enumerate means to name or list one after another, which is different from "explain briefly" or "tell in a few words"

Evaluate means to express worth, value, and judgment

Explain means to describe, with emphasis on cause and effect

Generalize means to arrive at a valid generalization from provided specific information

Identify means to state recognizable or identifiable characteristics

Infer means to forecast what is likely to happen as a result of information provided

Illustrate means to describe by means of examples, figure, pictures, or diagrams

Interpret means to describe or explain a given fact, theory, principle, or doctrine within a specific context

Justify means to show reasons with an emphasis on correct, positive, and advantageous

List means to simply name items in a category or to include them in a row or column without much description

Outline means to give a short summary with headings and subheadings

Prove means to present materials as witnesses, proof, and evidence

Relate means to tell how specified things are connected or brought into some kind of relationship

Summarize means to recapitulate the main points without example or illustrations

Trace means to follow a history or series of events, step by step, by going backward over the evidence

higher levels of cognition, and to stimulate discussion. It can also be similar to a multiple-choice type item.

Limitations. Remain alert for the student who has an alternative but valid rationale for her or his grouping.

Guidelines for use. To allow for an alternative correct response, consider making the item a combination grouping, short explanation type, being certain to allow adequate space to encourage student explanations.

Identification Type

Description. Unknown "specimens" are to be identified by name or some other criterion.

Example. Identify each of the food specimens on the table by its common name.

Advantages. This type of item is useful for authentic and performance assessments and allows students to work with real materials or symbolizations. It can measure higher-level learning, procedural understanding, and identification of steps in a process.

Limitations. This type takes more time than many of the other item types—both for the teacher to prepare and for the students to complete. Because of a special familiarity with the materials, some students may have an advantage over others. Therefore, be fair by ensuring that the specimens used are equally familiar or unfamiliar to all students.

Guidelines for use. Whatever specimens are used, they must be familiar to all or to none of the students, and they must be clear and not confusing (e.g., fuzzy photographs or unclear photocopies, dried and incomplete plant specimens, and garbled music recordings can be frustrating for students to discern). Consider using this item for a dyad or team rather than for individual testing.

Matching Type

Description. Several items are presented in a list of numbered items and the student is to match the items to a list of lettered choices or in some way connect those items that are the same or are related.

Example. In the blank space next to each description in column A (stem or premises column) put the letter of the correct answer from column B (answer or response column).

A (stem column)	B (answer column)
_____1. 20th Century U.S. president	A. Bill Clinton
_____2. U.S. past president	B. Thomas Jefferson
_____3. First U.S. president	C. George Washington

Advantages. Matching items can measure for ability to judge relationships and to differentiate between similar facts, ideas, definitions, and concepts. These items are easy to score and can test a broad range of content. They reduce guessing, especially if one group (e.g., the answer column) contains more items than the other, are interesting to students, and are adaptable for performance assessment.

Limitations. Although the matching item is adaptable for performance assessment, the items are not easily adapted to measuring for higher cognition. Because all parts must be homogeneous, it is possible that clues will be given, thus reducing the validity.

Guidelines for use. The number of items in the response or answer column should exceed the number in the stem column, but keep the number of stem items to 10 or less. Matching sets should have high homogeneity (i.e., items in both columns or groups should be of the same general category) and avoid mixing dates, events, and names. The answers in the response column should be short, about one or two words each and should be ordered logically, perhaps alphabetically or chronologically. If answers from the response column can be used more than once, which can help to avoid guessing by elimination, the directions should state that fact. Be prepared for the student who can legitimately defend an "incorrect" response. To eliminate the paper-and-pencil aspect and make the item more direct, use an item such as "from the materials on the table, pair up those that are most alike."

Multiple-Choice Type

Description. This type is similar to the completion item in that statements are presented (the stem) and are sometimes incomplete or have several options or alternatives. This type requires recognition or even higher cognitive processes than mere recall.

Example. Which one of the following is a pair of antonyms?

a. loud/soft
b. halt/finish
c. absolve/vindicate
d. procure/purchase

Advantages. This type of item can be answered and scored quickly. A wide range of content and higher levels of cognitions can be tested in a relatively short time. This type is excellent for all testing purposes—motivation, review, and assessment of learning.

Limitations. Unfortunately, because multiple-choice items are relatively easy to write, test authors tend to write items measuring only for low levels of cognition. Multiple-choice items are excellent for major testing, but questions should be of high quality and measure higher levels of thinking and learning.

Guidelines for use. Consider the following:

1. If the item is in the form of an incomplete statement, then it should be meaningful in itself and imply a direct question rather than merely lead into a collection of unrelated true and false statements.

2. Use a level of language that is easy enough for even the poorest readers and those with limited proficiency in English to understand; avoid unnecessary wordiness.

3. If there is much variation in the length of alternatives, arrange the alternatives in order from shortest to longest (i.e., first alternative is the shortest, last alternative is the longest). For single-word alternatives, the consistent use of the arrangement of alternatives is recommended, such as by length of answer or in alphabetical order.

4. Arrangement of alternatives should be uniform throughout the test and listed in vertical (column) form rather than in horizontal (paragraph) form.

5. Incorrect responses (distracters) should be plausible and related to the same concept as the correct alternative. An occasional humorous distracter may help relieve test anxiety, but in general they should be avoided. They offer no measuring value and increase the likelihood of the student guessing the correct response.

6. It is not necessary to maintain a fixed number of alternatives for every item, but the use of less than

three is not recommended. Although it is not always possible to develop four or five plausible responses, that number reduces chance responses and guessing, thereby increasing reliability for the item. If you cannot think of enough plausible distracters, include the item on a test the first time as a completion item. As the students respond, wrong answers will provide you with a number of plausible distracters that you can use the next time to make the item a multiple-choice type item.

7. Some mainstreamed students may work better when allowed to circle their selected response rather than writing its letter or number in a blank space.

8. Responses such as "all of these" or "none of these" should be used only when they will contribute more than another plausible distracter. Be sure that such answers complete the item. "All of the above" is a poorer alternative than "none of the above" because items that use it as a correct response must have four or five correct answers; also, if it is the right answer, knowledge of any two of the distracters will provide the cue.

9. Every item should be grammatically consistent. For example, if the stem is in the form of an incomplete sentence, it should be possible to complete the sentence by attaching any of the alternatives to it.

10. The stem should state a single and specific point, mean the same thing to every student, and must not include clues to the correct alternative. Here's an example: A four-sided figure whose opposite sides are parallel is called _____ . (Use of the word *parallel* clues the answer.)

a. an octagon
b. a parallelogram
c. a trapezoid
d. a triangle

11. The item should be expressed in positive form. A negative form can present a psychological disadvantage to students. Negative items are those that ask what is *not* characteristic of something, or what is the *least* useful. Discard the item if you cannot express it in positive terminology.

12. There must be only one correct or best response, which is easier said than done. You might consider providing space between test items for students to include their rationales for their responses, thus making the test a combination multiple-choice and short explanation item type. This form provides for the measurement of higher levels of cognition and encourages writing. It provides for the students who can rationalize an alternative that you had not considered plausible, especially possible today with

the diversity of cultural experiences represented by students. For example, recall the story about a math test question that asked, "If a farmer saw 8 crows sitting on a fence and shot 3 of them, how many would be left on the fence?" According to the answer key, the correct response was "5." However, one critical thinking student chose "none" and was marked wrong by the teacher. The student was thinking that the crows that were not shot would be frightened and would all fly away, thus "none" would remain on the fence.

13. Measuring for understanding of definitions is better tested by furnishing the name or word and requiring choice between alternative definitions than by presenting the definition and requiring choice between alternative words.

14. Avoid using alternatives that include absolute terms such as *never* and *always*.

15. Multiple-choice items need not be entirely verbal. Consider the use of realia, charts, diagrams, videos, and other visuals. They will make the test more interesting, especially to students with low verbal abilities or to those who have limited proficiency in English, and consequently, they will make the assessment more direct.

16. Once you have composed a series of multiple-choice items or a complete test of this item type, tally the position of answers to be sure they are evenly distributed, to avoid the common psychological habit (when there are four alternatives) of having the correct alternative in the third position. In other words, when alternative choices are A, B, C, and D or 1, 2, 3, and 4, unless the test designer is aware and avoids it, more correct answers will be in the "C" or "3" position than in any other.

17. While scoring, tally the incorrect responses for each item on a blank copy of the test. Analyze incorrect responses for each item to discover potential errors in your scoring key. If, for example, many students select B for an item for which your key says the correct answer is A, you may have made a mistake on your scoring key or in teaching the lesson.

Performance Type

Description. Provided with certain conditions or materials, the student solves a problem or accomplishes some other action.

Example. Write a retelling of your favorite ancient Greek fable or myth on the computer and create a diorama to accompany it.

Advantages. This type of item comes closer to direct measurement (authentic assessment) of certain expected outcomes than most other types. As indicated in discussions of the preceding question types, others can actually be prepared as performance type items, that is, when the student actually does what he or she is being tested for.

Limitations. This type can be difficult and time consuming to administer to a group of students. Scoring may tend to be subjective. It could be difficult to give makeup tests to students who were absent on test day.

Guidelines for use. Use your creativity to design and use performance tests, as they tend to measure well the important objectives. To establish a performance assessment situation, see the instructions in Figure 4.8. To reduce subjectivity in scoring, prepare distinct scoring guidelines (rubrics), as discussed in scoring essay type items and shown in Figures 4.9 and 4.10.[14]

Short Explanation Type

Description. The short explanation question is like the essay type but requires a shorter answer.

Example. Briefly explain in a paragraph how you would end the story.

Advantages. This type of item, like the essay type, assesses student understanding, but takes less

FIGURE 4.8   Steps for Establishing a Performance Assessment Situation with a Sample Rubric for Listening Skill and a Sample Checklist for Map Work

I. Specify the performance objective.

II. Specify the test situation.

III. Establish the criteria (scoring rubric) for judging the excellence of the process and/or product. Here is a sample rubric for assessing a student's skill in listening.

   A. Strong listener:

     Responds immediately to oral directions

     Focuses on speaker

     Maintains appropriate attention span

     Listens to what others are saying

     Is interactive

   B. Capable listener:

     Follows oral directions

     Is usually attentive to speaker and to discussions

     Listens to others without interrupting

   C. Developing listener:

     Has difficulty following directions

     Relies on repetition

     Is often inattentive

     Has short attention span

     Often interrupts the speaker

IV. Make a checklist by which to score the performance or product. The checklist is simply a list of the criteria you established in step III. For example, here is a brief checklist for map work:

Check each item if the map reaches the standard in this particular category.

_____ 1. Accuracy

_____ 2. Neatness

_____ 3. Attention to details

V. Prepare directions in writing, outlining the situation with instructions the students are to follow.

FIGURE 4.9   Sample Scoring Rubric for Student Research Paper

Parenthetical Reference	**14–15** All documented correctly. Paper's references document a wide variety of sources cited—at least five from bibliography.	**12–13** Most documented correctly. Few minor errors. At least three sources from bibliography are cited.	**11** Some documented correctly. Some show no documentation at all. May not correlate to the bibliography.	**1–10** Few to none are documented. Does not correlate to the bibliography. May be totally absent.
Bibliography and Sources	**14–15** Strong use of library research. Exceeds minimum of five sources. Bibliography is correctly formatted.	**12–13** Good use of library research. Exceeds minimum of five sources. Bibliography has few or no errors in format.	**11** Some use of library research. Meets minimum of five sources. Bibliography is present but may be problematic.	**1–10** Fails to meet minimum standards for library research. Bibliography has major flaws or may be missing.
Mechanics/Format	**14–15** Correct format and pagination. Neat title page, near perfect spelling, punctuation, and grammar.	**12–13** Mostly correct format and pagination. Neat. Few errors in title page, spellings, punctuation, and grammar.	**11** Errors in format and pagination. Flawed title page. Distracting errors in spelling, punctuation, and grammar.	**1–10** Incorrect format. Title page is flawed or missing. Many errors in spelling, punctuation, and grammar. Lack of planning is obvious. Paper is difficult to read.
Thesis	**9–10** An original and comprehensive thesis that is clear and well thought out. All sections work to support it.	**8** Comprehensive and well-focused thesis, which is clearly stated. All sections work to support it.	**7** Adequate thesis that is understandable but may be neither clear nor focused. It covers the majority of the issues found in the sections.	**1–6** Inadequate thesis that is disconnected from the research or may be too broad to support. May be convoluted, confusing, or absent.
Completeness/ Coherence	**18–20** Paper reads as a unified whole. There is no repetition of information. All sections are in place, and transitions between them are clearly developed.	**16–17** Paper reads as a unified whole with no repetition. All sections are in place, but transitions between them are not as smooth.	**14–15** Paper has required sections. Repetitions may be evident. The paper does not present a unified whole. Transitions are missing or inadequate.	**1–13** Paper lacks one or more sections and makes no attempt to connect sections as a whole unit. Sections may be grossly repetitive or contradictory.
Thinking/Analyzing	**23–25** Strong understanding of the topic. Knowledge is factually relevant, accurate, and consistent. Solutions show analysis of research discussed in paper.	**20–22** Good understanding of the topic. Uses main points of information researched. Solutions build on examination of research discussed in paper.	**18–19** General understanding of topic. Uses research and attempts to add to it; solutions refer to some of the research discussed.	**1–16** Little understanding of topic. Uses little basic information researched. Minimal examination of the topic. Solutions may be based solely on own opinions without support.

Source: Elk Grove School District, Elk Grove, California. Possible score = 100. Scorer marks a relevant square in each of the six categories (horizontal rows) and score for that category is the small number in that square.

FIGURE 4.10   Sample Scoring Rubric for Student Project Presentation

	14–15	12–13	11	1–10
Professional Presentation	Well organized; smooth transitions between sections; all enthusiastically participate and share responsibility.	Well organized with transitions, students confer/present ideas; group shows ability to interact; attentive discussion of research.	Shows basic organization; lacks transitions; some interaction; discussion focuses mostly on research.	Unorganized, lacks planning; no transitions; reliance on one spokesperson; little interaction; disinterest; too brief.
	14–15	12–13	11	1–10
Engagement of Audience	Successfully and actively engages audience in more than one pertinent activity; maintains interest throughout.	Engages audience in at least one related activity; maintains attention through most of presentation.	Attempts to engage audience in at least one activity; no attempt to involve *entire* audience. May not relate in significant way.	Fails to involve audience; does not maintain audience attention; no connection with audience. No relationship between activity and topic.
	18–20	16–17	14–15	1–13
Use of Literature	Strong connection between literature and topic; significant, perceptive explanation of literature; pertinent to topic. At least two pieces used.	Clear connection between literature and topic; clear explanation; appropriate to topic. Two pieces used.	Weak connection to topic; unclear explanation; one genre; one piece used.	No connection to topic; no explanation; inappropriate literature; no literature.
	18–20	16–17	14–15	1–13
Knowledge of Subject	Strong understanding of topic; knowledge factually relevant, accurate, and consistent; solution shows analysis of evidence.	Good understanding of topic; uses main points of information researched; builds solution on examination of major evidence.	Shows general understanding; focuses on one aspect, discusses at least one other idea; uses research, attempts to add to it; solution refers to evidence.	Little understanding or comprehension of topic; uses little basic information researched; forms minimal solution; relies on solely own opinions without support.
	18–20	16–17	14–15	1–13
Use of Media	Effectively combines and integrates three distinct forms with one original piece; enhances understanding; offers insight into topic.	Combines two forms with one original piece; relates to topic; connection between media and topic is explained.	Includes two or three forms but no original piece; media relates to topic. Explanation may be vague or missing.	One form; no original piece; connection between media and topic is unclear.
	9–10	8	7	1–6
Speaking Skills	Clear enunciation; strong projection; vocal variety; eye contact with entire audience; presentation posture; solid focus with no interruptions.	Good enunciation; adequate projection; partial audience eye contact; appropriate posture.	Inconsistent enunciation; low projection with little vocal variety; inconsistent posture.	Difficult to understand; inaudible; monotonous; no eye contact; inappropriate posture; interruptions and distractions.

Source: Elk Grove School District, Elk Grove, California. Possible score = 100. Scorer marks a square in each of six categories (horizontal rows) and score for that category is the small number in the square.

In a peer conference, students hand their papers to peers on the left, who offer suggestions for improvements.

time for you to read and score. By using several questions of this type, a greater amount of content can be covered than with a lesser number of essay questions. This type of question provides valuable opportunities for students to learn to express themselves succinctly in writing.

Limitations. Some students will have difficulty in expressing themselves in a limited fashion orally or in writing. They need practice, coaching, and time.

Guidelines for use. This type is useful for occasional reviews and quizzes and as an alternative to other types of questions. For scoring, establish a scoring rubric and follow the same guidelines as for the essay type item.

True-False Type

Description. A statement is presented and students are asked to judge its accuracy.

Example. T or F? Christopher Columbus discovered America in 1492.

Advantages. This type of item allows many items to be answered in a relatively short time, making broad content coverage possible. Scoring is quick and simple. True-false items are good as discussion starters, for review, and for diagnostic evaluation (preassessment) of what students already know or think they know

Limitations. This type can sometimes be difficult to write as purely true or false without qualifying them in such a way that clues the answer. Another

difficulty is writing an item that tests only one or two ideas with which the student should be familiar. In the previous example, a student has to consider more than one idea—Columbus, America, and 1492. Also, a student may question whether Columbus really did discover America or may misunderstand the meaning of "discovering America." Questions about the example are "Weren't people there already when he landed?" and "Where, exactly, did he land?" and "What is meant by 'America'?"

Other limitations are (1) much of the content that lends itself to the true-false type of test item is trivial; (2) guessing might be encouraged; and (3) this type of item lacks data about why a student misses an item. You realize that students have a 50% chance of guessing the correct answer, thus giving this item type both poor validity and poor reliability. You also realize that scoring and grading will give you no clue about why a student missed an item. Consequently, the limitations of true-false items far outweigh the advantages. *Therefore, we suggest that pure true-false items not be used for arriving at grades.*

Guidelines for use. For grading purposes, we suggest that you use modified true-false items (see guideline 11 that follows) where space is provided between items for students to write their explanations, thus making the item a combined true-false, short explanation type. Consider the following hints.

1. To prepare a false statement, first write the statement as a true statement, then make it false by changing a word or phrase.

2. A true-false statement should include only one idea.

3. Prepare close to an equal number of true and false items.

4. Proofread your items (or have a friend do it) to be sure that the sentences are well constructed and are free from typographical errors.

5. Avoid words that may have different meanings for different students.

6. Avoid using verbatim language from the student textbook.

7. Avoid trick items such as a slight reversal of numbers in a date.

8. Try to avoid using negative statements as they tend to confuse students.

9. Try to avoid using specific determiners (e.g., *always*, *all*, or *none*), because these words usually clue that the statement is false; also avoid words that may clue the statement as true (e.g., *often*, *probably*, and *sometimes*).

10. Rather than using symbols for the words *true* and *false* (sometimes teachers use symbols such as + and −) which might be confusing, or having students write the letters *T* and *F* (sometimes a student does not write the letters clearly enough for the teacher to be able to distinguish between them), have students either write out the words *true* and *false* or, better yet, have the students simply circle *T* or *F* in the left margin of each item.

11. To avoid wrong answers caused by variations in thinking and to make the item more valid and reliable, encourage the students to write in their rationales for selecting true or false and make the item a modified true-false item. Here's an exam-

ple: When a farmer saw 8 crows sitting on the fence surrounding his corn field, he shot 3 of them. Five were left on the fence. T or F?_____ . Explanation: _____

As stated earlier, for grading purposes, you may use modified true-false items, thus making the item a combined true-false, short explanation type and allowing for divergent and critical thinking. Another form of modified true-false item is the "sometimes-always-never" item in which a third alternative, "sometimes," is introduced to reduce the chance for guessing.

Now do Exercise 4.1 on pages 141 through 144 to begin the preparation of your assessment items for your ITU.

ASSESSING YOUR ITU BY FIELD TESTING

Once completed you will want to assess your ITU through field testing either on your own or as a member of a teaching team. You can begin with the teaching lessons you planned to initiate the ITU. As the unit continues, consider the ITU from daily perspectives. Write down the successes and failure experiences each day so you can make gradual, daily adjustments to your teaching, which is part of your formative evaluation of the unit. Gather information about the students' progress in the unit in various ways as discussed in this chapter. Collect information that relates specifically to your learning objective. For instance, you might consider developing an overall checklist about the information related to the unit for

A teacher can use a checklist to help assess students' participation in group work.

FIGURE 4.11   Sample Student Learning Assessment Checklist

Learning Assessment Checklist

Student _____   Date _____

Teacher _____   Time _____

_____ **1.** Can identify theme, topic, main idea of the unit

_____ **2.** Can identify contributions of others to the theme

_____ **3.** Can identify problems related to the unit of study

4. Has developed skills in:

_____ Applying knowledge	_____ Problem solving
_____ Assuming responsibility	_____ Reading text
_____ Classifying	_____ Reading maps and globes
_____ Categorizing	_____ Reasoning
_____ Decision making	_____ Reflecting
_____ Discussing	_____ Reporting to others
_____ Gathering resources	_____ Self-assessing
_____ Inquiry	_____ Sharing
_____ Justifying choices	_____ Studying
_____ Listening to others	_____ Summarizing
_____ Locating information	_____ Thinking
_____ Metacognition	_____ Using resources
_____ Ordering	_____ Working with others
_____ Organizing information	_____ Working independently
_____ Problem identification	_____ Others unique to the unit

Additional teacher and student comments:

your assessment record. It can be a place for recording notes about a student's participation, behavior, and development of conceptual and procedural knowledge, and about affective behaviors. The following sample checklist in Figure 4.11 would need to be modified to fit your purposes, but it is an example of a checklist that can be used in your ITU (to make additional blank copies, use Planning Master 4.1).

Each day you will reflect on that day's experiences and consider what went well and what needs to be changed, how it can be changed, and how soon the changes can be made. After the ITU has been taught, you should write what, if any, revisions you will make in the future, which is part of your summative evaluation of the unit. As discussed in Chapter 2, the best ITUs are never "set in concrete," but are ever changing.

When working as a member of a teaching team, on an agreed-upon date, the team members should present a synopsis of results of the lesson(s) each has taught. As the unit continues, the team can field test the ITU in various ways—members could trade classes or participate in team teaching. As an example, two members could combine their classes for instruction in the ITU, if the situation is possible within the school's facilities and scheduling arrangements.

During a common planning period (and periodically if needed), members should meet as a group to assess the progress of the ITU. During this time you will want to discuss recent pluses and minuses in the lessons, which is part of the team's ongoing formative assessment of the unit. Together, team members can brainstorm what they want to change in the ITU, how the changes should be introduced, and when such changes could occur. After the ITU has been completed, the team should reconvene to discuss what revisions in the ITU should be made for future use, which is part of the team's summative assessment of the unit.

SUMMARY

At this point in the guide, you have learned the importance of the assessment component of teaching and learning, of its ongoing nature, and of various techniques by which you and your students can discover what the students are learning and have learned. Many of these devices are information data-collecting techniques (such as checklists, journals, portfolios, and teacher logs), but others are more formal (tests). You realize that effective assessment begins with what students know or what they think they know about a topic and you will develop clear considerations about what it is the students should learn and then observe them as they are learning. Additionally, you will make judgments about the quality and quantity of their work both during and at the completion of their study. Quality assessment means "kid watching." Your observations and informal methods of assessment are central to the evaluation of meaningful learning, and for each student you must keep carefully annotated and well-organized records.

You have thought about and planned some of your assessment strategies. Now it is time for you to complete the development of your ITU, which you will do in Chapter 5.

QUESTIONS AND ACTIVITIES FOR DISCUSSION

1. Despite your best intentions, is it possible that there will be some students who fail to cooperate and to construct meaning in what they do? In what ways might this be determined in the classroom? How might it be remedied? Participate in a discussion of examples put forth by group members.

2. Some critics argue that different disciplines are not equivalent in importance and value or in the manner of the learning involved. In your opinion, are all disciplines equivalent? Why or why not? What helped you form your opinion? What methods would you use to determine which disciplines to include in an ITU? Discuss your suggestions with others in your group.

3. Other than a paper-and-pencil test, identify three alternative techniques for assessing student learning during or at completion of an interdisciplinary thematic unit.

4. Describe any student learning activities or situations that you believe should not be graded, but should or could be used for assessment of student learning.

5. Describe any prior concepts you held about assessment that changed as a result of your experiences with this chapter. Describe the changes.

6. Do you have questions generated by the content of this chapter? If so, list them and share the list with your colleagues to see if answers to your questions can be obtained.

EXERCISE 4.1

Preparing Assessment Items for My ITU

Instructions.   The purpose of this exercise is for you to practice your skill in preparing different types of assessment items, as you think about the various ways you will assess for student learning in your interdisciplinary thematic unit. Select from your ITU instructional objectives (as in Exercise 3.5) one objective, focus on the anticipated learning (not the conditions or performance level), and write assessment items for the objective for each category—preassessment (diagnostic assessment of what students know or think they know prior to your instruction), formative assessment (assessment of learning in progress), and summative (assessment of learning after instruction is completed). If you decide that a particular item type is not applicable for your particular grade level or for the assessment category, write "NA" next to the item, and then during review of one another's exercises, talk about your decision to obtain group consensus. Perhaps others may see how an item could be used. When completed, share this exercise with your colleagues for their feedback. If you need more space than provided here, use separate paper.

Tentative title of ITU:

Grade level:

Objective:

For Preassessment

1. Arrangement item:

2. Completion item:

3. Correction item:

4. Essay item:

5. Grouping item:

6. Identification item:

7. Matching item:

8. Multiple-choice item:

9. Performance item:

10. Short explanation item:

11. True-false or *modified* true-false item:

For Formative Assessment

1. Arrangement item:

2. Completion item:

3. Correction item:

4. Essay item:

5. Grouping item:

6. Identification item:

7. Matching item:

8. Multiple-choice item:

9. Performance item:

10. Short explanation item:

11. True-false or *modified* true-false item:

For Summative Assessment

1. Arrangement item:

2. Completion item:

3. Correction item:

4. Essay item:

5. Grouping item:

6. Identification item:

7. Matching item:

8. Multiple-choice item:

9. Performance item:

10. Short explanation item:

11. True-false or *modified* true-false item:

CHAPTER NOTES

1. J. Hickman and R. S. Bishop, "African-Americans: Journey to Freedom," *The Web,* 17(2), 19 (Winter, 1993).
2. G. E. Tompkins and K. Hoskisson, *Language Arts: Content and Teaching Strategies* (Upper Saddle River, NJ: Prentice Hall, 1991), p. 63.
3. S. J. Rakow, "Assessment: A Driving Force," *Science Scope,* 15(6), 3 (March, 1992).
4. See also H. Goodrich, "Understanding Rubrics," *Educational Leadership,* 54(4), 14–17 (December, 1996/January, 1997).
5. For information, contact Sunburst, 101 Castleton Street, PO Box 100, Pleasantville, NY 10570-0100. Phone 800-321-7511.
6. L. J. Gibbs and E. J. Earley, *Using Children's Literature to Develop Core Values* (Bloomington, IN: Fastback 362, Phi Delta Educational Foundation, 1994).
7. See E. A. Wynne and H. J. Walberg, "Persisting Groups: An Overlooked Force for Learning," *Phi Delta Kappan,* 75(7), 527–528, 530 (March, 1994).
8. See S. Kagan, "Group Grades Miss the Mark," *Educational Leadership,* 52(8), 68–71 (May, 1995); and D. W. Johnson and R. T. Johnson, "The Role of Cooperative Learning in Assessing and Communicating Student Learning," Chapter 4 in R. T. Guskey, (ed.), *Communicating Student Learning* (Alexandria, VA: ASCD Yearbook, Association for Supervision and Curriculum Development, 1996).
9. Software packages for the development of student electronic portfolios are becoming increasingly available, such as, for example, *Classroom Manager* from CTB Macmillan/McGraw-Hill, Monterey, CA, *Electronic Portfolio* from Learning Quest, Corvallis, OR, and *Grady Profile* from Aurbach and Associates, St. Louis, MO.
10. For a discussion of the biological importance and educational benefits of positive feedback, use of student portfolios, and group learning, see R. Sylwester, "The Neurobiology of Self-Esteem and Aggression," *Educational Leadership,* 54(5), 75–79 (February, 1997).
11. That grading and reporting should always be done in reference to learning criteria and never on a curve is well supported by research studies and authorities on the matter. See, for instance, the suggested readings at the end of this chapter, pages 18–19 in T. R. Guskey, and pages 436–437 in R. J. Stiggins.
12. For a presentation of other methods being used to report student achievement, See T. R. Guskey, *op. cit.*
13. See S. M. Brookhart, "Classroom Assessment: Pervasive, Pivotal, and Primary," *National Forum,* 77(4) (Fall, 1997) pp. 3, 5, 8. Baton Rouge, LA: The Honor Society of Phi Kappa Phi.
14. For a presentation on the importance of rubrics with samples, see M. Schmoker, *Results: The Key to Continuous School Improvement* (Alexandria, VA: Association for Supervision and Curriculum Development, 1996).

FOR FURTHER READING

Brookhart, S. M. (1997, Fall). Classroom assessment: Pervasive, pivotal, and primary. *National Forum* (Baton Rouge, LA: The Honor Society of Phi Kappa Phi), 77(4), 3, 5, 8.

Early, L. M., & LeMahieru, P. G. (1997). Rethinking assessment and accountability. In A. Hargreaves (Ed.), *Rethinking educational change with heart and mind* (pp. 149–168). Alexandria, VA: ASCD 1997 Yearbook, Association for Supervision and Curriculum Development.

Gondree, L. L., & Tundo, V. (1996, April). An alternative final evaluation. *Science Scope,* 19(7), 18–21.

Guskey, T. R. (Ed.). (1996). *Communicating student learning.* Alexandria, VA: ASCD Yearbook, Association for Supervision and Curriculum Development.

Hackman, D. G. (1996, March). Student-led conferences at the middle level: Promoting student responsibility. National Association Secondary School Principals *NASSP Bulletin,* 80(578), 31–36.

Haladyna, T. M. (1997). *Writing test items to evaluate higher-order thinking.* Needham Heights, MA: Allyn & Bacon.

Juarez, T. (1996, January). Why any grades at all, father? *Phi Delta Kappan,* 77(5), 374–377.

Krumboltz, J. D., & Yeh, C. J. (1996, December). Competitive grading sabotages good teaching. *Phi Delta Kappan,* 78(4), 324–326.

Lustig, K. (1996). *Portfolio assessment: A handbook for middle level teachers.* Columbus, OH: National Middle Schools Association.

McMillan, J. H. (1997). *Classroom assessment: Principles and practice for effective instruction.* Needham Heights, MA: Allyn & Bacon.

Miller, H. M. (1997, January). No more one-legged chairs: Sharing the responsibility for portfolio assessment with students, their peers, and their parents. *Middle School Journal,* 28(3), 242–244.

National Parent-Teacher Association. *National standards for parent/family involvement programs.* Chicago: Author, 1997.

Overturg, B. J. (1997, January). Reading portfolios reveal new dimensions of students. *Middle School Journal,* 28(3), 45–50.

Schmoker, M. (1996). *Results: The key to continuous school improvement.* Alexandria, VA: Association for Supervision and Curriculum Development.

Shaklee, B. D., Barbour, N. E., Ambrose, R., & Hansford, S. (1997). *Designing and using portfolios.* Needham Heights, MA: Allyn & Bacon.

Sills-Briegel, T., Fisk, C., and Dunlop, V. (1996, December/January). Graduation by exhibition. *Educational Leadership, 54*(4), 66–71.

Stiggins, R. J. (1997). *Student-centered classroom assessment* (2nd ed.). Upper Saddle River, NJ: Prentice Hall.

Wiggins, G. (1996, December/January). Practicing what we preach in designing authentic assessments. *Educational Leadership, 54*(4), 18–25.

SELECTED INTERNET ADDRESSES

Canadian Teacher-Librarians' Resource Pages (www.inforamp.net/abrown/). Information for those interested in children's books; updated each month.

Guiding Children through Cyberspace (www6.pilot.infi.net/carolyn/guide.html). Provides links to intellectual freedom issues, rating system, Internet use policies, and blocking software.

Junior Scholastic Interactive (http://scholastic.com/jsi) Features world events, geography skills, and citizenship.

CHAPTER 5

Completing Your ITU: Lesson Planning and Sample Units

Curiosity has its own reason for existing. Everything should be made as simple as possible, but not simpler. The most beautiful thing we can experience is the mysterious. It is the source of all true art and science. The important thing is not to stop questioning.

—Albert Einstein

INTERDISCIPLINARY AND INTEGRATED ACTIVITY: REAL-WORLD PROBLEM SOLVING AND DECISION MAKING

During any given day or specified time period, you and the students can look at a problem or subject of study from the point of view of many separate disciplines. Such an interdisciplinary approach to some matter of concern has been adopted not only by educators but also by other professionals. It is the mode of meaningful learning and real-life problem solving. As an example, consider the fact-finding and decision-making approach of public officials in Colorado when confronted with the task of making decisions about projects proposed for watersheds in their state. While gathering information, the officials brought in Dave Rosgen, a state hydrologist. Rosgen led the officials into the field to demonstrate specific ways in which he helped control erosion and rehabilitate damaged streams. He took the officials to Wolf Creek, where they put on high waders. Rosgen led the group down the creek to examine various features of that complex natural stream. He pointed out evidence of the creek's past meanders—patterns he had incorporated into his rehabilitation projects.

In addition to listening to this scientist's point of view, the officials listened to other experts to consider related economic and political issues before making final decisions about projects that had been prepared for watersheds in that state.

Just as Rosgen introduced information from hydrology to the state officials, you can (with the help of students and other teachers and adults) introduce experiences designed to foster ideas and skills from various disciplines. During this interdisciplinary approach, your students can study a topic and its underlying ideas to gain related knowledge and skills from different disciplines/areas on an ongoing basis. For instance, you can develop language arts skills through an ITU by stimulating communication skills through creative writing and other reading, writing, listening, and speaking projects. Throughout the unit, you can guide your students in exploring ideas related to different disciplines to integrate their learning.

Chapter 4 focused on various assessment techniques that can be used to enable you and your students to discover their progress in learning, generally by comparing what they are learning or did learn with what they were expected to learn. Students' personal inquiries are central to the process and much of the assessment of students' learning is done informally and continuously. It is now time for you to complete your ITU and try it out on students for whom it is designed. Your focus for this chapter is to prepare your lessons and put your ITU into its final shape for implementation, although you will make many modifications during its implementation and after. Like any good lesson plan, the best ITUs are never set in concrete.

ORGANIZATION OF THIS CHAPTER

To assist you in completing your unit, this chapter is organized into two parts. The first part of the chapter provides step-by-step guidelines and samples for preparing lessons. The second part provides sample interdisciplinary units. From the samples you will see ways that different teachers have planned their thematic units, provided here for your study, referral, and potential use. Rather than reading and studying all three, you may want to concentrate on only those of interest. Note that certain aspects of each sample ITU may be incomplete or omitted due to space constraints or to the nature of ITUs in general, which reflect the idea that one learning activity may lead to another and unforeseen activity.

As you complete your ITU, and as you refer to the samples, keep in mind what you learned in Chapter 3 about the common thread of four interwoven components that comprise the most effective ITUs: (1) the instruction is centered around a big and meaningful idea (theme) rather than on factitious subject areas; (2) you and the students share in the decision making and responsibility for learning; (3) the learning activities are selected so all students are actively engaged in their learning—they are both physically active with hands-on learning and mentally active with minds-on learning; and (4) there is steady reflection on and frequent sharing of what is being done and what is being learned.

The three sample ITUs are as follows:

1. *Civilizations: Dawn of a New Age in Ancient Greece.* For use in middle and secondary grades; the unit is divided into 11 lessons that may occur over a period of several weeks.
2. *Migrations: Early Newcomers to North America.* Adaptable for use in middle and secondary grades; the unit is divided into 10 lessons and may occur over a period of more than a week.
3. *Changes: Spring as a Time of Growth, Beauty, and Transformations.* For use in first through third grades; the unit is divided into 5 lessons that may extend over a period of more than a week.

LESSON PLANNING FOR INTERDISCIPLINARY THEMATIC INSTRUCTION

You will develop a personal system of lesson planning, a system that works best for you. If you are a beginning teacher, however, you may need a substantial framework from which to work. For that reason, this section provides a suggested lesson plan format (see Figure 5.1), which is the format used for the sample lesson plan in Figure 5.2. As you read this part of the chapter, several references will be made to the lesson plan in Figure 5.2.

In addition to the sample lesson plan that is provided, you will find alternative formats in the sample ITUs. Nothing is sacred about any of these formats and each has worked for some teachers. As

FIGURE 5.1   Sample Lesson Plan Format with Seven Components

1. Descriptive Data

Teacher _____ Class _____ Date _____ Grade level _____

Room number _____ Period _____ ITU _____

Lesson number _____ Topic _____

Time duration _____

2. Goals and Objectives
Instructional Goals:

Specific Objectives:
   Cognitive:

   Affective:

   Psychomotor:

3. Rationale

4. Procedure (includes modeling examples, transitions, practice, etc.)
Content (the exact number of activities in the procedures will vary):

_____ minutes Activity 1: Introduction

_____ minutes Activity 2:

_____ minutes Activity 3:

_____ minutes Activity 4: (final lesson conclusion or closure)

If time remains:

5. Assignments and Reminders of Assignments (if appropriate for grade level)

Special notes and reminders to myself:

6. Materials and Equipment Needed:

Audiovisual:

Other:

7. Assessment, Reflection, and Revision
Assessment of student learning:

Reflective thoughts about the lesson:

Suggestions for revision:

FIGURE 5.2   Lesson Plan Sample: Multiple-Day, Project-Centered, Interdisciplinary and Transcultural Lesson Using Worldwide Communication via the Internet

---

1. Descriptive Data

    Teacher _____   Class   __English/language arts/science__   Date _____

    Grade level __adaptable for grades 4–12_____   Room number _____   Period _____

    ITU __Changes: The Atmosphere_____   Lesson number _____

    Topic __Writing Response and Peer Assessment via Internet as Part of Investigative Research &__

    __Generative Writing__   Time duration: __several days__

2. Goals and Objectives

Instructional Goals:

2.1 One goal for this lesson is for students to collaborate and prepare response papers to peers from around the world who have shared the results of their own experimental research findings and research papers about ozone concentrations in the atmosphere.

2.2 Another goal for this unit is for students to prepare and publish worldwide the dissemination of a final paper about global ozone levels in the atmosphere to peers on the Internet.

Specific Objectives:

Cognitive:

a. Through cooperative group action, students will conduct experimental research to collect data about the ozone level of air in their environment. (application)

b. In cooperative groups, students will analyze the results of their experiments. (analyze)

c. Students will compile data and infer from their experimental data. (synthesis and evaluation)

d. Through collaborative writing groups, students will prepare a final paper that summarizes their research study of local atmospheric ozone levels. (evaluation)

e. Through sharing via the Internet, students will write response papers to their peers in other locations in the world. (evaluation)

f. From their own collaborative research and worldwide communications with their peers, students will draw conclusions about global atmospheric ozone levels. (evaluation)

Affective:

a. Students will respond attentively to the response papers of their peers. (attending)

b. Students will willingly cooperate with others during the group activities. (responding)

c. Students will offer opinions about the atmospheric level of ozone. (valuing)

d. Students will form judgments about local, regional, and worldwide ozone levels. (organizing)

e. Students communicate accurately their findings and diligently to the work of their worldwide peers. (internalizing)

Psychomotor:

a. Students will give commands on the computer so that their e-mail communications are transmitted accurately. (manipulating)

b. In a summary to the study, students will describe their feelings about atmospheric ozone concentrations and possible solutions. (communicating)

c. Students will ultimately create a proposal for worldwide dissemination. (creating)

3. Rationale

3.1 Important to improvement in one's writing and communication skills are the processes of selecting a topic, decision making, arranging, drafting, proofing, peer review, commenting, revising, editing, rewriting, and publishing the results—processes that are focused on in the writing aspect of this unit.

3.2 Student writers need many readers to respond to their work. Through worldwide communication with peers and dissemination of their final product, this need can be satisfied.

3.3 Students learn best when they are actively pursuing a topic of interest that has meaning for them. This unit provides an opportunity for students to brainstorm potential problems and arrive at their own topic(s) for problem solving.

3.4 Real-world problems are interdisciplinary and transcultural; involving writing (English/language arts), science, mathematics (data collecting, graphing, etc.), and intercultural communication; this unit is an interdisciplinary transcultural unit.

FIGURE 5.2   continued

---

4. Procedure (includes modeling examples, transitions, practice, etc.)
Content (the exact number of activities in the procedures will vary):

At the start of this unit, collaborative groups were established via Intercultural E-mail with other classes from schools around the world. These groups of students conducted several scientific research experiments on the ozone level of their local atmosphere. To obtain relative measurements of ozone concentrations in the air, students set up experiments that involved stretching rubber bands on a board, then observing the number of days until the bands break. Students maintained daily journal logs of the temperature, barometric pressure, and wind speed/direction and of the number of days that it took for bands to break.[1] After compiling their data and preparing single-page summaries of their results via the Internet, students exchanged data with other groups. From data collected worldwide, students wrote a one-page summary as to what conditions may account for the difference in levels of ozone. Following the exchange of students' written responses and their subsequent revisions based on feedback from the worldwide peers, students prepared a final summary report about the world's atmospheric ozone level. The intention is to disseminate worldwide (to newspapers and via the Internet) this final report.

Activity 1: Introduction *10* minutes

Today, in think-share-pairs, you will prepare initial responses to the e-mail responses we have received from other groups around the world. (teacher shares the list of places from which e-mail has been received).

Any questions before we get started?

As we discussed earlier, here are the instructions: in your think-share-pairs (each pair is given one response received via e-mail), prepare written responses according to the following outline: (a) note points or information you would like to incorporate in the final paper to be forwarded via the Internet; (b) comment on one aspect of the written response you like best; and (c) provide questions to the sender to seek clarification or elaboration. I think you should be able to finish this in about 30 minutes, so let's try for that.

Activity 2: *30* minutes
Preparation of dyad responses

Activity 3: *Undetermined* minutes

Let's now hear from each response pair. Dyad responses are shared with whole class for discussion of inclusion in response paper to be sent via the Internet.

Activity 4: *Undetermined* minutes

Discussion, conclusion, and preparation of final drafts to be sent to each e-mail corresponder to be done by cooperative groups (the number of groups needed to be decided by the number of e-mail corresponders at this time).

Activity 5: *Undetermined* minutes

Later, as students receive e-mail responses from other groups the responses will be printed and reviewed. The class then responds to each using the same criteria as before and returns this response to the e-mail sender.

Closure:

The process continues until all groups (from around the world) have agreed upon and prepared the final report for dissemination.

5. Materials and Equipment Needed

School computers with Internet access, printers, copies of e-mail responses

6. Assessment, Reflection, and Revision

Assessment of student learning for this lesson is formative; journals, daily checklist of student participation in groups; writing drafts

Reflective thoughts about lesson and suggestions for revision:

Special notes and reminders to myself:

---

[1]This information about the science experiment is from R. J. Ryder and T. Hughes, *Internet for Educators* (Upper Saddle River, NJ: Prentice Hall, 1997), p. 98, as is the Internet address for IECC (p. 96).

you review the suggested format and the alternatives, determine which appeals to your purposes and style of presentation and use it with your own modifications until you find or develop a better model. All else being equal, we encourage you to begin your teaching by following as closely as possible our format in Figure 5.1.

All plans should be written in an intelligible style. You have good reason to question teachers who say they have no need for a written plan because they have their lessons planned "in their heads." How many lessons will have to be planned in one's head for the periods in a school day that range from several to many, and for the numbers of students in each class? When multiplied by the number of school days in a week, a semester, or a year, the task of keeping so many plans in one's head becomes mind-boggling. Few persons could effectively accomplish such a feat. Until you have considerable experience, you will need to write and keep detailed plans for guidance and reference.

What you are going to be learning now is how to prepare a lesson plan, which could possibly be a daily plan. We do not use the term "daily lesson plan" but rather "the lesson plan." In some instances, as shown in the sample lesson of Figure 5.2 and in the first lesson of Civilizations: Dawn of a New Age in Ancient Greece that is shown later in this chapter, a single lesson plan may run for more than one class period or day, perhaps two or three or even more. In other instances, the lesson plan is, in fact, a daily plan and may run for an entire class period, or in instances of block scheduling, for less than the 2-hour block of time. In the latter case, more than one lesson plan may be used during that time.

ELEMENTS OF A LESSON PLAN

A written lesson plan should contain the following basic elements: (1) descriptive data, (2) goals and objectives, (3) rationale, (4) procedure, (5) assignments and assignment reminders, (6) materials and equipment, and (7) a section for assessment, reflection, and revision. These components are neither required in every written lesson plan nor presented in any particular or standard format. In addition, you can choose to include additional components or subsections or choose to delete a formal rationale for an ITU, although we suggest that you develop one. Figure 5.1 illustrates a format that includes the seven components and sample subsections of those components. It is placed alone so you may remove it and make copies for use in planning the lessons for your ITU.

Following are descriptions of the seven major components with explanations of why each is important, with examples.

Descriptive Data

This information represents demographic and logistical data that identify details about the class. Anyone reading this information should be able to identify when and where the class meets, who is teaching it, and what is being taught. Although the teacher knows this information, someone else may not. Members of the teaching team, administrators, and substitute teachers (and, if you are the student teacher, your university supervisor and cooperating teacher) appreciate this information, especially when asked to substitute, even if only for a few minutes during a class session. Most teachers find out which items of descriptive data are most beneficial in their situation and then develop their own identifiers. Remember that the mark of a well-prepared, clearly written lesson plan is the ease with which someone else (such as another member of your teaching team or a substitute teacher) could implement it.

For the sample lesson plan of Figure 5.2, descriptive data:

1. Name of course or class and grade level. These serve as headings for the plan and facilitate orderly filing of plans. Example:
   English/Language Arts/Science (integrated block course) Grades 4–12
2. Name of the unit. Inclusion of this detail facilitates the orderly control of the hundreds of lesson plans a teacher constructs. Example:
   English/Language Arts/Science Unit: Investigative Research and Generative Writing Grades, 4–12
3. Topics to be considered within the unit, also useful for control and identification. For example:
   English/Language Arts/Science Unit: Investigative Research and Generative Writing Topic: Writing Responses and Peer Assessment via the Internet

Anticipated Noise Level. You might include in the descriptive data, the category of anticipated classroom noise level such as high, moderate, or low. Its inclusion is useful to you during the planning phase of instruction when thinking about how active and noisy students might become during the lesson, and how you might prepare for that, and whether you should warn an administrator and teachers of neighboring classrooms. Inclusion of this item is sometimes requested by cooperating teachers and university supervisors.

Goals and Objectives

The instructional goals are general statements of intended accomplishments from that lesson. Teachers and students need to know what the lesson is designed to accomplish. In clear, understandable language, the general goal statement provides that information. From the sample of Figure 5.2, the goals are:

- To collaborate and prepare response papers to peers from around the world who have shared the results of their own experimental research findings and research papers about ozone concentrations in the atmosphere.
- For students to prepare and publish for worldwide dissemination a final paper about worldwide ozone levels in the atmosphere.

Because the goals are also in the unit plan, sometimes a teacher may include only the objectives in the daily lesson plan (as shown in Figure 5.2). For a beginning teacher, it is a good idea to include both.

Objectives of the lesson are included as specific statements detailing precisely what students will be able to do as a result of the instructional activities. Teachers and students must be aware of the objectives. Behavioral objectives provide clear statements of what learning is to occur. In addition, from clearly written behavioral objectives, assessment items can be written to measure whether students have accomplished the objectives. The type of assessment item used (discussed in Chapter 4) should not only measure for the instructional objective but should also be compatible with the objective being assessed. As discussed earlier, your specific objectives might be covert or overt or a combination of both. From the lesson shown in Figure 5.2, sample objectives are as follows:

- Through cooperative group action, students will conduct experimental research to collect data about the ozone level of air in their environment. (cognitive, application)
- Through the Internet, students will write and share response papers to their peers from other locations in the world. (cognitive, evaluation)
- Students will form judgments about local, regional, and world ozone levels. (affective, organizing)
- Students will create a proposal for worldwide dissemination. (psychomotor, creating)

Setting specific objectives is a crucial step in the development of any lesson plan. It is at this point that many lessons weaken. Related to specific objectives, teachers sometimes mistakenly list their intentions, such as "cover the next five pages" or "do the next 10 problems," and fail to focus on just what is the true learning objective in these activities—what the children will accomplish (performance) as a result of the instruction. When you approach this step in your lesson planning, ask yourself, "What should students learn as a result of this lesson?" Your answer to that question is your objective!

Rationale

The rationale is an explanation of why the lesson is important and why the instructional methods chosen will achieve the objectives. Parents, students, teachers, administrators, and others have the right to know why specific content is being taught and why the methods employed are being used. Teachers become reflective decision makers when they challenge themselves to think about *what* they are teaching, *how* they are teaching it, and *why* it must be taught. Sometimes teachers include the rationale statement in the front of the interdisciplinary thematic unit plan, but not in each daily lesson. At other times, the rationale is included within the introduction and goals of the unit.

Procedure

The procedure consists of the instructional activities for a scheduled time frame. You worked on this activity in Exercise 3.8 and will focus on it again in this chapter as you complete your ITU plans. You may want to refer back to your work on Exercise 3.8 as you continue through this chapter.

The substance of the lesson—the information to be presented, obtained, and learned—is the content. Appropriate information is selected to meet the learning objectives, the level of competence of students, and the requirements of the course. To be sure your lesson actually covers what it should, write exactly what content you intend to cover. This material may be placed in a separate section or combined with the procedure section. Having written the information, you now have a quick and easy reference tool. If, for instance, you intend to conduct the lesson using discussion, you can write the key discussion questions. Or, if you plan to introduce new material to older students in high school using a 12-minute lecture, then an outline of the content of that lecture is helpful.

The word *outline* is not used casually. You need not have pages of notes to sift through; nor do you need to read declarative statements to your students. You should be familiar enough with the content that an outline (detailed as much as you believe necessary) will be sufficient to carry on your lesson. Examine the following example of a content outline.

Causes of Civil War

A. Primary causes
   1. Economics
   2. Abolitionist pressure
   3. Slavery
   4. Other

B. Secondary Causes
   1. North-South friction
   2. Southern economic dependence
   3. Other

The procedure or procedures to be used, sometimes referred to as the instructional components, comprise the procedure component of the lesson plan. Appropriate instructional activities are chosen to meet the objectives, to match students' learning styles and special needs, and to ensure that all students have equal opportunity to learn. The procedure is the section in which you establish what you and your students will be doing during the lesson. Ordinarily, you should plan this section of your lesson as an organized entity having a beginning (an introduction or set), a middle, and an end (called the closure) to be completed during the lesson. This structure is not always needed if you plan the lessons to be simply parts of units or long-term plans and will carry on the activities mentioned in the units and plans. Still, most lessons need to include the following in the procedure section: (1) an **introduction,** which includes the process used to prepare students mentally for the lesson; sometimes referred to as the *set,* or *initiating activity,* or the *stimulus;* (2) a **lesson development** section, which details the activities that occur between the beginning and the end of the lesson; includes the transitions that connect the activities; (3) **coached practice** plans, which detail ways that you intend for students to interact in the classroom; sometimes referred to as the *follow-up* and includes individual practice, dyad practice, small-group work, and conferences or mini-lessons during which the students receive guidance and coaching from you and their peers; (4) the **lesson conclusion** or **closure,** which is the planned process of bringing the lesson to an end, thereby providing students with a sense of completeness and, with effective teaching, accomplishment and comprehension by helping students to synthesize the information learned from the lesson; (5) a **timetable,** which serves simply as a planning and implementation guide; (6) a **lesson extender** activity, which is a plan of action used if your students finish the lesson and time remains; and (7) **assignments,** which are what students are in-

structed to do as a follow-up to the lesson, either as homework or as in-class work, providing students an opportunity to practice and enhance their learning. Now we consider some of these important elements in further detail.

Introduction to the Lesson.   Like any good performance or piece of writing, a lesson needs an effective beginning. In many respects, the introduction sets the tone for the rest of the lesson by alerting students that the business of learning is to begin. The introduction should be an attention getter. If the introduction is exciting, interesting, or innovative, it can create a favorable mood for the lesson, which is sometimes referred to as a "hook." In any case, a thoughtful introduction serves as a solid indicator that you are well prepared. Although it is difficult to develop an exciting introduction to every lesson taught each day, you can implement a variety of options available to spice up the beginning of your every lesson. You might, for instance, begin the lesson by briefly reviewing the previous lesson, thereby helping students connect the learning. Another possibility is to review vocabulary words from previous lessons and to introduce new ones. Still another possibility is to use the key point of the day's lesson as an introduction and then again as the conclusion. Yet another possibility is to begin the lesson with a writing activity on some controversial aspect of the ensuing lesson. Sometimes teachers begin a lesson by demonstrating a discrepant event (i.e., an event that is contrary to what one might expect). At times, teachers select artifacts, audiovisual presentations, and children's books to start a lesson. At other times, computer simulations, displays, or newspaper articles help launch the learning. Still other times, paintings, problems, role playing, resource people, or replicas initiate a student discussion. The important thing is they are all attention getters.

Here are more examples:

* For social studies/language arts—a study of interpretations: As students enter the classroom, the state song, "I Love You, California," is playing softly in the background. The teacher begins class by showing on the overhead the state seal, and asks students to meet in dyads, discuss the object, and write down what they believe it is.
* For American history—a study of westward expansion: The teacher asks "Who has lived somewhere else other than (name of your state)?" After the students show their hands and answer, ask individuals why they moved to the state. The teacher asks the students to recall some of the reasons why the first European settlers came to the United States.

Use as a transition before the next activity about the westward expansion.

- For science—a study of adhesion or the process of predicting: The teacher takes a glass filled to the top with colored water and asks the students to meet in groups of two and discuss and predict how many pennies can be added to the glass before any water spills over the edge.

In short, you can use the introduction of the lesson to review past learning, tie the new lesson to the previous lesson, and introduce new material. The introduction can help you point out the objectives of the new lesson, help students connect their learning with other disciplines or with real life, and, by showing what will be learned and why the learning is important, induce in students motivation and a mind-set favorable to the new lesson.

The Lesson Development.   The developmental activities comprise the bulk of the plan and are the specifics by which you intend to achieve your lesson objectives. They include activities that present information, demonstrate skills, provide reinforcement of previously learned material, and provide other opportunities to develop understanding and skill. Furthermore, by actions and words, during lesson development the teacher models the behaviors expected of students. Students need such modeling. By effective modeling, you exemplify the anticipated learning outcomes. Activities of this section of the lesson plan should be described in some detail so (1) you will know exactly what it is you plan to do and (2) you will stay focused during the class meeting and not forget important details and content. It is for this reason you should consider, for example, noting answers (if known) to questions you intend to ask and solutions to problems you intend for students to solve.

Lesson Conclusion.   Having a clear-cut closure to the lesson is as important as having a strong introduction. The closure complements the introduction. The concluding activity should summarize and bind together what has ensued in the developmental stage and should reinforce the principal points of the lesson. One way to accomplish these ends is to restate the key points of the lesson, or to briefly outline them. Still another method is to repeat the major concept and have the students repeat the concept to one another, or have each student repeat the concept to you at the door as they leave the classroom. Sometimes the closure is not only a review of what was learned but also the summarizing of a question left unanswered that signals a change in your plan of activities for the following day. Regardless of the plan, the concluding activity is unusually brief and to the point.

The Timetable.   Estimating the time factors in any lesson can be very difficult. A good procedure is to gauge the amount of time needed for each learning activity and note that time alongside the activity and strategy in your plan, as shown in the preferred sample lesson plan format. Placing too much faith in your time estimate may be foolish—an estimate is more for your guidance during the preactive phase of instruction than for anything else. Beginning teachers sometimes find that their discussions and presentations do not last as long as expected. To avoid being embarrassed by running out of material, try to make sure you have planned enough meaningful work to consume the entire class period. Another important reason for including a time plan in your lesson is to give information to students about how much time they have for a particular activity, such as a quiz or a group discussion.

Assignments

When giving an assignment, make sure to note it in your lesson plan. When to present an assignment to students is optional, but never yell an assignment as an afterthought to students as they exit the classroom at the end of the period. When giving assignments— whether in-class or out-of-school assignments—it is best to write them on the writing board, in a special place on the bulletin board, or on a handout. Take extra care to be sure that assignment specifications are clear to the students.

It is also important that you understand the difference between assignments and procedures. An assignment tells students *what* is to be done, and procedures explain *how* to do it. Although an assignment may include specific procedures, spelling out procedures alone is not the same thing as an academic assignment. When the students are given an assignment, they need to understand the reasons for doing it and to have some notion of ways the assignment might be done.

Some teachers give assignments to their students on a weekly basis, requiring that students maintain an assignment schedule in their portfolios. When given on a periodic basis, rather than daily, assignments should still show in your daily lesson plans so you can remind students of them. Once assignment specifications are given, it is a good idea to not make major modifications to them, and it is especially important to not change assignment specifications several days after an assignment has been given. Last-minute changes in assignment requirements and procedures can be very frustrating to students who have already begun or completed the assignment; making changes shows little respect to those students.

Benefits of Coached Practice.   Allowing time in class for students to begin work on homework assignments and long-term projects is highly recommended; it provides opportunity for you to give individual attention to students. One contribution of block scheduling is that teachers have more time to provide coached practice. Being able to coach students is the reason for in-class time to begin assignments. The benefits of coached practice include being able to (a) monitor student work so a student does not go too far in a wrong direction; (b) help students to reflect on their thinking; (c) assess the progress of individual students; (d) provide for peer tutoring; and (e) discover or create a "teachable moment." For the latter, for example, while observing and monitoring student practice you might discover a commonly shared student misconception. You then stop the action and discuss that point and attempt to clarify the misconception or collaborate with students to plan a subsequent lesson or learning activity centered around the common misconception.

Special Notes and Reminders

Some teachers provide a place in their lesson plan format for special notes and reminders. Most of the time, you will not need such reminders, but when you do, it helps to have them in a regular location in your lesson plan so you can refer to them quickly. In that special section you can place notes to yourself concerning such things as announcements to be made, participation in school programs, and makeup work for certain students.

Materials and Equipment

Materials of instruction include the textbook, supplementary readings, media, and other supplies necessary to accomplish the lesson objectives. You must be certain that the proper and necessary materials and equipment are available for the lesson, which certainly takes planning. If you are busy during instructional time looking for materials that should have been ready before class began, then you may have to face some classroom control problems as a result.

Assessment, Reflection, and Revision

You must include in your lesson plan details of how you will assess how well students are learning (for-

mative assessment) and how well they have learned (summative assessment). For formative assessment, you can include informal checklists and comprehension checks that include both the questions you ask and those the students ask during the lesson. Questions you intend to ask (and possible answers) can be included in the developmental section of the lesson plan. For summative assessment, you can use tests, independent practice, or summary activities at the completion of a lesson. You also can use review questions at the end of a lesson (as a closure) or at the beginning of the next lesson (as a review or transfer introduction). We suggest again that your major questions for checking for comprehension should be detailed in your lesson plan.

In most lesson plan formats, there is also a section reserved for you to make notes or reflective comments about the lesson. Sample reflective questions you might ask yourself are as follows:

- How did I feel about my teaching today?
- If I feel successful, what student reactions made me feel that way?
- Would I do anything differently next time? If so, what and why?
- What changes to tomorrow's lesson need to be made as a result of today's lesson?

Writing and later reading your reflections can spark new ideas for a future lesson or lead to modifications of subsequent activities of the ITU. This type reflection also offers a catharsis, which eases the stress from teaching. To continue working effectively at a challenging task requires significant amounts of reflection. Proceed now to Exercise 5.1 on the following page, where you will analyze a lesson that failed; then, if appropriate for your group as indicated by your instructor, do Exercises 5.2 and 5.3 that follow at the end of the chapter.

SAMPLE INTERDISCIPLINARY THEMATIC UNITS

The remaining pages of this chapter provide three sample interdisciplinary units, namely (1) Early Civilizations: Dawn of a New Age in Ancient Greece; (2) Migrations: Early Newcomers in North America (both adaptable for middle and secondary grades); and (3) Changes: Spring as a Time of Growth, Beauty, and Transformations (for use in grades 1–4). From these examples, you will see ways that different teachers have planned their thematic units. Again, we emphasize that to conserve space in this book and to reflect the serendipitous nature of ITUs in general, certain aspects of each sample ITU may be incomplete or omitted. Sometimes when teaching an interdisciplinary thematic curriculum, you will find that your best prepared lesson may go untaught as the interests of students lead to uncharted areas, unforeseen discussions, or quickly planned activities.

As you review these sample ITUs, pay special attention to the margin notes, which are provided to help you focus your attention, to fill in possible gaps, and to provide additional information and resources. When related to management, the margin note is coded **(M)**; when related to technology and resources, it is coded **(T)**; and when related to student diversity, it is coded **(D)**.

Enjoy reading the following interdisciplinary thematic units as you appreciate the hard work of the teachers who created and contributed these lesson plans. When you have completed your reading, turn to Exercise 5.4 on pages 243 through 247 for a self-check on developing interdisciplinary thematic units.

Sample ITU 1

Early Civilizations: Dawn of a New Age in Ancient Greece*

Middle and Secondary Grades. This ITU revolves around several disciplines including geography, literature, mathematics, physical education, science, and social science. It was developed to facilitate and motivate students' learning about ancient Greece and to make comparisons between life today and life 2,000 years ago in Greece. As presented here, the unit could be taught by one teacher or, with modifications, by a team of teachers.

─D────────────

Activities should be varied and represent a holistic approach to the unit theme.

Unit Overview. This ITU includes a variety of multisensory activities involving language arts, mathematics, science, art, drama, social studies, health, and physical education. As presented, each lesson requires from 45 to 75 minutes, but with Lessons 1 and 11 each requiring at least 2 consecutive days. This unit will take at least 3 weeks. In addition to the 11 lesson plans are additional suggested activities. Originally designed for grades 5–9, it is adaptable for any grades 5–12.

*Source: Adapted by permission from unpublished contribution of Nancy Mortham.

The unit contains several cooperative learning activities that assume students have had prior experience working in cooperative groups. If students have not had such prior experience, then these lessons should be preceded by a discussion of the expected behaviors and responsibilities when working cooperatively with others. It is recommended that students be in teams of four at the start of the unit because this size group will facilitate an easy transition into group work and allow for a team-based behavior management system, if so desired.

To support the unit, an arranged environment should be created in the classroom(s). This supportive environment might include posters, artifacts, Greek music, trade and resource books, and simple toga costumes that can be worn during specific activities. Bulletin boards could be created utilizing students' myths from Lesson 4 and the vase art activity.

─M────────────

The actual time length of each lesson and number of class periods will depend on the intellectual level of your students and the nature of the scheduling at your school. Many of the activities will consume full class periods. You can incorporate any of the ideas in the margin notes for facilitating cooperative group activities or instituting the technology ideas.

To visually show the emphasis and the contributions of a particular discipline to some of the lessons in the unit, you can develop a web to focus on the integration of the different disciplines selected for the unit, such as the one that follows. It can be drawn on the writing board to discuss with the students if appropriate for your group.

Unit Goals. From California's History/Social Studies Framework, this unit is designed to incorporate these goals:

- Knowledge and cultural understanding
- Democratic understanding and civic values
- Skills attainment and social participation

More specifically, the unit is designed to explore the following:

- The changes in Greek society from 2000 to 400 B.C.
- Greek mythology
- The effects of Greece's geography on its people and their way of life
- How the early Olympic Games differ from those held today
- The social class structure in early Athenian society
- Greek architecture
- Two very different city-states: Sparta and Athens

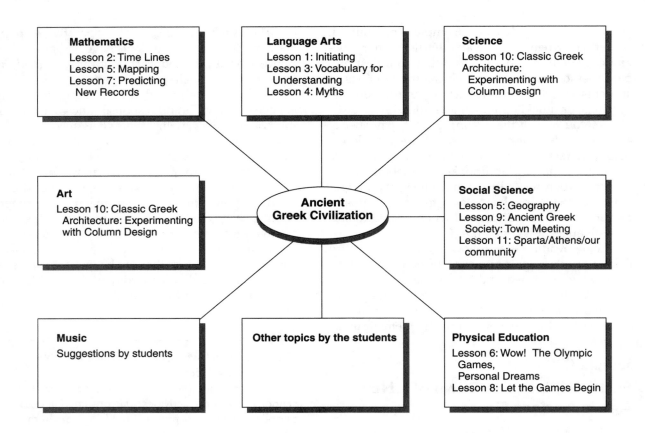

M

At various times, class meetings can be used to discuss goals and to establish class expectations, procedures, and consequences for inappropriate behavior.

Assessment of Student Learning. For this unit, there are three components for assessment of student learning: (1) students' portfolios, which include a unit assessment checklist, (2) a unit test, and (3) teacher's anecdotal notes. Additionally, students are encouraged to assess their own performances through self-assessment and group assessments.

M

Over 100 assessment tools are available in *Practical Aspects of Authentic Assessment: Putting the Pieces Together* (Norwood, MA: Christopher-Gordon, 1998) by Bonnie Campbell Hill and Cynthia A. Ruptic; additional class-tested forms and checklists for assessment are found in *Portfolios and Beyond: Collaborative Assessment in Reading and Writing* (Norwood, MA: Christopher-Gordon, 1993) by Susan Mandel Glazer and Carol Smullen Brown.

LESSON 1

Ancient Greece: Initiating Lesson

Objective

Students will demonstrate and share their learning about Grecian times by creating small-group presentations, which will be performed for the class.

Materials

Resource books, posters, artifacts, student texts

Procedure

"Today we are beginning an exciting unit on ancient Greece. We will participate in a wide variety of activities and have many opportunities to work in cooperative groups on special presentations and projects." Assess prior student knowledge by eliciting what they know about ancient Greece. Write their responses in a list. Then, with students, review the list to group similar entries, such as those related to clothing, shelter, and activities. Let the students "reserve" topics for personal inquiry. "Today we are going to form groups that will be in place for the remainder of the unit."

1. Put the students in teams of four (or three) students per team. Assign each team a topic to research from one of the following (depending on the number of students in your class, more than one team could have the same assignment): The Minoan Age; The Mycenaean Age; The First Olympics; The Age of Expansion; or The First Use of Coins.

Student teams create presentations to be performed in front of the class the next day or later, depending on the grade level, the complexity of their presentations, and the research needed. This may be done in the form of a play, newscast, report, discussion, and so forth.

2. Present and discuss assessment forms for the unit assessment, group presentations and listening skills checklist (not included here but modified forms are found in Figures 4.8, 4.9, and 4.10 of this guide).

3. The following day (or a later day), students present to the class.

4. Before, during, or immediately following each presentation, team members prepare an outline on the board to include who, what, when, where, and why or how.

5. Presenters respond to questions as the class takes notes on the information presented.

6. After the presentations, students evaluate their own listening behavior.

(Continued)

Students can create banners to hang from the ceiling over their groups. Each group decides on an appropriate name for their group and creates a banner made of butcher paper that depicts objects, mythological characters, or some other symbolism of ancient Greece. Students could research banners and their use or the procedures used in creating vases (see Lesson 3).

An excellent and long-standing Internet website from Athens for research about Greece is <http://www.ariadne-t.gr/>.

Students' ideas should be solicited with procedures for the research and presentations and task outcomes clearly identified and understood by students.

Video: *Conversations with Ancient Greeks* (Cinema Guild, 1992), grades 9 and above. Brings Socrates, Odysseus, Euripides, and other figures from ancient history into the present as the figures share their ideas in a conversational setting. They tell how their contributions affected the present. Includes breaks for student discussions.

LESSON 1

Ancient Greece: Initiating Lesson—Cont.

Closure

"What is something interesting that you learned from the presentations and that you didn't know before? Did your group have any problems while researching information or putting together your presentations?" Discuss cooperation when working in groups and the importance of giving each member of the group a chance to contribute ideas.

Assessment

Group presentations are teacher evaluated according to rubrics presented. Students individually self-assess their listening behavior using a checklist form (see item 2 in Procedures).

Socratic seminars are discussed as performance assessments in *The Performance Assessment Handbook, Volume I* by Bill Johnson (Larchmont, NY: Eye on Education, 1997).

Video: *Effective Listening Skills: Listening to What You Hear* (Cambridge Career Products, 1992), grades 10–12. Delivers information about the acronym DRIVE and the related skills for which the letters stand— deciding to listen, reading all stimuli, investing time wisely, verifying what was heard, and expending energy to listen.

You can model the expected behavior and send messages to students that acknowledge students' feelings, invite cooperation, give appropriate directions, and express feelings about a situation rather than about a student's character.

LESSON 2

Time Lines

Objective

Students will demonstrate and share their understandings of significant events and their time frame by creating and drawing time lines documenting significant events of ancient Greece.

Materials

Text as a resource; white, unlined paper; rulers; masking tape line on the classroom floor

Procedures

"As groups, you completed your presentations of information based on what was read about different events in early Greece. Today we are going to create a time line to give us a visual representation of the progression of events as they occurred over time in Greece."

1. Discuss the purpose of the time line, how to read it, and the meaning of B.C. and A.D.

2. Create a sample time line on the board using important personal dates offered by members of the class.

3. Point out the masking tape time line on the floor, and ask each group to select one person to stand at the correct spot on the time line that represents the event or period they presented yesterday, thus creating a "people time line."

4. After students are in place, they give a brief review of the information they presented yesterday. Stress the very long span of time in comparison to the history of the United States.

5. Students individually create their own time lines on paper, which include all of the dates represented by students on the people time line. These time lines, then, include dates for the Minoan Age, the Mycenaean Age, the first Olympics, and so on. Students place their completed time lines in their portfolios.

Closure

"We have been talking about events in Greece dating back to 2000 B.C. Raise your hand if you can tell us how many years ago that was. If a time line was written the same way as the number lines we see in math, how would we write the numbers that we refer to as B.C.?" (Those numbers would be negative numbers.)

Assessment

Observe students as they form the people time line and as they create their own time lines with the given information. Individual time frames will be reviewed from students' portfolios during individual conferences.

M

Students should primarily be instructed in small groups, and academically related discourse should be encouraged. There can be assigned academic tasks with intermittent teacher assistance.

D

Use the strategies indicated within the lesson procedures to provide additional opportunities to expand the study within each lesson to meet individual students or class needs.

LESSON 3

Vocabulary for Understanding

Objective

After completing a vocabulary coding exercise, students will define and illustrate relevant vocabulary words.

Materials

Vocabulary coding; textbook as resource

Procedure

"Early Greeks stored grain in large vases and examples of these are displayed around the room. Today you are going to color-code a vase based on the vocabulary from our unit."

1. Describe how students may color-code the vase (Figure 5.3), with the word and its definition colored the same color. Students may suggest other ways to match words with definitions.
2. Students should use the text as a resource.
3. Allow students time to complete the activity (about 15 minutes).
4. As students complete their coding, they may begin writing definitions and creating illustrations for each word. After beginning in class under the teacher's guidance, this activity should be completed as homework.

Word List

barter	democracy	tragedy	ephor
comedy	monarchy	sanctuary	turant
helot	oligarchy	city-state	

Closure

Questioning review: "Which of these words define a form of government? Which of these words are nouns that describe a person in ancient Greece? Two of the words are still used today to describe plays and other entertainment. Which are they?"

Assessment

The vocabulary coding and the definitions and illustrations are included in each student's portfolio.

D

Vocabulary words will vary depending on the grade level, English language skills, and intellectual maturity of students.

D

Students could research the procedures for creating vases.

D

The "coding with coloring" activity asks students to complete a higher-level task—to match terms and their definitions. This activity both supports a need for LEP students and sequences appropriate conceptual growth in building knowledge about ancient Greece.

LESSON 3

Vocabulary for Understanding—Cont.

FIGURE 5.3 Vocabulary Coding with Color

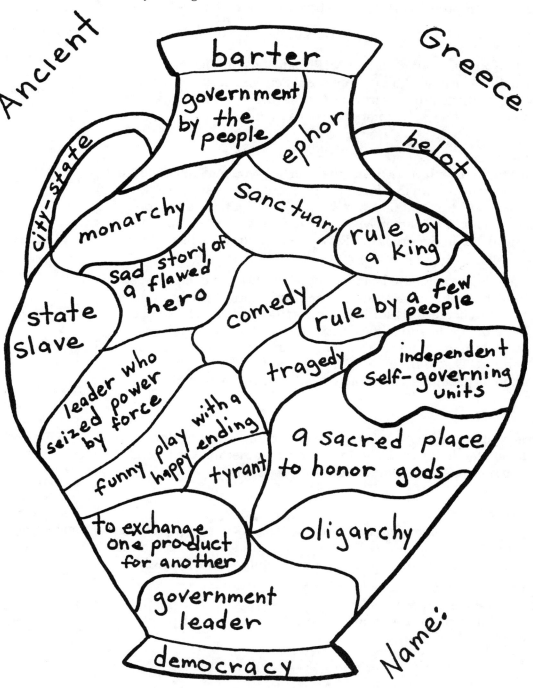

LESSON 4
Myths

Objective

After listening to and reading Greek myths and discussing what constitutes a myth, students will create their own myths.

Materials

Prometheus and the Story of Fire by I. M. Richardson (New Jersey, Troll Associates, 1983); overhead transparency of "Perseus Meets the Medusa" adapted by Lanette Whitnell from *D'Aulaires' Book of Greek Myths;* visual display that illustrates the components of a myth.

Procedure

"I'd like to share with you a poster that will help you remember the major components of a myth." Present and discuss the poster depicting a large black cauldron, entitled "Brew Up a Myth." On the cauldron are cards that read Imagination, Mystery, Pre-Science Explanation of Nature, and Belief in Supernatural Powers. Have students listen for the components as a myth is read aloud.

1. Read aloud *Prometheus and the Story of Fire.* Discuss components.
2. While brainstorming, students compare/contrast myths and legends. Teacher records student ideas on the board and then encourages students to add to the descriptions on the myth cauldron.
3. Students participate in a choral reading of "Perseus Meets the Medusa." Discuss.
4. Students begin their first rough drafts of their own myths.

Closure

"Raise your hand if you think you can explain why the stories we heard and read today are classified as myths rather than as legends." Students may refer to the myth poster for assistance.

Assessment

After the students complete their rough drafts, they receive feedback from their peers using the myth checklist as a guide (Figure 5.4). Final drafts are teacher evaluated using a rubric similar to the following:

The myth demonstrates a belief in higher powers (Greek gods/goddesses)	12.5 points
The myth explains something in nature	12.5 points
Writing skill	75.0 points

T

Activity center material: *Greek Mythology* (Tapes 'n Books for Gifted Education, 314-350 Weinacker Ave., P.O. Box 6448, Mobile, AL 36600), grades 5–12. Includes task cards with activities keyed to Bloom's taxonomy with an emphasis on student tasks related to classification of the cognitive domain.

D

More advanced literature can be substituted according to students' reading level.

M

It is important that you communicate to students that you know what is occurring in the classroom through nonverbal interactions (handshakes, smiles) as well as emphasize procedures, expectations, rewards, and consequences with the understanding that the responsibility for good behavior rests with each student individually.

LESSON 4

Myths—Cont.

Assessment of the writing skill considers purpose, mode, audience, effective elaboration, consistent organization, clear sense of order and completeness, and fluent and effective language (see criteria for Figure 4.2 of this guide).

FIGURE 5.4 Myth Assessment Checklist

Myth Checklist

1. Does this myth demonstrate a belief in
   higher powers (Greek gods/goddesses)   yes _____   no _____

2. Does this myth try to explain something
   in nature?   yes _____   no _____

3. In this myth I like:

4. Suggestions:

Author of the myth:

Peer reviewer:

M

You should strive to promote cooperative group work and to provide support for students' assessment of one another's work.

LESSON 5

Mapping, Geography, and Communities

Objective

Students will demonstrate further understanding of ancient Greece as they create a physical map of Greece, discuss how geography played an important role in the development of Greek society, and complete information retrieval charts. Through Socratic questioning, students will make connections about their own communities with what they have learned about early Grecian communities.

Materials

One map per cooperative learning group (CLG); paper maché; glue; retrieval charts

Procedure

"Today, in your cooperative learning groups, you are going to make a physical map of Greece. Each of you can contribute. When the map is complete, place it on the display table. Show the locations of city-states on the map."

1. Groups complete their maps.
2. In groups, students read the section of the text (or other sources) that deals with the geography of Greece.
3. As a class, students brainstorm how the geography affected
   a. farming (only a quarter of the land was suitable for growing grain; Greeks also grew grapes and olives)
   b. development of city-states (isolated, close-knit communities developed because of mountains and sea)
   c. trade (people traded by sea for goods they could not grow or make)
   d. culture (trade led to extensive contact with people from other cultures, which led to the spread of products and ideas)
4. Students complete their individual retrieval charts (see Figure 5.5).

Closure

"Let's share our ideas from the retrieval charts." Students volunteer to share their responses. "Although both the geographic terrain and climate affect a culture, it takes people working together to build a community. The people who successfully settled in the Aegean region formed tightly knit communities to build and shape their civilization. How does the geography of the Aegean region compare with our own? Is your community a tightly knit one? Why or why not? What kinds of things determine how close members of a community feel?" Continue with other questions generated by the students.

D

Rather than creating a physical map, you may prefer that students draw individual maps of Greece.

T

CD-ROM: *Geopedia* (Encyclopedia Britannica Ed. Corp., 1993), grades 5–8. This program has references, resources, and student activities (brain teasers) about Greece and other countries, regions, and cities of the world. Includes excellent photographs and video clips.

Video: *Europe: Southern Region* (EBED, 1994), grades 6–12. This is an overview of Greece and southern Europe and the effects of the Mediterranean Sea on the climate of the region.

Web Site: *Nueva Center for Learning* Nueva School, Hillsborough, CA (www.nueva.pvt.k12.ca.us/ ~debbie/library/). K–12. This site, managed by D. Abilock, librarian, lets students type in bibliographic information for an item being researched. Search Engine lets students do different searches such as web pages from a geographic region, e.g., Greece.

LESSON 5

Mapping, Geography, and Communities—Cont.

Assessment

The geography retrieval charts are added to students' portfolios. Students' responses and thinking that they demonstrated are informally evaluated.

FIGURE 5.5   Retrieval Chart: Ancient Greece

Ancient Greece Retrieval Chart

How did geography and climate influence ancient Greece in the following areas?

Farming:

Development of city-states:

Trade:

Culture:

Use the following space to record any important ideas you discover during this discussion:

M

Discuss: Socrates' instruction was known as Socratic Method. It is a form of cross-examination during which Socrates would pretend to know nothing of the subject under discussion. It consists of a series of carefully directed questions to make the other person find out the truth independently. He used inductive argument and arrived at general conclusions through examples from the life of the common people. Encourage students to ask questions to make others discover connections between early Grecian and today's communities.

T

If you and your students so choose, this closure could take awhile, and could lead students into a long-term study of their own community.

D

This lesson complements science. Students make connections of geographic location and climate, which also affect suitability for farming.

LESSON 6

Wow! The Olympic Games, Personal Dreams

Objective

After comparing and contrasting the early Olympic Games with the present day and watching a video of Olympic heroes from the past, students will brainstorm and determine qualities they deem important in an Olympic athlete.

Materials

Video: *The Olympic Challenge*

Procedure

"What did you see in the video about the personal qualities of the athletes? Raise your hand if you can tell us something about the attitudes of the athletes you watched."

1. Ask students how many have watched the Olympic Games. What are their thoughts about the games?
2. Discuss with students these aspects of the ancient Olympic Games:
   a. The purpose was to honor the gods.
   b. War ceased while the games were played.
   c. Only men participated.
   d. Games were held every 4 years.
   e. The Olympics began with just a 200-yard footrace and later included other races, boxing, wrestling, discus throw, horse racing, and chariot races.
3. Write the following question on the board and ask students to think about it as they view the video: "What personal qualities are often found in Olympic athletes?"
4. Students view the video and take notes if appropriate for the group.
5. Make a list on the board as students share the qualities that make an Olympic athlete (e.g., dreams, goals, perseverance, talent, pride, dedications, determination, courage, endurance, failure, fear).

Closure

"Many of the qualities that make a successful Olympic athlete are also the qualities of any successful person. What do you think this means?" Discuss goal setting, dreams, and so on. Remind students of the television commercial with Michael Jordan talking about how many times he has failed. Discuss the life of Wilma Rudolph. Perhaps students would like to pursue projects related to the dreams, trials, failures, and successes of famous people.

Assessment

The quantity of student contributions and the level of student thinking are recorded in the teacher's log.

The first modern Olympic games were held in Athens in 1896; the Olympic games in Athens in the year 2004 should be particularly useful for this or a similar lesson. You may suggest students read *Coubertin's Olympics: How the Games Began* (Lerner, 1995) by Kristy Davida or *Wilma Unlimited: How Wilma Rudolph Became the World's Fastest Runner* (Harcourt, 1996) by Kathleen Krull. Davida's text recounts how the games were revived to an international level and Krull's biography portrays Rudolph's achievement as the first American woman to win three gold medals in a single Olympics.

Using a think-write-pair-share activity, students brainstorm their perceptions of the personal qualities of Olympic athletes.

Procedures can be based on teacher lecture or student research.

LESSON 7

Predicting New Records

Objective

After observing you create a bar graph on the board as a model, students will design a bar graph that graphically displays Olympic discus records.

Materials

Graph paper; overhead transparency; list of Olympic records

Procedure

"Let's take a vote to find out which fruit is the favorite of most class members. Raise your hands if apples are your favorite. Oranges? Bananas?" You write information on the board and create a bar graph to display the results and think aloud to tell students, as you create the graph, what you are doing. "The neat thing about a bar graph is that we don't have to look at the actual numbers to know at a glance which fruit is the favorite. We need only to compare heights on the bar graph."

1. Students work individually to create a bar graph of Olympic discus records, given the following figures:

Year	Distance in Feet	Year	Distance in Feet
1896	96	1972	211
1912	148	1988	226
1932	162	1996	227.6
1956	185		

2. Students make a prediction for the next summer Olympic Games based on previous years and then graph their predictions.
3. Students write a short paragraph explaining the reasons for their predictions.
4. Students discuss if they would like to make further predictions by collecting data and making more bar graphs.
5. If appropriate, repeat the previous graph activity or engage students in developing a variety of graphs with selected information about the top three medal-winning countries in the summer Olympic Games.

Past Medal Winners

1928: United States with 22 gold medals (G), 18 silver (S), and 16 bronze (B); Germany with 10 G, 7 S, and 14 B; Finland with 8 G, 8 S, and 9 B.

1932: United States with 41 gold medals (G), 32 silver (S), and 30 bronze (B); Italy with 12 G, 12 S, and 12 B; Finland with 5 G, 8 S, and 12 B.

(Continued)

LESSON 7

Predicting New Records—Cont.

1936: Germany with 33 gold medals (G), 26 silver (S), and 30 bronze (B); United States with 24 G, 20 S, and 12 B; Italy with 8 G, 9 S, and 5 B.

1948: United States with 38 gold medals (G), 27 silver (S), and 19 bronze (B); Sweden with 16 G, 11 S, and 17 B; France with 10 G, 6 S, and 13 B.

1952: United States with 40 gold medals (G), 19 silver (S), and 17 bronze (B); Soviet Union with 22 G, 30 S, and 19 B; Hungary with 16 G, 10 S, and 16 B.

1956: Soviet Union with 37 gold medals (G), 29 silver (S), and 32 bronze (B); United States with 32 G, 25 S, and 17 B; Australia with 13 G, 8 S, and 14 B.

1960: Soviet Union with 43 gold medals (G), 29 silver (S), and 31 bronze (B); United States with 36 G, 26 S, and 28 B; Germany with 12 G, 19 S, and 11 B.

1964: United States with 45 gold medals (G), 28 silver (S), and 34 bronze (B); Soviet Union with 30 G, 31 S, and 25 B; W. Germany with 7 G, 14 S, and 14 B.

1968: United States with 45 gold medals (G), 28 silver (S), and 34 bronze (B); Soviet Union with 29 G, 32 S, and 30 B; Hungary with 10 G, 10 S, and 12 B.

1972: Soviet Union with 50 gold medals (G), 27 silver (S), and 22 bronze (B); United States with 33 G, 31 S, and 30 B; E. Germany with 20 G, 23 S, and 23 B.

1976: Soviet Union with 49 gold medals (G), 41 silver (S), and 35 bronze (B); United States with 34 G, 35 S, and 25 B; E. Germany with 40 G, 25 S, and 25 B.

1980: Soviet Union with 80 gold medals (G), 69 silver (S), and 46 bronze (B); E. Germany with 47 G, 37 S, and 42 B; Bulgaria with 8 G, 16 S, and 17 B.

1984: United States with 83 gold medals (G), 61 silver (S), and 30 bronze (B); W. Germany with 17 G, 19 S, and 23 B; Romania with 20 G, 16 S, and 17 B.

1988: Soviet Union with 55 gold medals (G), 31 silver (S), and 46 bronze (B); E. Germany with 37 G, 35 S, and 30 B; United States with 36 G, 31 S, and 27 B.

1992: Unified Team (Soviet Union) with 45 gold medals (G), 38 silver (S), and 29 bronze (B); United States with 37 G, 34 S, and 37 B; Germany with 16 G, 22 S, and 16 B.

LESSON 7

Predicting New Records—Cont.

Closure

"When we create and read bar graphs, we are more interested in making comparisons and observing for trends than in knowing the exact numbers that are graphed. How do the previous discus records help us in predicting what will happen in next summer's games?" Because the number of years between each discus record fluctuates, students must make their predictions by taking into account that there is only a difference of 8 years from the 1992 entry to the 2000 Olympics. "What else would you like to predict on the basis of your collection of data and the creation of a bar graph?"

Assessment

The bar graphs are included in each student's portfolio. Students also respond to the open-ended question, "Can discus records continue to increase indefinitely?"

Internet use suggestions are found in expanded lists of Internet resources in *K–12 Resources on the Internet: An Instructional Guide* (New York: Library Solutions, 1998) by Gail Junion-Metz. This book comes with a disk that has more than 350 links to K–12 resources on the Web.

Management suggestions include recognizing the effect of your response to one student's misbehavior on students whose behavior is appropriate, and to your ability to be alert in class and to redirect potential student misbehavior.

Make students accountable for researching Olympic records, by women and men, and creating bar graphs. Assessment could extend to performance assessment of students' creating bar graphs.

LESSON 8

Let the Games Begin

Objective

After discussing proper exercise procedures, computing target aerobic heart rates, and creating pulse-rate graphs, students will monitor and record their pulse rates while voluntarily participating in movement activities and drawing conclusion about what it means to be physically fit and how regular exercise helps maintain fitness.

Materials

16 Frisbees; straws; participation awards; graph papers; target heart rate bulletin board; watch with second hand; blue, red, green crayons

Procedure

"When is the last time you participated in a physical activity for at least 15 minutes that made your heart beat faster and your body sweat? Today we are going to learn how to exercise safely and effectively so that we can be physically fit."

1. Students brainstorm the meaning of physical fitness, and why it is important to exercise regularly.
2. Introduce the physical activity sequence: warm-up, stretch, aerobic activity, cool down.
3. Explain how maximum heart rates and target heart rates are calculated:

   maximum rate = 220–age
   target heart rate = 60%–80% of maximum rate

4. Students calculate their target heart rates, and then you introduce the target heart rate bulletin board (Figure 5.6).
5. Students create line graphs (Figure 5.7) to record the following color-coded data:

   Resting pulse rate (in blue)
   Aerobic pulse rate (in red)
   Recovery pulse rate (in green)

6. Teach students proper procedure for taking and recording a 10-second pulse and record resting pulse rates.
7. Students voluntarily participate in the following activities: (Note: students who choose or for a reason cannot participate in the exercise activities can serve as teacher helpers—keeping time, recording, and so on.)

   warm-up—fast walk around 0.1-mile course
   stretch—legs, arms, back
   aerobic—modified kickball, in which one entire team runs the bases while the outfield passes the ball and runs to form a circle at a designated place.

M

Teachers who are most effective are those who specify task outcomes, have high expectations for students, and use active teaching behaviors.

LESSON 8

Let the Games Begin—Cont.

FIGURE 5.6   Target Heart Rate Bulletin Board Display

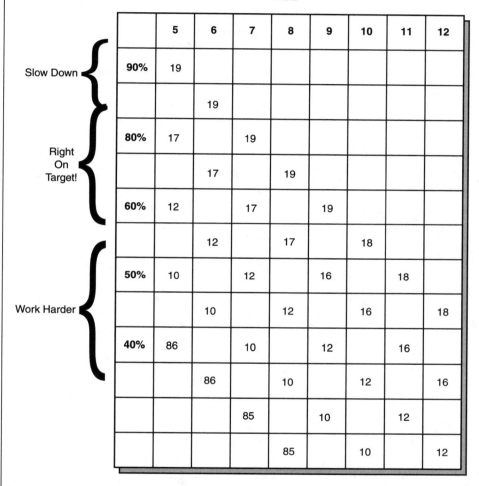

AGE

		5	6	7	8	9	10	11	12
Slow Down {	**90%**	19							
			19						
Right On Target! {	**80%**	17		19					
				17	19				
	60%	12		17		19			
			12		17		18		
Work Harder {	**50%**	10		12		16		18	
			10		12		16		18
	40%	86		10		12		16	
			86		10		12		16
				85		10		12	
					85		10		12

8. During activity, students take their aerobic pulse rates.
9. After a cool-down walk of about 5 minutes, students take their recovery pulse rates.
10. Both pulse rates are recorded on students' graphs (Figure 5.7).
11. Students participate in a fun Olympic activity:

    Javelin throw using straws
    Discus throw using Frisbees

(Continued)

Teachers and students have rights in their classrooms to expect appropriate student behavior. Consequences for persistent inappropriate behavior should be stated, clearly understood, and quickly applied.

LESSON 8

Let the Games Begin—Cont.

FIGURE 5.7 Sample Line Graphs of Pulse Rates

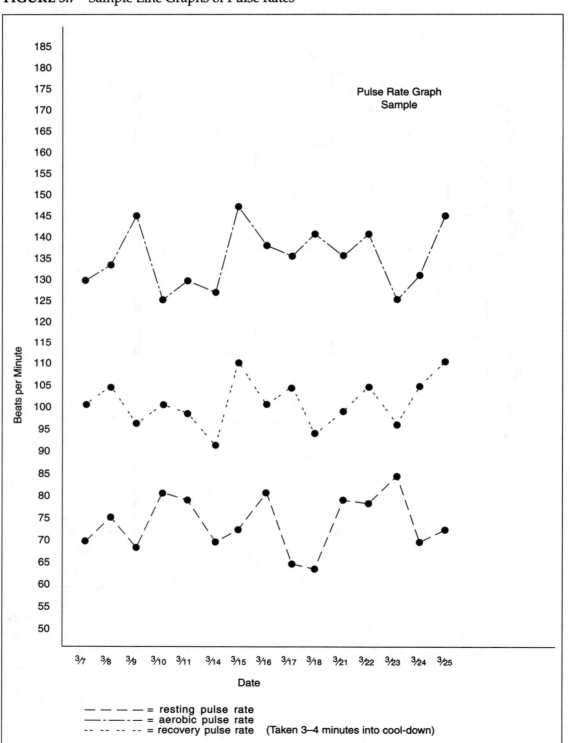

Pulse Rate Graph
Sample

Beats per Minute

Date

———— = resting pulse rate
—·—·— = aerobic pulse rate
-- -- -- = recovery pulse rate   (Taken 3–4 minutes into cool-down)

LESSON 8

Let the Games Begin—Cont.

Closure

"Raise your hands if you can tell us the proper sequence of physical activity. Why is it important to warm up and stretch before an aerobic activity? Who can explain how we calculate our target heart rates? We will be keeping track of our pulse rates for the rest of this month as we participate in physical education activities. As you begin to exercise regularly, what do you hypothesize that we will discover? We should find that your resting pulse rate will become lower and your recovery rate will be quicker."

Assessment

Pulse rate graphs are added to each student's portfolio. Students are encouraged to monitor their own improvement. Students who participate in the movement activities receive an award for participation, which is worth points at the end of the unit (Figure 5.8). An alternate award activity will be decided for students who cannot participate in the movement activities.

FIGURE 5.8 Participation Award (Sample)

Ancient Greece

Games Day

Participation Award

LESSON 9
Ancient Greek Society: Town Meeting

Objective

After discussing the four classes of Athenian society, students demonstrate their knowledge as they participate in a simulated town meeting and complete their retrieval charts.

Materials

Retrieval charts; role play description sheet; game cards for citizen, family of citizen, metic, slave; identification necklaces for children, accused slave, accusing metic, and wife of citizen

Procedure

As students enter the room, hand each a game card, which will identify his or her role in the simulation. Explain briefly that the students will be participating in a role play and that they are to stay in character until the town meeting is finished. (Note: Depending on the number of students in your class, cards should be divided proportionately as follows: 15% citizens, 48% family of citizens, 12% metics, and 25% slaves.)

1. Arrange the classroom for a town meeting.
2. Explain the following four levels of ancient Greek society.

   Citizens. Men over 18 years of age. They may vote, hold office, speak at town meetings, own slaves, and they are protected by laws.
   Family members of citizens. Wives and children. They may not vote or speak at town meetings and have no rights, privileges, or protection under law.
   Metics. Foreigners, tradesmen, shopkeepers, and craftsmen. They may not vote or hold office, but they may speak at town meetings and are protected under law.
   Slaves. Prisoners of wars and other captives. They may not vote or hold office. They have no protection under the law and no job choice, although they may have a family only with their master's permission.

3. Students read the scenario from the role play description sheet (Figure 5.9).
4. Reiterate the roles and powers.
5. Students hold the town meeting.
6. Students form groups of three or four to complete the information retrieval chart (Figure 5.10).

Closure

"How would you differentiate among the roles of citizens, family members of citizens, metics, and slaves? Which would you prefer to be? How would you compare and contrast the democracy of ancient

LESSON 9

Ancient Greek Society: Town Meeting—Cont.

Greece with democracy in the United States? Are there town meetings held in our country? Have you or your parents ever attended one? Are they similar to those of ancient Greece? Different? How?"

Assessment

The retrieval chart is a required element for the student folder. Students will also be assessed according to participation in the simulation.

FIGURE 5.9   Role Play Description Sheet

Town Meeting in Ancient Greece

Setup

Eight chairs should be placed in the front of the room for the key characters in this simulated town meeting: five citizens, one metic, one wife of citizen, and one slave. Other chairs can be arranged in rows for those members of the town not allowed to speak in the meeting. Other metics should sit closest to the key characters in case they wish to speak.

Scenario

While at the busy town center where metics were selling their wares earlier in the day, turmoil erupted. A slave who was accompanying the family members of a citizen was accused of stealing food from one of the metics. The only one who actually saw this happen was the metic, who accuses the slave of stealing, and the wife of the slave owner, who claims it was not the slave but another thief who is at fault. Since slaves have no legal rights and are not citizens, a crime such as stealing can result in severe fines for the slave owner and possible banishment or even death for the accused slave.

   The slave owner is called to a town meeting and he is accompanied by the rest of his family. All other citizens and people of the town are present at this meeting. They listen to arguments from both the metic's and the slave owner's points of view. The slave owner's wife quietly supplies her husband with information but is not allowed to speak to the assembly. The accused slave is not allowed to speak. The slave owner, since he is a citizen, is the only one who can speak on behalf of the slave. The metics may speak, but they cannot vote as to the guilt or innocence of the accused slave.

   After all arguments have been heard, the citizens take a vote to determine the verdict.

T

Perhaps students will want to attend a town meeting or some similar meeting in their community, which could quite possibly lead to a community service project.

M

In discussion, point out that prosecution against Socrates was based on his view that there were weaknesses in the Greek democracy (i.e., that it did not require proof of special knowledge of its leaders; that it surrendered people's destinies to those without adequate experience in democratic government; and that it treated all opinions of citizens as equal in value and neglected the morality or justice of a particular policy).

(Continued)

LESSON 9

Ancient Greek Society: Town Meeting—Cont.

FIGURE 5.10   Greek Society Information Retrieval Chart

Greek Society

Level	Description	Rights	Responsibilities
Citizens			
Family of Citizens			
Metics			
Slaves			

Compare democracy in United States today with the democracy of ancient Greek society. List the similarities and differences.

Similarities	Differences

LESSON 10

Classical Greek Architecture: Experimenting with Column Design

Objective

Students will demonstrate skill in hypothesizing and experimenting to determine which column designs will support the most weight.

Materials

Data collection form; 9" × 12" construction paper; tape; rulers; supplemental teaching information form; pictures illustrating the three architectural styles

Procedure

"Let's take a minute to look around the room at the pictures of ancient Greece that show us examples of their architecture. Raise your hand if you think you can tell me something about how the early Greeks built structures. Are there examples of that kind of architecture today?"

1. Encourage students to share what they already know or think they know about architectural design.
2. Using the supplemental teaching information (Figure 5.11) as a resource, discuss the three orders of Greek architecture: Doric, Ionic, and Corinthian. Show examples of each.
3. Discuss the scientific method and why it should be thought of as a cyclic rather than a linear process (i.e., as new data come in, an earlier conclusion may be thrown out, and the process repeats or cycles all over again).
4. Describe the experiment students will conduct and clarify any questions they may have about it. Then give students the instructions for the column experiment (Figure 5.12).
5. Put students in their cooperative learning groups and assign the following roles: recorder, gatekeeper, thinker.
6. Allow students enough time to conduct their testing and to record their results.

Closure

Ask groups to share their results and then write those results on the board. Discuss the need to make multiple trial tests when conducting an experiment. Ask students to calculate the average result for each tested column using the data from the board.

Assessment

The completed experiment forms are included in each student's portfolio. Each student's level of understanding is assessed by reviewing the student's conclusions and by further questioning, perhaps in individual conferences.

(Continued)

LESSON 10

Classical Greek Architecture: Experimenting with Column Design— Cont.

FIGURE 5.11   Classical Greek Architecture: Supplemental Teaching Information Sheet

Classical Greek Architecture

General Information

The earliest buildings of Greece were made of sun-dried bricks, timber and decorative terra-cotta. Later, stone and marble became the chief materials. Mortar was rarely used, the finely cut blocks being held by metal dowels and clamps. Although Greek architects were aware of the arch and vault, their approach was relatively conservative. The megaron, with its portico entrance and low-pitched roof, was the model for Greek temples. The earliest temples were timber; their forms were later translated into mud-brick and finally, stone. The two basic elements of timber structures, vertical supports (columns) and horizontal members (entablatures), were transformed into the three carefully proportioned orders, or styles, of Greek architecture: the Doric, Ionic, and Corinthian.

The Doric: The earliest and simplest of the classical orders. The fluted columns stand firmly on their platform without intermediate bases. The abacus is deep and plain.

The Ionic: This elegant order is recognized by the capital (head of the column) of spiral-shaped scrolls called volutes.

The Corinthian: The last and most elaborate order. The tall fluted column was capped by an elaborate stylized carving of acanthus plants. The decorative character of this order made it popular.

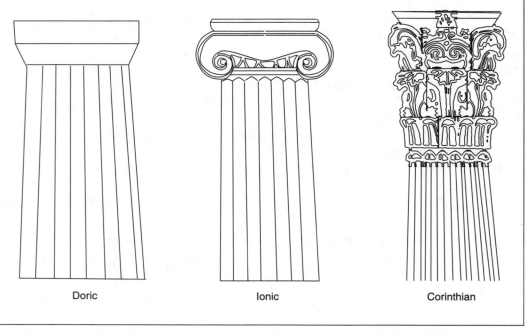

Doric   Ionic   Corinthian

Source: Adapted from *The Book of Buildings: A Traveler's Guide* by Richard Reid, Michael Joseph Limited, 1980.

LESSON 10

Classical Greek Architecture: Experimenting with Column Design—Cont.

FIGURE 5.12   The Column Design Experiment

Column Experiment

Focus question: Will a single sheet of paper support a heavy book? Try this experiment to find out.

Purpose: What do I want to find out?

　　　　　　Which of the tested columns will support the most weight?

Experiment:

　1. Roll a 9" x 12" piece of construction paper so that it is 9 inches long and has a diameter of 1 inch.

　2. Stand the paper on end to form a 9-inch high column.

　3. Add math books to the column until the column collapses.

　4. Repeat with the following column specifications: 9 inches long with a 2-inch diameter; 6 inches long (folded in half) with a 1-inch diameter; and 6 inches long (folded in half) with a 2-inch diameter.

Analysis: Collect and interpret data

Relative Strengths of Various Columns

Number of math books

	9 x 1	9 x 2	6 x 1 (doubled)	6 x 2 (doubled)	
12					
11					
10					
9					
8					
7					
6					
5					
4					
3					
2					
1					
0					

Conclusions: What did I learn?

What questions do I now have? (This will lead to a new purpose, perhaps a new experiment)

LESSON 11

Sparta/Athens/(name of our community)

Objective

After discussing selected terms, students will do team research on an assigned or selected topic and report on it to the class.

Materials

Text; resources already available in classroom

Procedure

"When we discussed the geography of Greece, we talked about the development of city-states. What is a city-state? Are there any in existence today?" (Note: Singapore was, until 1997, a modern city-state.) "Which city would have been a better place to live, Athens or Sparta?"

1. Discuss these terms: *government, economy, lifestyle, monarchy, oligarchy,* and *democracy.* For background, use the information sheet (Figure 5.13).
2. Assign or have each cooperative learning group select one of the following topics. There are 15 topics listed; depending on the number of students in your class you may want to modify the topics or assignment.

Arts/Athena	Arts/Sparta	Arts/our town
Government/Athena	Government/Sparta	Government/our town
Education/Athena	Education/Sparta	Education/our town
Economy/Athena	Economy/Sparta	Economy/our town
Lifestyle/Athena	Lifestyle/Sparta	Lifestyle/our town

3. Student teams research their topics, perhaps over a period of several days.
4. Groups present their information to the class with a visual outline. The focus should be on comparing and contrasting Athens and Sparta.
5. Students ask questions of the presenters and take notes on the information given.

Closure

"What were some ways that Sparta and Athens differed? How might we account for these differences? In what ways did they differ from our own community? Where would you rather live—Sparta, Athens, or in our town? Why?"

Assessment

Students complete self-assessments and group assessments (Figure 5.14) on their presentations. The student presentations are evaluated with regard to content accuracy and completeness.

LESSON 11

Sparta/Athens/(name of our community)—Cont.

FIGURE 5.13   Athens and Sparta: Supplemental Teacher Information Sheet

Athens

Government. In ancient Greece, Athens was a monarchy, ruled by one king. In time, the nobles were depended on more and more to help defend the land and thus began to demand more power in return. By the end of the Dark Ages, an oligarchy developed with power in the hands of a few. As the population grew in this society where much of the land was unsuitable for farming, food shortages occurred and people began to look for change. After a period of tyranny, an early form of democracy appeared, around 510 B.C. The entire process took several centuries. The democracy included a council of 500 members, who were chosen at random each year. The council proposed new laws and were paid for their service. An assembly included all citizens that met every 9 days to vote on laws. Courts were made up of citizens who were paid to serve as jurors.

Economy. The main activity in the Athens area was farming. Most citizens had just enough land to support their families. The wealthy few had estates with slaves. Some tenant farmers rented land. Until 500 B.C., trading depended on bartering; around 570 B.C., the government began to make gold and silver coins. By 600 B.C., Athens had become an international trade center. The monetary system and trade led to wealth, but the wealthy were expected to give large sums of money to the government to support projects resulting in a flow of money back to the citizens.

Education. Boys from wealthy families began their formal education at age 7. They lived at home, unlike the Spartans. They were taught reading, writing, math, poetry, music, dance, and athletics. They had a much more liberal education than the Spartans. At age 18, men joined the army for 2 years of military service. The wealthy men attended academies and studied throughout their lives. Girls received no formal education in Athens.

Lifestyle. Boys were more prized than girls. Upon birth, infant girls were sometimes left abandoned outside the city gates. Men managed farms and estates and participated in the government. Boys lived at home during their schooling. Girls received no training and often were married by age 15. Women cared for the home and raised the children. Athenians enjoyed greater freedom than the Spartans and entertained themselves with myths, plays, and poetry.

Sparta

Government. The government of Sparta began as a monarchy with two kings and gradually moved toward an oligarchy with power in the hands of a few. The 30-member senate consisted of men who were over the age of 60. The senators were elected by the citizens, who were male landowners over the age of 30. Members of the citizen's assembly could not propose laws but could vote yes or no on the laws proposed by the senate or the ephors. The senate and the ephors really had the power to ignore a vote if they chose and power was concentrated in the hands of a few families.

Economy. Sparta had a military economy and the men were required by law to be soldiers. As a result, people in the surrounding communities provided trade and craft items, although luxury goods were forbidden. Every citizen was given a plot of land by the government, and helots (state slaves) were assigned to farm the land. The helots were given crops as payment. The owner was required to give the government crops in exchange for daily meals; if he was unable to do so, he lost his rights as a citizen.

Education. Because Sparta was a militaristic city-state, education focused on military training, athletics (jumping, boxing, and wrestling), discipline, reading, and writing. At age 7, boys left their families to live in military barracks. Conditions in school were very harsh, as it was believed that hardship would create stronger character.

Lifestyle. Much can be understood by knowing that government inspectors were sent upon the birth of a child to determine whether the child would live or be abandoned in a cave to die. Male children lived in barracks from the age of 7 and at age 18 were expected to devote their lives to the army. At the age of 30 they gained full citizenship but were expected, even if married, to eat all meals with the soldiers in the mess hall. It can be inferred from this that family life was not as strong a value as military life. Entertainment consisted of religious festivals, chorus contests, and dance contests.

LESSON 11

Sparta/Athens/(name of our community)— Cont.

FIGURE 5.14   Form for ITU Student Self-Assessment and Group Assessment

---

Unit Self-Assessment and Group Assessment

Please evaluate your contributions to your group by placing an X at the location that most accurately reflects your own performance.

1. While creating the group banner, I
   did not take part   took responsibility for some
                                                  part of the project

   1   2   3   4   5

---

2. During the paper column experiment, I
   did not work cooperatively or share
   with others   worked cooperatively with
                                                  others

   1   2   3   4   5

---

3. When working with my group, I
   usually failed to stay on task   Worked to the best of my
                                                ability

   1   2   3   4   5

---

4. In a few sentences, explain what you enjoyed most about the ancient
   Greece unit.

5. Which activity did you like the least? Why?

6. List some problems you and your group experienced while working on
   the assigned projects.

7. List some successes you and your group enjoyed while working on the
   assigned projects.

ADDITIONAL SUPPLEMENTAL RESOURCES

Other CD-ROM and laser disc resources include:

- *Ancient Lands* (by Microsoft, for grades 5–12, CD-ROM for Mac or Windows)
- *Early Civilizations* (by BFA, for grades 4–12, Laserdisc or VHS videotape)
- *History of Civilization* (by Queue, for grades 8–12, CD-ROM for IBM)
- *Recess in Greece* (by Electronic Arts/Morgan Interactive, for grades 5–10, CD-ROM for Mac)
- *The Story of Civilization* (by Compton's/World Library, for grades 7–12, CD-ROM for IBM or Windows)
- *World History Illustrated: Ancient Greece* (by Queue, for grades 6–12, CD-ROM for Mac or IBM)

For middle grade children (grades 4–8), special education, and ESL students, as well as for independent reading, see *Favorite Greek Myths*, a Scholastic Smart Book (Scholastic) by Mary Pope Osborner, with illustrations by Mary Howell, on CD-ROM for Macintosh computers. Available from Educational Software Institute, 4213 South 49th Street, Omaha, NE 68127.

For older students (grades 9 and up), consider using *Theseus: Caught in the Maze of Minoa* (Compton's New Media/Westwind), a CD-ROM for Macintosh computers. With this medium, students can experience the fun and fascination of mythological lore as they follow the adventures of Theseus and his encounters with dozens of authentic characters. The program's giant database allows students to summon accurate information on gods, goddesses, and heroes and to quickly hunt down detailed maps and genealogical charts. This in-depth study of Greek literature, history, and foreign culture tells the tales of gods and heroes with illustrations, narration, music, and sound effects. Requires Macintosh system 7.0 or greater and color. Available from Educational Software Institute, 4213 South 94th Street, Omaha, NE 68127.

Summative Unit Assessment. Summative assessment of student learning for this unit will be based on the teacher's anecdotal records, each student's unit assessment checklist from the student's portfolio (see Figure 5.15), and the student's performance on the unit test (Figure 5.16).

FIGURE 5.15 Unit Assessment Checklist

Item	Point Value	Student Self-Evaluation
Write your own myth	10	_____
Myth checklist (you are the reviewer)	5	_____
Group banner with a clear theme	5	_____
Vocabulary scribble	5	_____
Definitions and illustrations	5	_____
Retrieval chart (geography)	10	_____
Participation in games day	10	_____
Discuss bar graph	10	_____
Paper column experiment	10	_____
Retrieval chart (levels of Greek society)	10	_____
Debate (knowledgeable participation)	10	_____
Self-assessment and group assessment	10	_____
Total	100	_____

FIGURE 5.16   Example of Unit Test

Unit Test

1. Compare the Olympic Games in ancient Greece to the Olympic Games held today. How are they alike? How are they different?

2. Write the letter of the correct definition after each vocabulary word.

oligarchy _____	a. rule by a few people
barter _____	b. independent self-governing unit
helot _____	c. government by the people
sanctuary _____	d. state slave
democracy _____	e. sad story of a flawed hero
city-state _____	f. a sacred place to honor gods
monarchy _____	g. rule by a king
tragedy _____	h. exchange one product for another

3. How did the geography of Greece affect the following (choose any two and explain):
   a. farming

   b. the development of city-states

   c. trade

   d. culture

4. We learned that there were four classes of people in ancient Athens. What type of people belonged to each class and what rights did people of each class have?

5. Compare life in Athens with life in Sparta. Outline the differences. Where would you rather live? Explain why.

Sample ITU 2

Migrations: Early Newcomers in North America*

Middle and Secondary Grades. This interdisciplinary thematic unit about Native people, early explorers, and colonists in North America can be adapted for students in middle and secondary schools as part of an integrated program about the development of the United States.

Unit Overview. Through selected learning activities, students can develop a meaningful understanding of the United States as they study about people with different background, ideas, and ways of life. In this unit, students become better acquainted with the early explorers, the study of the early settlement of the colonies, the people who lived there, and some of the reasons newcomers came to North America. You can guide students as

*Source: Adapted by permission from *A Resource Guide for Elementary School Teaching: Planning for Competence* (4th edition) (Merrill/Prentice-Hall, 1997) by R. D. Kellough and P. L. Roberts.

they compare that time period with present-day events, developing new insights which for a selected group of students can be expanded for whatever period of time that seems appropriate. By necessity, some of the lessons will last several days.

To visually graph the emphasis and show the contributions of a particular discipline to some of the lessons in the unit, you can develop a web to show the integration of the different disciplines selected for the unit such as the following. It can be drawn on the writing board to discuss with the students if appropriate for your group.

Unit Goals. From California's History/Social Studies Framework, this unit is designed to explore

- selected early explorers
- early settlement of colonies, the people who lived there, and reasons why they came to North America and how those reasons are similar and different from the reasons newcomers today come to America.
- effects of the environment on people and their food, clothing, and shelter
- how the concept of colonization compares with that of today

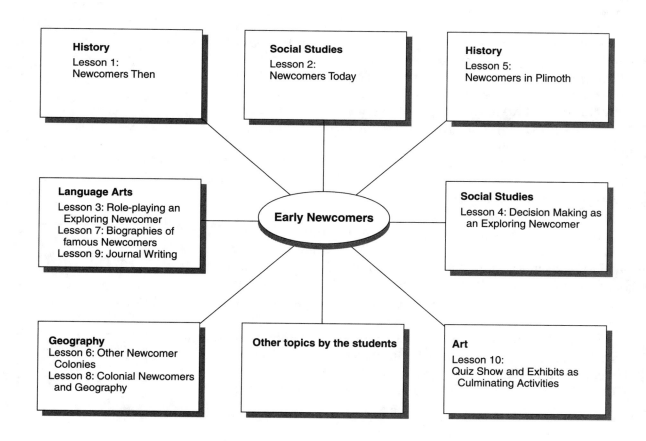

LESSON 1

Newcomers Then

Objectives
- Given a biography, the student will interpret a concept of "newcomer," describe the ideas of others, and demonstrate active listening skills.
- Students will willingly cooperate with others during group activities.
- Students will describe their feelings about the topic.

Materials
My Name Is Pocahontas (Holiday House, 1992) by William Accorsi or *The Double Life of Pocahontas* (Putnam, 1983) by Jean Fritz; paper, pencils, writing board or overhead transparency; students' portfolios

Procedure
"Today you are going to hear about newcomers to the culture of a Native American princess, Pocahontas. Listen to find out what the princess did to help in events that happened between her culture and the newcomer's culture."

1. Introduce the concept of early English settlers as newcomers by reading aloud excerpts from *My Name Is Pocahontas* (Holiday House, 1992) by William Accorsi. This fictionalized biography is told by the princess beginning in her childhood. She tells of her friendship with Captain John Smith, her marriage to John Rolfe, and her trip to England as Rolfe's wife. Another read-aloud choice is *The Double Life of Pocahontas* (Putnam, 1983) by Jean Fritz. This biography focuses on the role the princess played in the events between two cultures. Discuss ways Smith and Rolfe were newcomers in Pocahontas's culture.

2. Write the word *newcomers* on the board or overhead transparency. Ask the students to identify important ideas, understandings, concepts, or feelings (from their own point of view or reference material) related to the topic of newcomers. Write their suggestions on the board in a list and invite students to write/copy their own lists at their desks or in small groups.

You may want to guide students toward an interdisciplinary focus with such questions as, "What in the biography tells us someone used mathematics in a certain way? Art? Science? Music? How could math help us learn about colonial newcomers? Art? Science? Music?"

3. Ask the students to rank order the concepts from the most general to the most specific (mathematics).

4. Arrange the general concept words in a graphic web on the writing board in a web format. Invite the students to draw their own concept web at their desks. If appropriate, circle the general concept words. Arrange the general concept words so that the most specific

---

T

For grades K–6, sample lesson and unit plans on American civilization can be viewed on the Internet at <http://www.trinity/edu/departments/education/core/lessons/amerplan html>.

D

Engage students in effective instructional conversation (EIC), which means that students build on what others say so each statement expands, clarifies, or challenges previous statements. EIC has been demonstrated as highly relevant to the linguistic, cognitive, and academic development of linguistically and culturally diverse students.

T

Also see *Pocahontas: Powhatan Peacemaker* by Anne Holler (Chelsea, 1993) in *Multicultural Friendship Stories and Activities for Children, Ages 5–14* (Scarecrow Press, 1998) by Patricia L. Roberts.

M/D

Working in small groups supports students' understanding of a particular concept as well as contributes positively to their understanding of self and their acceptance of others.

LESSON 1

Newcomers Then—Cont.

concept words and related ideas can be connected to them with radiating lines (as in a web).

5. Invite students to discuss and define the connections between the related ideas.

6. Engage students in defining selected terms from the concept web in the following ways: (1) by reading a definition from the dictionary, glossary, thesaurus, or textbook, (2) by pantomiming or demonstrating something about the term, (3) by describing something about the term, and (4) by displaying an illustration related to the term.

7. If appropriate to emphasize various disciplines further, discuss with students any or all of the following:

   a. What can we see in this story of Pocahontas that shows a relationship between someone's behavior and his or her beliefs? (anthropology)
   b. What economic problems can we see in this story? Resolutions of the problems? (economics)
   c. How could we show what we know about Pocahontas through the visual and performing arts (art, music, dance, sculpture, and so on)? (art)
   d. In what ways do you believe geography influenced the life of Pocahontas? (geography)
   e. How have ways we receive information about this topic changed over time? (history)
   f. In what ways could we express what we know about newcomers through math? (mathematics)
   g. What scientists bring us more information about this topic? (science)
   h. How did the people in this time period organize themselves? (political science)
   i. In what ways can we participate to resolve a real problem related to the topic (newcomers)? (sociology)

Closure

"Let's share our ideas about the concept of newcomers." Invite students to volunteer the information they gained about this concept and have them describe the ideas of others that they hear. To encourage them to demonstrate their listening skills, engage students in expanding some of the sentences they hear, in clarifying others, and if appropriate, in challenging still others.

(Continued)

LESSON 1

Newcomers Then—Cont.

Assessment

- Engage students in individual written assessments of what they learned from listening to (reading aloud) the biography and have them sketch or finish incomplete sentences with their own words. The following sentences are examples that the students could complete individually with their words or sketches:

    My idea of the concept of newcomer is _____.

    What I learned most about newcomers was _____.

    Here is one idea about newcomers that I heard from someone else: _____ .

- Have students place their written assessments in their portfolios.
- Keep teacher observations on a checklist regarding student participation in developing the concept map, in ranking the concepts, and in defining terms. Have students begin a journal related to this unit and describe the most important thing they learned from the lesson and how they could apply what they learned to their lives in some way.
- Prepare a guideline related to assessing a student's skill in listening. You can assign a score if needed. Example: _____ (student name) is a strong listener who demonstrates the following:

    a. an immediate response to oral directions. (5 points)
    b. a focus on the one who is speaking.
    c. an appropriate attention span.
    d. an attention to what others are saying.
    e. interaction by expanding, clarifying, or questioning what others are saying.

LESSON 2

Newcomers Today

Objective

Students will demonstrate further understanding about the concept of the word *newcomers* today as they look for news articles about contemporary newcomers. Students will make connections of similarities and differences about today's newcomers and early newcomers and report their findings back to the group.

Materials

Copies of different newspapers, paper, pencils, venn diagram

Procedure

"Just as John Smith and John Rolfe were newcomers to the culture of Pocahontas, there are people today who are newcomers to your culture. Look at the newspapers you are given, and with your partner, look for articles (photographs and headlines) about newcomers today. Get ready to tell the whole group about something similar and different about today's newcomer and a colonial newcomer."

1. Distribute copies of different newspapers to the students and ask them to work with partners and look for articles about newcomers today. Younger students can look for photographs and read headlines. Older students can read the articles and look for similarities and differences between the newcomers of today and the colonial newcomers. Have the students report back to the whole group about the similarities and differences they found.

2. Demonstrate the use of a Venn diagram to show the similarities and differences between colonial newcomers and contemporary newcomers. Have the students develop the diagram as a group. If appropriate, engage more able students in working with partners to complete their own venn diagrams to show similarities and differences in the two groups of newcomers.

3. Invite students who developed their own diagrams to show them and report on what they wrote about similarities and differences.

4. If appropriate to further emphasize various disciplines, discuss the following:

   a. How can we show what we know about these newcomers to America through art, music, dance, and sculpture? (expressive arts)
   b. What experiences have we had that would help us understand the way these newcomers lived? (anthropology)
   c. In what ways did geography influence the newcomers? (geography)

(Continued)

M

You can structure learning groups around selected skills or content in ad hoc groups for special assistance.

LESSON 2

Newcomers Today—Cont.

d. What can we do to find out what newcomer groups settled in our area? How is their influence shown today? (history)

e. How can we participate in our community today to resolve a problem related to today's newcomers? (sociology)

Closure

Engage students in discussing, "What meaning does this have for us today?" Engage the students in dictating a paragraph about the two newcomer groups for a group chart. If appropriate, engage more able students in writing individual paragraphs about the similarities and differences of the two groups.

Assessment

- In a group, ask students an oral assessment type question, "Now that you've thought about what it was like to be a colonial newcomer and what it is like to be a contemporary newcomer, what could we do in the future to assist newcomers?" List all of the responses on a class chart, an overhead transparency, or bulletin board, for later reference. Have students copy the list and place their copies in their portfolios.

  Teacher observation on student participation:

  a. While developing a group diagram (or written paragraph) the similarities and differences of the two newcomer groups can be kept. Have students place copies of the diagram (or individual paragraphs) in their portfolios.

  b. While recording responses to oral assessment question, consider a teacher observation checklist, as shown in Figure 5.17.

  c. While reading and reporting on newspaper articles, you can develop a checklist about a student's reporting to the group, as shown in Figure 5.18.

- Have students write in a journal related to the unit and describe the most important thing they learned about newcomers and how they can use the information to relate better to newcomers who come into their lives in some way.

LESSON 2

Newcomers Today—Cont.

FIGURE 5.17   Sample Teacher Observation Checklist

Teacher Observation Checklist

Observation period _____ for _____

The following is the number of times the students demonstrated participation in group work.

Student name	**in group diagram**	**in response to questions**
1. Pat		

FIGURE 5.18   Sample Checklist of a Student's Oral Report to a Group

Checklist of a Student's Oral Report to a Group

Date _____

The student _____ (name) did the following:

	sometimes	**always**	**needs work**
spoke up so all could hear			
finished sentences			
appeared confident before group			
gave good introduction			
was informed about topic			
explained clearly			
stayed on topic			
gave good ending			
was interesting			
gave good answers to questions			

LESSON 3

Role-Playing an Exploring Newcomer

Objective

After discussing the role of what it means to be an exploring newcomer, students will participate in role playing activities and draw some conclusions about what it means to be in that role.

Materials

Samples of edible foods/plants (ordered from a local producer) unique and unfamiliar to the students, writing journals, pencils, sketch paper, crayons

Procedure

"We can play the part of exploring newcomers who have the responsibility of finding some edible plants for the rest of the colony. To begin, who will suggest some ways we can play the roles of newcomers who are exploring the area and looking for plants for food that the colonists can eat."

1. With the whole group, discuss ways of portraying the role(s) related to being exploring newcomers. Elicit suggestions about playing the roles from the students and write their ideas on the board.

2. Discuss questions such as those in Figure 5.19 that are related to role playing for information purposes and problem solving before students are asked to play the roles. You can list the questions for the students to use during the role playing exercise. Later the list can be reused by the students as a reference for their class discussion after the role playing events.

FIGURE 5.19   Sample List of Role Playing Questions

Role Playing List

What's your persona?

What do you look like?

Where are you?

What does the setting look like?

Why are you there?

What could happen?

How are you feeling?

What are you thinking?

What will you say?

How will you act toward the other person?

How can you make the relationship stronger with someone?

LESSON 3

Role-Playing an Exploring Newcomer— Cont.

3. Invite two partners to role-play two exploring newcomers looking for edible plants. Give each partnership one of the unique and unfamiliar foods or plants to use in the role playing exercise. Have two other partners be the audience. Then have them change roles so each student can play the part of an exploring newcomer.

4. *Stop the Action 1 for Journal Writing.* Stop the students and ask them to write in their journals what they are thinking and feeling. As part of the study of the topic, invite them to include any words and actions they particularly liked during the role play.

5. After writing, invite the students to meet with new partners and resume the role play with two other partners as an audience. Have them trade roles.

6. *Stop the Action 2 for Sketching.* Stop the role play and engage the partners in making a sketch of something related to the role play— have them make the object lifesize or larger. Ask them to write a dedication to a friend in the class for their sketches: "To_____ from your exploring newcomer friend _____." Let students give their sketches to the person to whom they wrote the dedication.

7. After sketching, invite the students to trade partners still another time and resume role playing again. Have them trade roles so each student can be an exploring newcomer.

8. *Stop the Action 3 for Discussion.* Ask the partners to meet with another pair of partners and discuss ways the role playing stimulated their curiosity about wanting to know more about being an exploring newcomer. Have them each make a copy of their list:

   What We Are Curious About
   1.

9. After list making, invite the students to trade partners and resume role playing again. Have them trade roles so each student can play all the roles in this situation.

10. *Stop the Action 4 for Suggestions.* Back in the whole group, debrief the role playing by having students suggest ways the role playing helped them learn more about what it was like to be an exploring newcomer. Ask volunteers to tell the ways the role playing stimulated their curiosity about wanting to know more about the theme, topic, or particular event that was selected. They can refer to their lists entitled "What We Are Curious About." Elicit any additional experiences that the students have had related to the role playing. Discuss.

11. If appropriate, discuss with students any or all of the following:
   a. What can we show through art, music, dance, sculpture to indicate what happened when newcomers were searching for food? (expressive arts)

(Continued)

T

Laserdisc: *The First Thanksgiving* (Clearvue/eav), grades 1–3; *Pilgrims at Plymouth* (Clearvue/eav), grades 4–6.

D

Instructional conversation emphasizes the teacher's role in facilitating and guiding student learning through verbal interactions.

M

Class expectations, matters of behavior, and consequences can be established with student input through class meetings.

LESSON 3

Role-Playing an Exploring Newcomer— Cont.

b. Which scientists can we invite to class to tell us about edible plants? (biology)
c. Who could lead us on a field trip to investigate the quantity of edible plants in our area? (science)

Closure

"All the items in our role playing list are items to help us understand what it means to be an exploring newcomer. Which item (items) helped you the most? Why?" Discuss ways students participated in the role playing activities and engage them in drawing some conclusions about what it means to be in that role.

Assessment

- Ask students to record what they learned about the topic by writing paragraphs in their journals to tell what they learned from the role playing activity. Encourage them to write about ways in which they learned more than just mere facts (about personalities, feelings, attitudes, facial expressions, body language, points of view).
- Further, encourage students to refer to their lists of "What We Are Curious About" and follow their curiosity into areas related to this unit that interest them by engaging in independent research when they finish class assignments or during library time. The lists and paragraphs can be placed in the students' portfolios.
- Teacher observations of student participation in role playing can take the form of a checklist (see Figure 5.20).

FIGURE 5.20   Sample Role Playing Observation Form

Teacher Observation for Role Playing

Observation Period _____

Student Name	cooperates	contributes	is consistent
1. Dick			

LESSON 4

Decision Making as an Exploring Newcomer

Objectives

- Students will participate in decision making, cooperate in discussion and small-group work, and sketch what they have learned about testing an unfamiliar food for edibleness.
- Students will respond attentively, willingly cooperate with others during group activities, and create a proposal for decision making related to the safety of eating unfamiliar foods.

Materials

Squanto and the First Thanksgiving (Carolrhoda, 1983) by J. K. Kessel; samples of edible foods/plants (ordered from a local producer) unique and unfamiliar to the students; writing journals, pencils, sketch paper, crayons

Introduction

Squanto, a Paatuxet Indian, taught the pilgrims ways to survive the harsh winter in Massachusetts. They relied on Squanto's knowledge to help them survive. Suppose they did not have Squanto to help them and thus were exploring newcomers who had to search for food among unfamiliar plants—what would they have done to determine which foods were safe for them to eat?

We can imagine we are colonists and have no one—not even Squanto—to tell us which food is safe to eat. We can play the part of exploring newcomers who have the responsibility of finding some edible plants for the rest of the colony. We can show how we made decisions as exploring newcomers who had the responsibility of finding safe, edible plants for the rest of the colony.

Procedure

1. Read aloud excerpts related to the Native Americans' survival skills from *People of the Breaking Day* (Atheneum, 1990) by M. Sewall. Discuss what the Native Americans did to survive and gather food in their environment.

2. Have students get in small groups and imagine they are exploring newcomers who do not have the knowledge that the Native Americans had, but who have the responsibility of finding some edible plants for the rest of the colony.

3. Distribute some unfamiliar edible foods to the groups. Suggestions include bok choy leaves, watercress leaves, cilantro, Ugli™ fruit (also called star fruit), and radicchio. Ask the groups to act out finding

(Continued)

A rich resource about Plimoth Plantation is on the Internet at <http://www.plimoth,org/>

LESSON 4

Decision Making as an Exploring Newcomer—Cont.

their food items. Have students play the role of exploring newcomers who have not seen the foods before and are concerned about eating them. Their challenge is to make decisions about the safety of eating the unfamiliar food their group has been given. They should discuss what they would do to determine the food's safety for the colony. What would they do?

4. Have the groups engage in making decisions about testing the safety of the food.

5. Back in the whole group, have a reporter from each group tell the group's decisions about determining the safety of the food for the colony. Write the group's decision-making proposals on the board or on an overhead transparency. Discuss each decision.

6. Ask the students to brainstorm additional ways that the exploring newcomers could have "tested" an unfamiliar food to determine the extent to which it was safe for humans to eat. Write their suggestions on the board or transparency.

7. Have the students make posters depicting the most interesting and valuable information they have learned about testing unfamiliar foods. On the back, ask them to write (or tell) an explanation about what they learned.

8. Related to the topic of decision making, discuss any or all of the following and ask them to suggest an individual or small-group project that is related.

   a. How can we show the acquired food of the Native Americans of this time period through art, music, dance, or sculpture? (expressive arts)
   b. What experiences have we had about acquiring food that will help us understand what decisions the Native Americans had to make to acquire food? (anthropology)
   c. In what ways did geography affect the food of the Native Americans? (geography)
   d. How can we participate in our community today to help resolve a problem related to acquiring food for those who need it? (sociology)

Closure

Invite students to offer suggestions in regard to improving any future decision-making activity, cooperating in discussion and small-group work, and making sketches about what was learned when testing an unfamiliar food.

M

Many schools have discovered ways of scheduling opportunities for teams of teachers to work together and of providing longer blocks of time for students to actively pursue meaningful learning.

LESSON 4

Decision Making as an Exploring Newcomer—Cont.

Assessment

- If appropriate for your group, introduce the idea of circle assessment, during which the members of each group sit in a circle and respond in turn to your assessment questions. Possible questions include, "What did you learn from this activity?" and "What do you still want to know?"
- Teacher observation on a checklist of student participation in role-playing an exploring newcomer, in discussing the decisions, and in drawing their posters to show information can be kept. Also include information about students participating in decision making, cooperating in discussion and small-group work, and making sketches about what was learned when testing an unfamiliar food.
- Have students also write in their journals related to this unit and draw a picture or describe the most important thing they learned from the lesson and how they could apply what they learned to their lives in some way.
- Have students place their work in their portfolios.

LESSON 5

Newcomers in Plimoth

Objectives
- Given information, students will identify responsibilities of the colonists, discuss and describe their lives, and demonstrate listening skills in partnership and group work.
- Students will offer opinions and justify their ranking choices about the topic.
- Students will describe their feelings about the topic.

Materials
The Pilgrims of Plimoth (Macmillan, 1986) by M. Sewall

Procedure
"You are going to hear about the children, women, and men who were the newcomers who lived at Plimoth Colony. Listen to find out what their lives and responsibilities were like."

1. Divide the class into three groups. Have one group listen and report back on the responsibilities of the children, a second group on the lives and responsibilities of the men, and the third, the lives and responsibilities of the women at Plimoth.

2. When the groups report, list their responses on the board. From the list, have students identify or infer any problems the colony newcomers had.

3. Review the problems and help students classify similar problems together under student-suggested headings such as "Problems of Shelter" and "Problems Getting Food." Ask the students to list the problems on paper and then rank order them with the greatest problem being number one, and so on.

4. Ask students to meet with partners and justify their choices and their rankings to one another. Ask the partners to give written feedback about their agreement or disagreement with any of the rankings.

5. Back in the whole group, discuss the rank ordering and what was needed to help resolve some of the problems the colonial newcomers had.

6. Related to the topic of Newcomers in Plimoth, discuss with the students any or all of the following:

   a. How can you show some of the daily responsibilities of these newcomers in Plimoth through art and sculpture, dance, or music? (expressive arts)

LESSON 5

Newcomers in Plimoth—Cont.

   b. What experiences have *you* had that help you understand the newcomers' problems of getting shelter and food? (anthropology) How can you share this experience with others? What are your feelings about this?

   c. In what ways can you show others how geography influenced the shelter available to the newcomers? (geography)

   d. How could you participate in your community today to help newcomers acquire shelter and food? (sociology)

Closure

"Many of the responsibilities of the colonists are also the responsibilities people face today. What do you think are some of these responsibilities?" Have the students identify responsibilities of the colonists. Encourage them to expand on what they say and discuss and describe what went on in the colonists' lives. Encourage them to demonstrate listening skills toward others in the group.

Assessment

- Ask students to place their list of problems, rankings, and written feedback in their portfolios.
- Teacher assessment can be done by observing the students' participation in the discussion and activity and noting demonstration of listening skills as they respond to others.
- Reports of students back to the group can be assessed with a set of guidelines you have established (see Figure 5.21).
- Have students write in a unit journal and describe what they learned about the lives and responsibilities of the newcomers at Plimoth and how they could apply what they learned to their lives in some way.

LESSON 5

Newcomers in Plimoth—Cont.

FIGURE 5.21   Sample Oral Report Guidelines

Teacher Guidelines for Oral Report

_____ (student name)   _____ (date)

_____ (topic)

Excellent presentation (5 points for each of the following)
a. Made good eye contact with audience.
b. Spoke loudly so all could hear.
c. Spoke for scheduled time.
d. Appeared confident.
e. Introduced report well.
f. Covered important information.

Adequate presentation (3 points for each of the following)
a. Made eye contact sometimes with audience.
b. Spoke but not all could hear all of the time.
c. Spoke but not for allotted time.
d. Appeared uneasy and not always confident.
e. Vaguely introduced report.
f. Covered information but not always important.

Disorganized presentation (1 point for each of the following)
a. Made no or limited eye contact.
b. Spoke but not all could hear most of the time.
c. Spoke for brief time.
d. Appeared uneasy.
e. Failed to introduce report.
f. Covered unimportant information.

LESSON 6
Other Newcomer Colonies

Objectives

- Students will transform information into an art form, will research reasons for the establishment of colonies, and will organize and summarize information.
- Students will cooperate with others during the activities and demonstrate communication skills.

Materials

Map, reference materials, paper, pencils

Procedure

"You are going to read about other newcomers who lived in other colonies. Read to find out several reasons why newcomers started their colonies."

   1. With a map, point out the location of the northern, middle, and southern colonies.

   2. Ask students to identify one group of colonies to research. In their research, ask them to consider the following questions:

> a. What reason(s) can you give for why newcomers started the colonies of Rhode Island, Connecticut, and New Hampshire?
> b. Were the middle colonies started by newcomers for the same (or different) reasons?
> c. For what reasons were the southern colonies started by new-comers?
> d. What main idea or statement can your group make from this information?

   3. Have students in small groups follow their individual inquiries about their colony group with class resources, the school library, computer programs, and so on.

   4. Ask the group members to together organize and summarize the information they have gained.

   5. In the whole group, have students report on the main idea or statement from each group related to the previous study questions.

   6. Back in the small groups, have students transfer their information into an art form and make a mural to illustrate the information each student considers as the most valuable. Have students display the mural to others and answer any questions the other students might have about the mural and its information. Ask for feedback about cooperation of group members during the group work.

(Continued)

M

You may prefer to teach selected skills, such as map skills, in mini-lessons for ad hoc groups as a break-out instructional technique.

T

Historic maps can be obtained from the USGS; see the USGS website at <http://www.usgs.gov/>.

T

Laserdisc: *The Geography of the New England States* (SVE), grades 4–8. This disc could be useful for both teacher and students. Other resources are *Map Skills for Beginners* and *Map Skills* (Coronet/MTI), grades K–5 and 3–6, respectively; and *Latitude and Longitude* (National Geographic), grades 4–9.

T

Video: *Colonial Williamsburg* (Videotours, 1993), grades 7 and up. This documentary shows the physical development of the colony. CD-ROM: *PilgrimQuest* (Decision Development Corporation), grades 4–12. This is an excellent multimedia resource about the colonies.

LESSON 6

Other Newcomer Colonies—Cont.

7. Regarding the topic of newcomer colonies, engage students in suggesting individual or group projects related to any or all of the following:

    a. How can you show some of the similarities or differences of the northern, middle, and southern colonies through art and sculpture, dance, or music? (expressive arts)

    b. What experiences have *you* had that help you understand the way these colonists lived? (anthropology) What can you tell about these experiences to others?

    c. In what ways do you think geography influenced the site of the colonies? (geography)

    d. What can you do in your community today to find out which newcomer groups settled in your area? (history)

    e. What can you do to improve your own relationships with newcomers? (sociology)

    f. How can you express what you know about newcomers through mathematics (e.g., collect data about ethnic groups)? (mathematics)

8. As an option for a mini-lesson, suggest to students that they gather additional information about the colonies from reading maps further: "We will locate some major places and use the rulers to measure distances. We will review map symbols to locate latitude lines and match a color code to locate specific colonies." Help the students respond to a worksheet similar to that in Figure 5.22 to help them work on their map skills. Guide those who need assistance as they respond to information. Assessment of this mini-lesson is based on students' responses to the worksheet and on the ways they demonstrate that they can locate places, determine distance, identify latitude, and read map symbols and color codes.

Closure

"Many of the reasons why the colonists had to establish their colonies are also the reasons why people immigrate to other countries today. What do you think are some of these reasons?" Have the students identify reasons for the establishment of the colonies and write them on the board. Encourage them to expand on what they hear others say in the discussion. Encourage them to demonstrate communication skills toward others in the group.

Assessment

• Teacher observations are recorded and kept as to the students' participation in individual inquiry, organizing, and summarizing information with a small group, reporting on a main idea, and illustrating valuable information on a group mural.

Software: *National Inspirer* and *Geography Search* (Tom Snyder Productions), grades 4–12 and 5–9, respectively.

Some teachers introduce students to a breakout instructional technique of scheduling mini-lessons in ad hoc groups to teach skills, such as selected map skills.

LESSON 6

Other Newcomer Colonies—Cont.

- Have students write in a journal about ways their own relationships with newcomers could improve, about the colonies they would have liked to belong to if they had lived during this period, and about how they could apply what they learned to their lives in some way.
- Make checklist of student names to indicate which students transformed information into the mural art form, which researched and recorded reasons for the establishment of colonies, which organized and summarized their information, which cooperated with others during the activities, and which demonstrated communication skills.

FIGURE 5.22   Sample Map Skill Individual Worksheet

Map Skill for Individual Student Activity

Student _____   Date _____

Teacher _____   Period _____
Map I

Find the map on page _____ of your textbook (Atlas, Information sheet). Complete the following items:

1. Locate the English colony of Roanoke Island. Write the name of the ocean that surrounds the island.

    _____

2. Calculate the miles to the inch with your ruler and measure the distance from the colony on Roanoke Island across the ocean to Raleigh Bay.

Map II

Find the map. Complete the following items:

3. Locate the colony on Roanoke Island again. Between which two lines of latitude was this colony located? _____ and _____

4. Study the map symbols to find out which group had the rights to the land where this colony started.

Map III

Find the map on page _____ of your textbook. Complete the following items.

5. Review the color code on the map and write the names of the colonies that were known as the New England Colonies.

    _____

6. Which colonies were known as the Middle Colonies?

7. Which colonies were known as the Southern Colonies?

LESSON 7

Biographies of Famous Newcomers in the Colonies

Objectives
- Students will identify specific events in a biography as most important, and will participate in partnership and group activity.
- Students will describe their feelings about the contributions of this famous person.

Materials

Biographies of famous newcomers in the colonies (some choices are Peter Stuyvesant, William Penn, Anne Hutchinson, John Smith, John Rolfe)

Procedure

"You are going to read about famous newcomers who made contributions to the people's lives in the colonies. As you read, write some specific events in the person's life that you found important to you and put the information in a letter to the famous person. Then, you'll meet with a partner and read your letter aloud and ask for questions."

1. Ask each student to choose and read a biography about a famous newcomer who lived in one of the colonies.

2. After reading, have students engage in the individual activity of writing a letter to that person and mentioning specific events in the person's life that were most important to the student. Then, have students meet with partners to read their letters aloud to one another and to ask their partner if they have any questions about the famous newcomer in the colonies.

3. Have students describe the biography they read to their partners and have them tell what contributions the newcomer made to life in the colonies. Have them conclude their partnership activity by telling one another what they learned that helped them appreciate the contributions of the famous newcomer.

4. Back in the whole group, have students tell what they learned from each other during their partnership activity.

5. Regarding the topic of famous newcomers in the colonies, ask the students for their suggestions about individual or group projects related to any or all of the following:

    a. How can you show the contributions of some famous newcomers in the colonies through art and sculpture, dance, or music? (expressive arts)

Vocabulary words, especially those related to famous people in this lesson, can vary depending on the grade level, English language skills, and intellectual maturity of the students.

The more diverse the students, the greater the need for integrated curriculum and active learning with partners and small groups.

LESSON 7

Biographies of Famous Newcomers in the Colonies—Cont.

b. What experiences have *you* had that help you appreciate the contributions of some of the famous colonists? (anthropology)
c. In what ways can you apply what you learned about these famous colonists to your own lives? (sociology)

Closure

"Many of the contributions of some famous colonists are contributions people also make to their communities and the people around them today. What do you think are some of these contributions?" Have the students identify contributions of some famous newcomers. Write the students' ideas on the board, a chart, or overhead transparency. Encourage students to expand on what they hear others say by writing a paragraph to report what they learned that helped them appreciate the contributions of the famous newcomers in the colonies.

Assessment

- Have students write a paragraph and report what they learned that helped them appreciate the contributions of the famous newcomer in the colonies.
- Keep teacher observation on a checklist of student participation related to reading a biography, writing a letter to a famous person, meeting with a partner, and participating in asking and answering questions.
- Have students write in a journal on the unit and describe the most important thing they learned from reading the biography and how they could apply what they learned to their lives in some way.
- Have students place their final summarizing paragraphs in their portfolios.

LESSON 8

Colonial Newcomers and Geography

Objectives
- Students will willingly cooperate in small groups to research and report on the geography of the colonies—the New England colonies, the middle colonies, or the southern colonies.
- Students will offer opinions and judgments about the topic.

Materials
Maps related to the sites of selected colonies

Procedure
"Imagine that you are one of the colonists who is to choose a land site for the new settlement. You will read maps to make decisions about selecting a site. What kind of land site will your colony need? What clues on the map will help you make a decision?"

1. Have students research and report back to the group which colonies were known as the New England colonies, which ones were known as the middle colonies, and which were known as the southern colonies.

2. Divide students into six groups. Distribute a map related to the site of the New England colonies to two groups, a map related to the site of the middle colonies to two groups, and a map related to the site of the southern colonies to two groups.

3. When the students have their maps, ask them to use the information on the map (legend, color code, etc.) and imagine that they are the council members who will decide on a site for their colonies. Have them use the maps as the basis for a discussion about the best site for the colonies to build (near water, building materials, land to grow crops, etc.)

4. Have them report back to the whole group and announce the selected sites on their maps and the reasons for the selection.

5. Back in the small groups, have students research the sites of the original colonies and compare the sites *they* selected with the actual sites of the colonies.

6. Ask students to write individual paragraphs about what they learned from this activity about selecting a site for a community (colony or city) to live.

7. Regarding the topic of colonial newcomers and geography, ask the students for their suggestions about individual or group projects related to any or all of the following:

    a. How can you show the geography of the colonies through art and sculpture, dance, or music? (expressive arts)

LESSON 8
Colonial Newcomers and Geography— Cont.

b. What experiences have *you* had that help you appreciate the affect of geography on where people live? (geography)

c. In what ways can you apply what you learned about newcomers in the colonies and geography to your own lives? (sociology)

Closure

"Many of the effects of geography on the colonists are similar to effects that people also feel today in their communities. What do you think are some of these effects?" Have the students identify effects of geography on the newcomers. Write the students' ideas on the board, a chart, or overhead transparency. Encourage students to expand on what they hear others say by writing a paragraph to report what they learned that helped them appreciate the effect of geography on the people in the colonies.

Assessment

Have students place their paragraphs in their portfolios. Teacher observation on a checklist of student participation can be kept. Have students write in a journal on the unit and describe the most important thing they learned from the lesson and how they could apply what they learned to their lives in some way.

Software: *Colonization* (Tom Snyder Productions), grades 5–12. This program is useful for exploring modern-day decision making about establishing colonies in space.

LESSON 9

Journal Writing

Objectives
- Students will demonstrate interest in bookmaking (journal making).
- Students will interpret information in an analysis/synthesis, and demonstrate communication skills.
- Students will respond attentively to the writing of their peers.

Materials
Students' journals; writing materials, materials for bookmaking (journal making)

Procedure
"You are going to have time to analyze what you have learned in this unit of study by rereading your journals. To show that you took time to analyze what you read, you are to write a final paragraph as a synthesis about what you have learned about early newcomers in North America. First, I'll show you how I would write a brief paragraph—a synthesis—about what I learned. Then, when your paragraph is finished, you can complete your journals in a bookmaking (journal making) activity by making covers, writing in page numbers, writing a table of contents, sketching any extra illustrations you want to add, and putting an index in the back of your journal."

1. Have students write a description of what they have learned in their journals. You can model writing a brief analysis on the writing board or on an overhead transparency. Have students read and study the entries they wrote or sketched in their journals on the topic. Ask them to analyze and then write a final paragraph about what they learned. If needed, guided practice to help students write their paragraph of analysis can be scheduled.

2. Have the students meet with partners and trade their paragraphs. Have them read one another's work and write one question concerning something in the paragraph that they do not understand. Have each student give the question to his or her partner who can attempt to answer it, if possible, and who can respond with another question about the paragraph he or she has just read. Repeat the question/answer activity until students run out of questions or class time ends. The paragraphs are then returned to the original authors.

3. For an additional activity, have students make covers for their journals, write in page numbers, develop a table of contents, sketch additional illustrations, and add an index of their topics at the back of the journal.

LESSON 9

Journal Writing—Cont.

4. When appropriate throughout the unit, an individual student can "reserve" an inquiry and report on a topic of his or her choice related to a diversity of heritages reflected by people's lives during this time period. Figure 5.23 is a bibliography of multiethnic children's books that emphasizes the diversity of heritages with selections from a range of grade levels. Due to limited space in this guide, this list is not an exhaustive, comprehensive compilation of all the books on the topic and you and the students are encouraged to add related books that you discover.

Several activities for these books include the following:

a. Have the students read more than one book to promote more than the traditional view of this time period. For example, engage the students in discussing the time period from the perspectives of Native Americans, Latino-Hispanics, Asians, and Africans.

b. Encourage students to read and compare stories of families of diverse heritages set in the time period of this bibliography (1600s with some overlap to the 1700s) with stories of families today. Have the students note differences and similarities in societies and personal attitudes.

c. Encourage the students to suggest other books about life in the 1600s that they have found in their library searches; ask them to mention books written by authors of various heritages. Add the titles to Figure 5.23.

5. To provide additional classroom service to blind and visually impaired students, consider requesting Braille materials, talking books, raised relief maps, magnifiers, and large-type printed materials. For information about products, reports, films, and publications, write to the American Foundation for the Blind, Consumer Products Department, 15 West 16th Street, New York, NY 10011.

6. To provide additional classroom service to deaf and hearing-impaired students, consider requesting assistance from a signing adult, classroom aide, or interpreter as needed. Use visuals and the overhead projector for writing questions and responses. For information and a catalog of products, write to Gallaudet University.

7. To provide additional classroom service to ESL students, invite the students to work with students who have strong oral skills. When appropriate, children's books related to the unit can present people of different ethnic and cultural groups and can be read aloud. Selections can be made from a source such as *Cultural Cobblestones: Teaching Cultural Diversity* (Scarecrow, 1994) by Lynda Miller, Theresa Steinlage, and Mike Printz or *Multicultural Friendship Stories and Activities for*

(Continued)

LESSON 9

Journal Writing—Cont.

FIGURE 5.23   Multitext Reading: Diversity of Heritages

Diversity of Heritages: A Bibliography

Accorsi, W. *My Name Is Pocahontas,* Ill. by author (Holiday House, 1992). This book is the life story of the Indian princess who was the daughter of the Indian leader, Powhatan. Biography. Native American heritage. Grades K–2.

Anderson, J. *The First Thanksgiving Feast,* Ill. by G. Ancona (Clarion, 1989). This book is a first-person account of life at Plymouth in the 1620s. The photographs are taken by Plimoth Plantation, a Living History Museum. Nonfiction. European heritage. Grades 3–6.

Asimov, I. *Henry Hudson* (Gareth Stevens, 1991). In this account, Hudson (?–1611), a British sea captain, is sent on the *Hopewell* by the English Muscovy Company in 1607 to find a passage to the east around North America. The book focuses on Hudson's voyages, his crew, and his troubles, including his last voyage in 1611. The crew mutinies and places Hudson, his son, and loyal sailors adrift in a small boat and they are never heard from again. Labeled drawings of Hudson's ships and a glossary are included. Nonfiction. European heritage. Grades 3–4.

Bowen, G. *Stranded at Plimoth Plantation, 1626* (HarperCollins, 1994). This book is the fictionalized diary of a young colonist, Christopher Sears, who writes about the problems of living at Plimoth Plantation. Woodcuts for illustrations. Historical fiction. European heritage. Grades 4–7.

Brebeuf, Father Jean de. *The Huron Carol* (Dutton, 1993). This text tells the story of the birth of Christ as set in the Huron world and told by a missionary, Father Jean de Brebeuf, in the 1600s. Folk literature. Native American heritage. Grades 4 up.

Bulla, C. R. *Squanto, Friend of the Pilgrims* (Scholastic, 1988). This story is about the life of the Native American who helped the European pilgrims survive in the New World. Biography. Native American heritage. Grades 2–5.

Chow, O., and Vidaure, M. *The Invisible Hunters* (Children's Book Press, 1987). This book narrates the impact of the first European traders on the life of the Miskiot Indians in Nicaragua in the 17th century. Historical fiction. Hispanic heritage.
Grades 4–7.

Christian, M. B. *Goody Sherman's Pig* (Macmillan, 1990). This story is based on historical facts about Goody Sherman, who started a legal battle over her runaway pig in 1636. Historical fiction. European heritage. Grades 3 and up.

Fisher, L. E. *Colonial Craftsman* (Marshall Cavendish Corporation, 1997). This informational text explores the lives, times, and occupations of colonists in America and presents history through illustrations. One of a series that includes *The Glassmakers, The Silversmiths, The Cabinetmakers, The Schoolmasters, The Doctors, The Shipbuilders, The Peddlers, The Shoemakers, The Weavers,* and *The Homemakers.* European heritage. Grades 4 up.

Fleischman, P. *Saturnalia* (HarperCollins, 1990). Set in December 1681, a 14-year-old Indian boy from the Narraganset people searched for evidence of his past. Historical fiction. Native American heritage. Grades 7 and up.

Fradin, D. *Anne Hutchinson* (Enslow, 1990). This book is the life story of Hutchinson who preaches that true religion is the following of God's guidance through an "Inner Light." Biography. European heritage. Grades 3–5.

M

You should select books that are well written, emphasize human relations, and cause a reader to consider the actions of the characters.

T

Video: *Catch the Whisper of the Wind* (Horizon 2000, 1993), grades 7 and up. This has quotations and songs of American Indians in tribal languages.

M

Select a highly motivated, well-written book that relates to the topic being studied and read it aloud to students to create interest and discussion that lead to further investigation.

M

For creative activities with bibliographies for children, turn to *Hooray for Heroes! Books and Activities Kids Want to Share with Their Parents and Teachers* (Scarecrow, 1994) by Dennis Denenberg and Lorraine Roscoe.

D

Minority children are affirmed by seeing members of their ethnic or linguistic groups pictured or described in literature. Note the story of Japanese colonists in the 1600s in *The Coming of the Bear.*

LESSON 9

Journal Writing—Cont.

FIGURE 5.23 Continued

Fritz, E. I. *Anne Hutchinson* (Chelsea, 1991). This life story describes Anne's early life, education, and finally her banishments from the colony. Biography. European heritage. Grades 3–5.

Iannone, C. *Pocahontas: The True Story of the Powhatan Princess* (Chelsea, 1995). This text details the princess's brief life and includes original sketches, paintings, and quotes from primary sources that include *The General Historie of Virginia, New England and the Summer Isles* by John Smith. Biography. Native American heritage. Grades 4–7.

Kagan, M. *Vision in the Sky: New Haven's Early Years 1636–1783* (Shoestring Press, 1989). Kagan presents aspects of colonial life with a focus on the strict Puritan values by which the colonists lived, and their relations with Native Americans. Nonfiction. European heritage. Grades 4–8.

Lasky, K. *A Journey to the New World: The Diary of Patience Whipple* (Scholastic, 1996). Based on facts, this text narrates what the experience of journeying on the *Mayflower,* settling in Plymouth, and attending Thanksgiving was like for a young girl. Historical fiction. European heritage. Grades 4 and up.

Namioka, L. *The Coming of the Bear* (HarperCollins, 1992). In a parallel colonization in the 1600s, two samurai, Zenta and Matsuzo, escape to Ezo (now Hokkaido) and confront the warlike tension between the Aimu who live there and Japanese colonists who try to settle the land. Historical fiction. Asian heritage. Grades 5 and up.

Petry, A. *Tituba of Salem Village* (HarperCollins, 1991). Tituba, an intelligent black slave is vulnerable to suspicion and attack from the witch hunters in Salem. Historical fiction. African heritage. Grades 5 and up.

Raphael, E., and D. Bolognese. *Pocahontas: Princess of the River Tribes,* Ill. by the authors (Scholastic, 1993). This life story is a brief account that lists facts about selected events in the life of the Indian princess who died in England in 1617. Biography. Native American heritage. Grades 1–3.

Sewall, M. *People of the Breaking Day* (Atheneum, 1990). Sewall's book portrays the Wampanoags as a people, proud and industrious, living in southeastern Massachusetts before the colonists arrived. Nonfiction. Native American heritage. Grades 2–4.

Stone, M. *Rebellion's Song* (Steck-Vaughn, 1989). This collection has six life stories about people living in colonial times. Multiple Biography. European heritage. Grades 3 and up.

Van Leeuwen, J. *Across the Wide Dark Sea: The Mayflower Journey,* Ill. by T. B. Allen (Dial, 1996). A 9-year-old boy journeys with others as newcomers. Historical fiction. European heritage. Grades 2–4.

Walters, K. *Samuel Eaton's Day: A Day in the Life of a Pilgrim Boy* (Scholastic, 1993). Set in 1627 at Plimoth Plantation, this book shows the activities in the daily life of Samuel, a 7-year-old boy. He checks his animal snares and gathers wood before he eats his breakfast of curds, mussels, and parsley. Historical fiction. European heritage. Grades 2–6.

Water, K. *Tapenum's Day: A Wampanoag Boy in Pilgrim Times,* Ill. by R. Kendall (Scholastic, 1996). This fictionalized story is about Tapenum and his family. It describes each member's responsibilities in regard to acquiring food and providing clothing and shelter. Photographs are taken at a recreated Indian homesite at Plimoth Plantation, Massachusetts. Glossary of Wampanoag words. Nonfiction. Native American heritage. Grades 2–4.

(Continued)

T

CD-ROM: *Black American History: Slavery to Civil Rights* (Queue, Inc., 1994), grades 7 and up.

M

Additional sources include *The Native American in Long Fiction: An Annotated Bibliography* (Scarecrow, 1996) by J. Beam and B. Branstad; *The Best of the Latino Heritage: A Guide to the Best Juvenile Books about Latino People and Cultures* (Scarecrow, 1996) by I. Schon; *African-American Voices in Young Adult Literature: Tradition, Transition, Transformation* (Scarecrow, 1994) edited by K. P. Smith; and *Tales from Gold Mountain: Stories of the Chinese in the New World* (Macmillan, 1990) by P. Yee.

T

Website: Mayflower: Caleb Johnson's Mayflower Web Pages includes such sections as "Girls on the Mayflower" and "Women on the Mayflower" and "Pilgrim Clothing": members.aol.com.calebj/m ay flower.html

D/T

Taking an imaginary journey into history via literature, particularly historical fiction and biography, creates student interest in distant lands, the people who lived there, and other time periods.

LESSON 9
Journal Writing—Cont.

Children, Ages 5–14 (Scarecrow, 1997) by Patricia L. Roberts. Further, provide the students with bilingual materials as needed and, when appropriate, bicultural materials. Write for information to the National Clearinghouse for Bilingual Education, 1300 Wilson Boulevard, Suite B2-11, Rosslyn, VA 22209 and to Gryphon House, 37 Otis House, P.O. Box 217, Mount Ranier, MD 20822 (multiethnic books).

8. To provide additional classroom service to physically impaired students, establish a buddy system to help them in using materials, equipment, and other resources. To inquire about reading programs, write to the National Library Service for the Blind and Physically Handicapped, Library of Congress, Washington DC 20542 and to Telesensory Systems, Inc., 3408 Hillview Avenue, P.O. Box 10099, Palo Alto, CA 94304.

9. To provide additional classroom service to gifted and talented education students, provide them with computer programs and extensive reading related to the topic and, if appropriate, to the diversity of heritages related to the topic. Engage the students in using their reading to lead to independent inquiry, biographical research about key figures, and class reports. Provide the students with computer programs, reference material, texts, and library books as resources for the unit. If appropriate, the students can respond to questions recorded in a unit study guide.

10. To provide additional classroom service to students with learning modalities, provide them with access to a wide range of materials at room sites (perhaps study centers at tables or desks) and allow scheduled time for individual or free choice at the centers. For example, audio-oriented students could select the audiovisual table and gain information about the topic of early settlers as newcomers with the filmstrip *The Pilgrims of Plimoth* (Weston Woods, Weston, CT) by M. Sewall.

Assessment
- Teacher's summative assessment can be based on the portfolios, journal writings, responses to questions during the culminating activity, and ways students demonstrate their interests in their journals and how they shared information about the unit.
- A scoring rubic such as the following can be created for any of the previous items:

   Worth 5 points each
   1. Highly inventive
   2. Presence of characteristics expected (very successful communication of ideas)
   3. Presence of predetermined criteria

LESSON 9

Journal Writing—Cont.

Worth 4 points each
1. Fairly successful communication of ideas
2. Some details and some predetermined criteria
3. Some presence of expected characteristics

Worth 3 points each
1. Communication of ideas is unsuccessful
2. Little or no presence of predetermined criteria
3. Little or no presence of expected characteristics

- In addition, a behavior checklist (Figure 5.24) based on teacher observations throughout the unit can be developed.

FIGURE 5.24   Sample Checklist for Teacher Observations of Group Work

---

Example of Group Work Checklist

_____ (student name) _____ (date)

1. Participated in group task

    _____ always _____ often _____ sometimes _____ seldom _____ never
    Comments:

2. Participated in helping others

    _____ always _____ often _____ sometimes _____ seldom _____ never
    Comments:

3. If appropriate, participated in writing or copying learning plan and giving a copy to the teacher

    _____ always _____ often _____ sometimes _____ seldom _____ never
    Comments:

4. Participated in decision making

    _____ always _____ often _____ sometimes _____ seldom _____ never
    Comments:

(Continued)

LESSON 9
Journal Writing—Cont.

FIGURE 5.24   Sample Checklist for Teacher Observations of Group Work

Example of Group Work Checklist—Continued

5. Participated in collecting and recording information

_____ always _____ often _____ sometimes _____ seldom _____ never

Comments:

6. Participated in group discussion

_____ always _____ often _____ sometimes _____ seldom _____ never

Comments:

7. Participated in organizing information collected by the group

_____ always _____ often _____ sometimes _____ seldom _____ never

Comments:

8. Participated in drawing a conclusion by the group

_____ always _____ often _____ sometimes _____ seldom _____ never

Comments:

9. Participated in preparing materials needed for group to present its findings

_____ always _____ often _____ sometimes _____ seldom _____ never

Comments:

10. Participated in making a presentation to others

_____ always _____ often _____ sometimes _____ seldom _____ never

Comments:

Other added by the teacher or students

LESSON 10

Quiz Show and Exhibit as Culminating Activities

Objectives

- Students will use information gained to prepare questions and answers for a quiz show format, will form judgments related to appropriate questions to prepare, and will demonstrate active listening skills.
- Students will willingly cooperate with others during the group activities.
- Students will create materials for a quiz show or an exhibit.

Materials

Students' review materials related to the topic

Procedure

"You are going to have an opportunity to prepare for a culminating quiz show. You can make it similar to the TV show, *Jeopardy*, and choose your own categories. In groups, discuss what you learned about the early newcomers in America. Review any information you need, such as the facts in your journals and portfolios." Model a way to do this and show students how to use some materials to prepare a few categories, questions, and answers.

1. Divide students in small groups for discussion about what they learned related to the unit. Ask students to prepare for the culminating quiz show and prepare clues about famous newcomers, places, or events related to the unit.

2. In a quiz show format, have the students take turns describing or giving clues about a particular famous newcomer, a place, or event related to the topic. They can select students to answer. A correct answer gives the answering student an opportunity to describe or give clues related to the unit.

3. Further, regarding this unit of early newcomers in North America, ask any students who have prepared individual or group projects to exhibit items for the group. The following questions are suggestions for discussion.

   a. Who has an exhibit that reflects what we know about these newcomers to America through journal writing? (expressive arts)
   b. Who has charts or graphs that show some information we know about newcomers? (mathematics)
   c. Others suggested by the students.

(Continued)

LESSON 10

Quiz Show and Exhibit as Culminating Activities—Cont.

Closure

"Many of the descriptions and clues related to early newcomers in North America help us understand the way these newcomers lived. The descriptions and clues also help us understand the following:

   a. How being a newcomer has changed (or stayed the same) over time
   b. How newcomers acquire food, shelter, and work in the economy
   c. How newcomers organize themselves especially in conflict situations
   d. How people from newcomer groups have contributed to society
   e. How newcomers have cultural roots, language, and customs to share with others

Assessment

- Teacher assessment can be based on the students' participation in group work. You can meet with the small groups and observe and make notes. As you meet with groups and observe, make notes that will go in a folder for each student.
- A sample checklist (Figure 5.25) can indicate students' participation in preparing questions and answers, in demonstrating listening skills, and in participating in the quiz show activity.
- Assessment also is based on students' responses to the quiz show and the way(s) they demonstrate that they can share information about the topic.

LESSON 10

Quiz Show and Exhibit as Culminating Activities—Cont.

FIGURE 5.25   Sample Checklist for Individual/Group Work

Student _____   Date _____

Teacher _____

	often	sometimes	seldom
The student participated in:			
the task of the group	_____	_____	_____
helping others	_____	_____	_____
decision making	_____	_____	_____
discussing information	_____	_____	_____
organizing information	_____	_____	_____
drawing conclusion(s)	_____	_____	_____
preparing materials to present findings	_____	_____	_____
discussing positive contributions of others	_____	_____	_____
making a positive contribution to the group	_____	_____	_____
respecting others' opinions	_____	_____	_____
other	_____	_____	_____

A teacher's responsibility is to ensure that the thematic instruction incorporates the school, district, and state's frameworks, content, and skill-related goals, as well as objectives for the grade level.

Assessment of Student Learning.   For this unit, individual learning of students is assessed through teacher observations, portfolios, journals, and student participation in the collaborative and cooperative activities. There is daily, ongoing observation/assessment of the students' progress as well as a cumulative assessment at the completion of all the lessons.

M

Journals provide opportunities for personal reflection, expression, and organization of thoughts.

Sample ITU 3

Changes: Spring as a Time of Growth, Beauty, and Transformations*

Primary and Middle Grades.   This interdisciplinary thematic unit revolves around several disciplines, including science and literature. It was developed to facilitate and motivate students' learning about changes in the environment around them and to make comparisons between seasons they experience. It is hoped the instruction will gradually enlarge the students' perspective of changes from the school's own environment during a selected season to other environments and seasons. As presented here, the unit could be taught by one teacher or, with modifications, by a team of teachers.

Unit Overview.   This ITU was developed for use mainly in the primary grades and as presented, reflects some recommendations of Project 2061, a science literacy project, as published in *Science for All Americans*. The unit consists of five lessons, the first of which can be taught immediately following a rainstorm or anytime when water puddles are on the ground. The unit contains several cooperative learning activities that facilitate developing an understanding of the concept of cycles of changes. This concept relates to several of the national science content standards for grades K–4: characteristics and changes in populations; changes in environments; organism and environments; and change, constancy, and measurement.

To visually graph the emphasis and illustrate the contributions of a particular discipline to some of the lessons in the unit, you can develop a web similar to the following to show the integration of the different disciplines selected for the spring unit. This diagram will help in making decisions about selecting activities you want to add, change, or delete in the unit.

Unit Goals.   Related to national science content standards and Project 2061, this unit is designed to incorporate the following goals:

- To become familiar with the natural world and recognize its diversity and its unity
- To understand some key concepts of science
- To gain skills in predicting and observing
- To understand the connections among water, rain, and evaporation
- To understand how plants grow and what is needed for plant growth
- To understand the importance of water
- To understand diversity in nature
- To gain knowledge about rainbows
- To understand cycles and change in nature and life
- To make presentations to others

Assessment of Student Learning.   For this unit, individual learning of students is assessed through ongoing (formative assessment) teacher observation of student participation in the activities. Assessment and rubrics are to be developed with the children as the unit progresses.

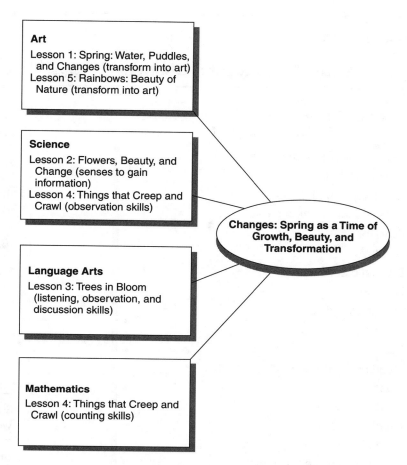

Art

Lesson 1: Spring: Water, Puddles, and Changes (transform into art)
Lesson 5: Rainbows: Beauty of Nature (transform into art)

Science

Lesson 2: Flowers, Beauty, and Change (senses to gain information)
Lesson 4: Things that Creep and Crawl (observation skills)

Language Arts

Lesson 3: Trees in Bloom (listening, observation, and discussion skills)

Mathematics

Lesson 4: Things that Creep and Crawl (counting skills)

Changes: Spring as a Time of Growth, Beauty, and Transformation

Source: Adapted by permission from unpublished work submitted by Stephanie Carington, Nancy Giboney, Suzanne Cantlay, and Kevin MacDonald.

The culminating activity is designed to be a major feature of this unit. After completing the five lessons, students will select a theme topic for continued pursuit. They can select this topic individually, in pairs, or in small groups. This pursuit can entail further research, investigation, and a presentation to the class at some later date or a community service project of the whole class. The only requirements for the culminating unit activity (see Figure 5.26) are that (1) it must be an activity selected by the student(s), and (2) it must deal in some way with the central theme of Changes: Spring as a Time of Growth, Beauty, and Transformations. The culminating activity also involves a summative assessment.

M

Matters of learning expectations, classroom procedures, and consequences are best established in class meetings, rehearsed over and over with students, and then applied consistently.

LESSON 1

Spring: Water, Puddles, and Changes

FIGURE 5.26   Examples of Culminating Activities

Audiovisual Presentations
Children's books
Computer simulations
Creating information games
Dioramas
Displays
Dramatic activities
Learning centers
Newspaper display
Paintings
Problems
Reading reader scripts
Replicas
Resource people
Retelling a story
Role playing
Performing a prepared play
Performing shadow puppet theater
Transparencies
Writing new words to familiar tunes
Others suggested by the students

T

You can introduce a final activity with a puppet presentation that offers facts about the topic with suggestions from *Leading Kids to Books Through Puppets* (American Library Association, 1998) by C. F. Bauer; or relate children's literature to many thematic units used in today's elementary schools with *Literature Frameworks: From Apples to Zoos* (Linworth, 1997) by S. L. McElmeel. Each letter of the alphabet is linked to a theme along with basic background information.

D

Students can observe how weather changes throughout the week (month, semester, year) and draw conclusions about its effect on people's lives.

LESSON 1

Spring: Water, Puddles, and Changes—Cont.

Objective

Students will share their learning about what happens to water in puddles over a period of time, the different aspects of water, some of the connections among water, rain, and evaporation and will make comparisons and predictions.

Materials

Water puddles, plastic bags, chalk, art paper, crayons or markers

Procedure

"Today after the rain storm, we will go outside to find where the ground is wet and look for water puddles. To keep our feet dry, we will cover our shoes with baggies and fasten the baggies around our ankles with rubber bands." Assess prior student knowledge by eliciting what they know about different aspects of water.

- What do you think the water in a puddle will do when you walk through it? (spread out) Why do you think so?
- What do you think will happen when you walk away from the puddle? (make wet prints) Why do you think this is so?
- Do you think the shoeprints will last forever? Why or why not?

1. List their responses as predictions (guesses, hunches) on the board, a class chart, or an overhead transparency. Tell students the responses can be confirmed later when they return from outside.

2. Outside, have students walk through the water puddles. (If appropriate, you can spray water from a hose to make additional puddles.) Ask the students to observe what happens to the puddles when they walk through them and what happens after they walk away from the puddles.

3. Distribute chalk pieces to each student and have them draw around the puddles so they can compare the sizes. Which is largest? Smallest? About the same?

4. With students back in the classroom, point out the earlier responses (predictions, guesses, hunches) suggested by the students. Have them check their predictions and confirm the appropriate ones.

5. Invite the students to draw two pictures—one showing what the puddles looked like when they walked through them outside and another showing what they think the puddles will look like in 2 hours.

6. After 2 hours, students go outside to check the puddles and discuss what has happened. Explain that the puddles will eventually recede as they evaporate, becoming smaller and smaller until they dry up.

M

Active teaching fosters students' engagement in the learning tasks and includes student involvement, appropriate instructional pacing, and monitoring of student participation and progress.

D

Strategies to help introduce nonreaders to reading in English include the use of real objects, talking about pictures, reading aloud, demonstrating meaning, reciting poetry in choral groups, creating chart stories, playing word games, and making class dictionaries and word files.

D

Students can be assigned to partners to complete selected activities. ESL students can be assigned to work with students who have strong oral skills.

T

CD/Audio cassette: "Sing a Song of Seasons" by Rachel Buchman or "When the Rain Comes Down" on *A Cathy and Marcy Collection for Kids* (both Rounder Records, 1997 and 1994, respectively), grades K–2.

LESSON 1

Spring: Water, Puddles, and Changes—Cont.

7. During the lesson, play background songs that relate to the unit, and invite the children to listen to stories from children's literature and sing along with such songs as "If Only the Raindrops were Lemon Drops" on Raffi's *Evergreen, Everblue* (Troubador, 1990), grades K–2, a cassette that includes environmental theme music.

Closure

"What is something interesting that you learned today that you didn't know before? What would you like to continue learning about?" Discuss the idea of a final—culminating—activity and show examples of what might be done. Present the two requirements for the activity: (1) it must be an activity selected by the student(s), and (2) it must deal in some way with the central theme of Changes: Spring as a Time of Growth, Beauty, and Transformations. Have the students announce who will work individually, in pairs, or in small groups. Suggest to them that they can do further research or investigation, prepare a presentation to the class, or take part in preparing a class exhibit for the school or a community service project.

Assessment

You can keep anecdotal notes about students and ways they demonstrated and shared their learning about what happens to water in puddles over a period of time. You can ascertain students who noticed the different aspects of water and connections among water, rain, and evaporation. You also can note student's pictures to determine the extent to which they predicted a change in the puddle they observed and can make comparisons. This is also an opportunity to assess individual psychomotor skills and to record observations on a teacher checklist. If appropriate for the group, have students begin portfolios to keep samples of their work and insert their pictures about predicting changes in water puddles.

D

When appropriate, read aloud selections of children's literature that present different ethnic and cultural groups. For example, you might choose *Bringing the Rain to Kapiti Plain: A Nandi Tale* by Verna Aardema (Dial, 1981). This accumulating story from Kenya is about a herdsman who wants to make things better for his people, the drought environment, and the effect on living things.

T

If appropriate for the group, have the students focus on the following interdisciplinary features:

- Anthropology: "How does our national community of scientists share information about weather changes in the spring (seasons) with us?"

- Economics: "What work is done by others to bring us information we need to study changes in spring (other seasons)?"

- Geography: "What geographical influences affect changes in spring (other seasons)?"

- History: "How has our community changed from one spring to another? Over several years?"

- Political science: "How do the scientists organize themselves to study changes in the seasons?

- Sociology: "What community cooperates to bring us information and services related to changes in the seasons?"

LESSON 2

Flowers, Beauty, and Change

Objective

Students will participate in touching, observing, smelling, and planting flower seeds and sharing their view about what is needed for flower growth.

Materials

Art paper, circles, scissors, printed leaves and stems, glue, seed, soils, and cups

Procedure

"Today, look at the examples of flowers here in the room and touch and smell them." Elicit the students' descriptions of the flowers. If desired, write their descriptions on index cards and place the cards by each display of flowers.

1. Show students different types of flower seeds. If appropriate, place the seeds on the stage of an overhead projector so students can discuss the different shapes and sizes.

2. Elicit from the students a point of view similar to that of a botanist. Ask what they think is important for seeds to grow and develop into flowers (soil, water, sunlight, wind, and other ways seeds travel and disperse). Write their responses on the board.

3. Students plant their own seeds in paper cups (or clear plastic cups) so they can eventually observe the life phenomena exhibited by the plants (observations botanists use). Point out that since the seeds

An ITU can be initiated any number of ways, though the approach taken should be one that will engage the students' interest in the topic. Here, students observe the preparation of an avocado for a simulated hydroponics activity.

(Continued)

D

Through real-life experiences, primary grade students can increase their skill in using their senses to gain information.

D

Active teaching includes communicating directions clearly, presenting new information clearly, maintaining students' involvement in tasks, communicating expectations, and monitoring students' progress.

T

Video: *Look What I Grew: Windowsill Gardens* (Intervideo/Pacific Arts Video, 1992), grades K–4. Students are introduced to hydroponics in *Wonders of Growing Plants* (Churchill Media, 1993), grades K–4. Diverse children explore ways plants are propagated with seeds, cuttings, succulent leaves, and roots.

LESSON 2

Flowers, Beauty, and Change–Cont.

are all different, each student will eventually have a unique flower that can grow in his or her region (botanists are interested in plant life in various regions). Discuss the idea that the flower seeds depend on the students for care.

4. After the students have planted the seeds, have them use scissors, glue, and art paper or printed leaves and stems to create their original ideas of blooming flowers and sketch themselves caring for the plant in some way.

5. Discuss the many changes in a flower before it blooms (from the students' point of view) and the questions, "Do flowers last forever?" "Why do you think that way?"

Closure

Discuss what was learned today and write high points of the discussion on the board. Remind students of the culminating activity requirements (an activity selected by the student and related to the central theme of Changes: Spring as a Time of Growth, Beauty, and Transformations). Possibly begin brainstorming ideas for this activity—encourage a flow of ideas by all the students and discourage any judgments of the ideas; keep a record of the ideas and elicit who will work individually or with someone else and display the information, adding to the record during the lessons that follow.

Assessment

You can keep anecdotal notes about students and ways they participated in discussion, planting seeds, and caring for their flowers before they bloomed. With a checklist, you also can assess student's pictures to determine the extent to which they transformed their information into an art form to make their pictures of blooming flowers. If students are keeping portfolios, have them insert their pictures of blooming flowers.

T

Audio cassette/book: *Miss Rumphius* (Puffin Books, 1994), grades K–2. An independent elderly lady follows her grandfather's advice to make the world more beautiful and plants lupine seeds around her small village on the sea coast.

T/D

CD-ROM: *A World of Plants* (National Geographic Society, 1993), grades K–3. This program offers nature study about the parts of a plant and includes the topics of "What Is a Seed?" "A Tree Through the Seasons," and "Plants Are Important." Pronunciation and parts of speech are in English and Spanish. Spoken instructions are available in Spanish.

T

Students who select culminating activities related to caring for the environment may benefit from interacting with selected children's books in *100+ Integrated Language Arts-Environmental Awareness Books and Activities for Children, Ages 5–14* (Hamden, CT: The Shoe String Press, 1998) by P. L. Roberts.

LESSON 3

Trees in Bloom

Objective

Students will demonstrate listening and observation skills and share their learning about parts of flowering trees and observing trees in various ways.

Materials

Chart paper, rulers, microscopes or magnifying glasses, samples of tree pieces

Procedure

"Today we are going to arrange parts of flowering trees—such as the almond tree and the cherry tree—on the display table near the rulers and microscopes. Take turns to measure the tree parts, look at the parts through the scopes, and then pass around the parts to one another to touch, smell, and observe them with magnifying glasses. As you are passing around the parts of the flowering trees, listen to the story of *The Giving Tree* (HarperCollins, 1964) by Shel Silverstein to find out why he named the tree, "a giving tree."

1. Before reading *The Giving Tree* aloud, elicit the students' thoughts about the book title (i.e., what the title means to them) and some of the illustrations (i.e., what they think will happen in the story). Write their thoughts on the board.

2. Read the story aloud and then discuss the students' initial thoughts written on the board and compare their thoughts with what happened in the story. Write the comparisons on the board or a class chart in two lists:

What we thought:	What happened in the story:
1.	1.

Ask volunteers to tell the group what they heard in the story that told them why the author named the tree, "a giving tree."

3. Ask students to recall how the tree in the story produced its leaves and flowers (and what happened) and then explain that different types of trees do not produce leaves and flowers at the same time. Ask students why they think that leaves would develop at different times (temperature, sunlight, water, and other environmental conditions). Ask students further questions:

   a. Do you think that all the leaves come out at the same time on the same tree? Why or why not? (Perhaps compare branches and leaves of flowering trees in the classroom to see if all the leaves have come out.)

(Continued)

LESSON 3

Trees in Bloom—Cont.

b. Do you think that all trees produce flowers at the same time? Why or why not? (Perhaps compare flowers of trees shown in the classroom to see if both types of trees have produced blooming flowers.)

c. Do you think a tree's flowers are beautiful? Why or why not? (Perhaps hold up branches of flowering trees on the display table.) What makes something beautiful to you?

d. Do you think that tree blooms last forever? Do you think trees last forever? Why do you think that way?

e. What do you think will happen if we put these tree blooms in colored water in a vase in the room for several days? Why do you think that way?

T

Video: *My First Science Video* (Sony Kids' Video, 1992), grades K–4. This video is based on *My First Science Book* (Knopf, 1990), with 15 easy science experiments including how colored water travels through stems into petals.

Closure

"Let's share our ideas about what we learned today." Discuss and record the students' remarks on a class chart, overhead transparency, or the writing board. Next, remind students of the culminating activity requirements. If appropriate, elicit students' ideas for their culminating activities and have them tell the group what they are going to work on and if they will work individually or with someone else. Record the information they give the group:

Name of student(s)	Topic related to spring
1.	1.

Assessment

Informally, assessment can be conducted by observing students who participated in group activities and by listening to their contributions to the discussion. This information can be recorded in anecdotal notes in a teacher's log. Further, a checklist can provide a record of those students who demonstrated listening and observation skills and shared their learning about parts of flowering trees and observing trees. Students can copy the group's remarks about what they learned today from the board, class chart, or overhead, and place in their portfolios.

LESSON 4

Spring Creatures that Creep and Crawl

Objective

Students will participate in acting out movements of different animals seen in the area in spring, in observing specimens of earthworms, ants, and spiders, in sharing what they have learned including counting, and in telling why the creatures seem to be quite active in spring.

Materials

Earthworms in soil, spiders in jar, ants in ant farm, miscellaneous objects such as seashells for counting

Procedure

"Today, let's act out the movements of some springtime creatures that creep and crawl." Elicit suggestions from students—ants, spiders, worms—and have them act out the movements of different creatures seen in the region in the springtime. For instance, a student can crawl to portray a crawly creature moving across the floor in the front of the room and ask the others to predict the name of the creature being portrayed. If appropriate, ask the moving student to exaggerate the motions and invite the rest of the students to join in and mimic the motion of the leader. After identifying creatures seen in the spring, ask the students to get into small groups and observe some actual specimens.

1. Divide the students into small groups and distribute specimens of worms in soil, ants, spiders, and other creatures in inexpensive plastic glasses covered with clinging plastic wrap. Ask them to observe and discuss the different creatures.

2. Ask a student-facilitator in each group to pass around the creatures in the plastic glasses, one by one, for students to observe. If appropriate, have the facilitator write the observations on index cards.

3. Back in the whole group, have the students respond to the following:

    a. What did the earthworms seem to do when they were in the soil? Why do you think they were showing this behavior?
    b. What did the ants seem to do in the soil in their ant farm?
    c. What did the spider seem to do in the plastic glass?
    d. What else would you like to know about these creepy crawly creatures? How could you find out?

4. Invite students to go outside with small plastic shovels and dig for similar small creatures to bring back to the classroom for display and discussion. Have students sort out and count their ants, earthworms, spiders, and so on. You can have the children use circular disks as counters.

(Continued)

D

You can arrange the day or part of the day so students work on group activities in small groups. Positive cross-cultural interactions take place when students work together to complete their learning tasks.

M

Class time can offer active learning experiences that students pursue independently or with others.

T

Depending on the students' interests, longer-term student-centered projects (such as a culminating activity) might develop as a result of this type of discussion.

LESSON 4

Spring Creatures that Creep and Crawl—Cont.

5. At the completion of the counting and discussion about what was found, have students return their small creatures to their original habitat and replace all dirt and grass as it was originally.

6. In the classroom, initiate a discussion about the importance of not disturbing habitats, of leaving the environment an even better place than when found, and of life cycles and change.

7. Invite the students to mention what they learned about animals seen in the springtime and write their suggestions on the board.

Closure

Continue discussing what has been learned; remind students of the culminating activity requirement; continue eliciting the students' ideas about what they will be preparing for their final activity.

Assessment

Assessment of student learning can be conducted by monitoring the students, eliciting their responses to questions, and observing their participation in the lesson activities. Checklists can record the students' behaviors related to acting out movements of different animals seen in the spring; observing specimens of earthworms, ants, and spiders; counting; discussing; and participating in small-group and whole-group work.

T

The discussion about disturbing and not disturbing natural habitats could lead to an extended project study of the students' choice.

T

Perhaps an assignment could be in order to have students observe, classify, and count plant and animal life in their neighborhoods; perhaps each student could be responsible for observing a square meter of their backyard or a one-square block of their community. Have them report back to class and tell their findings.

LESSON 5

Rainbows: Beauty of Nature

Objective

Students will name the colors seen in a rainbow, transform information about rainbows into artwork representing the colors, read color words in sentences, and construct individual books of sentences.

Materials

Art paper, tempera paints, brushes, white construction paper (18 inches wide), sentence strips, and pocket chart

Procedure

"Who will tell us when they have seen a rainbow and what time of year they saw it? What is the 'prettiest' feature of a rainbow from your point of view? Why do you think that way? What are the names of the colors you saw in a rainbow?"

1. With the whole group, show examples on art paper of the seven primary colors found in a rainbow. Discuss the color names. Ask the students to use paints, crayons, or markers to draw rainbows using the seven colors. Display the artwork in the room.

2. Have the students suggest sentences about the colors in the rainbow and write their lines on cardboard sentence strips. Read the lines aloud individually and as a group. For a second reading, invite all the students to read along chorally.

3. If appropriate for the group, prepare photocopied duplicates of the sentences and have students construct individual books with pages of the sentences. Ask them to illustrate each sentence.

Closure

With the group, engage students in summarizing what they learned in the lesson and connect it back to information they learned in previous lessons about changes and other topics about spring. Discuss the process for finalizing the culminating unit activity and announce which student(s) will share their project on what day and at what time. Set a time line for the activity's completion.

Assessment

- Assessment of student learning relates to the students' participation in rainbow artwork, choral reading of the sentences, and completion of the students' books of sentences.
- Summative assessment of student learning for this unit will be based on the teacher's anecdotal records, the student's performance during activities through the unit, and each student's unit assessment checklist from the student's portfolio. Figure 5.27 is an example of a unit assessment checklist.

(Continued)

LESSON 5

Rainbows: Beauty of Nature–Cont.

FIGURE 5.27   Sample Spring Unit Assessment Checklist

_____ (unit)

_____ (student name) _____ (date)

	yes	no	sometimes
I participated in the following:			
Sharing my knowledge about what happens to water in puddles over a period of time			
Discussing the different aspects of water			
Discussing water, rain, and evaporation			
Making comparisons and predictions			
Touching, observing, and smelling flowers			
Planting flower seeds			
Sharing my view about what is needed for flower growth			
Learning to listen			
Using magnifying glass to observe items			
Learning about parts of flowering trees			
Copying remarks of what I learned			
Acting out movements of different animals seen in the area in spring			
Observing specimens of earthworms, ants, and spiders			
Counting creatures active in spring			
Transforming information about rainbows into artwork			
Choral reading of a book of sentences			
Using color words			
Preparing a culminating final activity			

Comments about what I learned during the unit:

SUMMARY

Now that you have reviewed the examples of interdisciplinary thematic units, note the various ways that you can develop a unit for an integrated curriculum.

- Turn your attention to selected sources related to ITUs in "For Further Reading" to gain additional information from this list at the end of the chapter.
- Further, now review Exercise 5.4 on pages 235. Share your results with the instructor.

This guide began by providing an introduction to the value of integrated curriculum and within that concept, interdisciplinary thematic units. It then proceeded to provide you with data about initiating an interdisciplinary thematic unit, developing objectives, learning activities, and assessment tools for a unit, up to this point, where you are now ready for the application level—as a teacher who wants to develop and implement an interdisciplinary thematic unit for your students. From your previous self-check in Exercise 5.4, in what ways do you feel you are ready? Not ready?

We wish you the best during your educational adventure developing an interdisciplinary thematic unit and in the continued use of integrated curriculum. Occasionally, you may want to return to this guide for reference.

P. L. R.

R. D. K.

QUESTIONS AND ACTIVITIES FOR CLASS DISCUSSION

1. Explain the importance of the idea that all teachers are teachers of reading, writing, studying, and thinking. Do you agree or disagree with this idea? Why?
2. Describe the way(s) you have attended to student learning styles and student learning strengths (or weaknesses) in your ITU.
3. Give at least two reasons why both a student teacher and a first-year teacher need to know how to prepare detailed lesson plans, especially when a textbook program you are using provides them.
4. Although we have not discussed the topic of student safety fully in this guide, describe specific considerations you should give to student safety when preparing unit and lesson plans. Share your ideas with others in your group.
5. What classroom observations and experiences have your peers had related to the use of ITUs in the classroom? Ask them to share their observations with you in small-group or whole-group discussions. Take notes on the discussion, and with the group members, suggest any guidelines for teaching with ITUs you infer from your notes.
6. What questions do you have about developing ITUs? Offer your question(s) to peer volunteers to write on a question map located on the board. Copy the final question map and use one of the questions to start your own individual inquiry about ITUs. Report what you find to others in a culminating group meeting.
7. In what ways would you recommend more computer usage in the learning process related to an ITU? In what ways could you include more computer usage for students with special needs? How could you find out more about this? Report your findings to the group.
8. What suggestions do you have for the use of ITUs with diverse populations (e.g., gifted and talented students, students at risk, and students with special needs)? What resources will help you find out more about this issue?
9. The use of community resources can add a great deal to your students' background of knowledge and frame of reference for learning. What suggestions for community involvement in an ITU for your students can you offer?
10. If you desire disciplinary soundness for an interdisciplinary thematic study in your classroom, you will need a sure grasp of what is current in each of the disciplinary fields in your unit. Team up with others to collect information about what is current in various disciplinary fields. Select disciplines that you may need when developing an ITU. What suggestions do you have for getting started on this research project? Plan a brief report about what you found and present it to others during a culminating group meeting.
11. Read an article in the current literature about some disciplinary advocates. Perhaps choose an article in the current literature about the social studies advocates who would draw the topics for thematic study from such sources as the National Council of Social Studies Standards document, the NCSS History Standards Task Force, and the curricular frameworks in *Social Education*. Report what you learned from the articles in a small-group or whole-group setting as part of a culminating activity.
12. Although you have the best intentions of fostering opportunities for cognitive challenges through an ITU, is it possible that there will be students who can both construct and fail to construct meaning in what they do? In what ways might this be determined in the classroom? Participate in a discussion of examples mentioned by group members.

13. In small groups, discuss the complex and challenging tasks of collaborative learning, risk taking, developing hypotheses, and creating visual graphics (such as question maps) as teaching-learning processes that can be part of an ITU approach. Each member in the group can be responsible for presenting information about one of the tasks. Discuss the uses of each one, and if time allows, any abuses you know about from your experience.

14. One criticism about the importance of content is related to the trade book–required content connection. Consider, for example, that the students in your classroom are participating in a demonstration related to the color unit mentioned earlier in this chapter. A volunteer pours milk into a clear pie plate or cake pan until it reaches about one-third up the side of the pan. Place the container on the overhead projector and turn on the light to show the ingredients on the screen. Invite a student to put a few drops of an inexpensive green dish detergent into the milk. (Note: Avoid using the expensive lemon, lime, or grease-cutting detergent.) Invite some other students to put a few drops of two or three different colors of food coloring into the mixture. Invite the children to listen to several poems about colors read aloud as one or two class volunteers watch the clock to note how much time elapses before something happens in the mixture. Speculate what is happening and what color combinations make what colors. Add more detergent when the activity in the mixture decreases. In your opinion, should the students study a unit about colors? Or should they be introduced to this type of activity *only* if this content is mandated by school, district, and state documents? What resources would help you determine the content in children's books that relates to the content of this unit? To content required by your school? In what ways can you ensure that your students are being introduced to content required by your school, district, and the state?

15. Support for developing and implementing ITUs is available in professional literature about educational theory, especially constructivist theory, and related research. Volunteer to report on one or more of the entries in the bibliography to a small group or the whole group.

16. Some critics have serious concerns about the kinds of thematic units (and the underpinnings) discussed in much of the literature currently available. For example, one concern is that the in-depth studies in ITUs may be about topics that are *neither* meaningful nor personally and academically powerful to the learner and the teacher. If a parent expresses this concern, in what way(s) would you assure that parent that the selected topic(s) in your classroom has personal and academic value for the student(s)?

17. Other critics have mentioned that different disciplines should be handled differently in ITUs because all disciplines are not parallel in importance and value. In your opinion, are all disciplines parallel? Why or why not? What helped you form your opinion? In what ways could you determine which disciplines to include/not include in your classroom ITU?

18. Still other critics point to the issues in this area—the bifurcation in philosophical camps between disciplinary and social studies pundits. They form groups and throw verbal rocks at one another related to the topics for theme study. One philosophical camp consists of social studies advocates who lean toward the themes recommended by the National Council of Social Studies Standards document drafted in 1993, those recommended by the NCSS History Standards Task Force in 1992, and those presented in the curricular frameworks in such journals as *Social Education*. Review the curriculum materials for your grade that are recommended/used by your school, district, or state and determine if the curriculum material seems to advocate this approach toward themes. If the approach appears to be unclear, in what way could you find out more about this issue?

19. What other questions do you have about developing and implementing an ITU in your classroom? How can you find some answers to your questions?

20. Congratulations! You have completed this guide about developing a unit; we hope that for you it has been a professionally rewarding experience. As mentioned, if you have questions generated by the content of this chapter, list them and share the list with your classmates for helpful assistance. We wish you the best of success in implementing your interdisciplinary thematic unit.

EXERCISE 5.1

Analysis of a Lesson That Failed

Instructions.   The planning and structure of a lesson can be a predictor of the success of its implementation. The purpose of this exercise is to read the following report of a lesson implementation and to use the report as a basis for class discussion about its outcome.

The setting: Seventh-grade biology class; 1:12–2:07 P.M., spring semester.

Actual events as they took place:

1:12	Bell rings.
1:12–1:21	Teacher directs students to read from their text, while he takes attendance.
1:21–1:31	Teacher lectures on "parts of a flower," showing pictures of flower parts by holding up pages from a college botany text.
1:31–1:37	Teacher distributes to each student a ditto; students are to now "label the parts of a flower."
1:37–1:39	Teacher verbally gives instructions for working on a real flower (e.g., compare with ditto); can use microscopes if they wish.
1:39–1:45	Teacher walks around room distributing to each student a real flower.
1:45	Chaos. Teacher writing referrals, sends two students to the office. Much confusion, students wandering around, throwing flower parts at each other.
1:45–2:07	Teacher flustered, directs students to spend remainder of period reading text. Two more referrals written during this time.
2:07	End of period (much to the delight of the teacher).

Questions for discussion:

1. Do you believe this teacher had a prepared lesson plan? If it appears so, what (if any) were the good points of it? the problems with it?

    Good Points: _____

    _____

    _____

    _____

    _____

    _____

    Problems: _____

    _____

    _____

    _____

    _____

    _____

2. From what you can infer from the scenario, and from what you can infer about his lesson plan, was chaos predictable? Why or why not? _____

_____

_____

_____

_____

_____

3. How might the lesson plan have been prepared to more likely avoid the chaos? _____

_____

_____

_____

_____

_____

_____

4. Choosing to use this "traditional" lesson plan format, what behaviors could the teacher have performed that might have avoided the chaos? _____

_____

_____

_____

_____

_____

_____

5. Within this 55-minute period, students were being expected to operate high on the learning experiences ladder. Consider this: 9 minutes of reading; 10 minutes of hearing; 6 minutes of reading and labeling; 2 minutes of hearing; 6 minutes of action (the only direct experience); and 22 minutes of reading. In all, about 49 minutes (89%) of abstract verbal and visual symbolization. Is that a problem? _____

_____

_____

_____

_____

_____

_____

_____

EXERCISE 5.2

Preparing Lesson Plans for My ITU

Instructions. Using the lesson plan format of Figure 5.1 or an alternative format that is approved by your instructor, prepare two _____ -minute lesson plans. The length should be decided in your class according to grade level and other factors. Prepare the lessons for a grade level of your choice and plan them to be the first and second lessons of your ITU. As you prepare these plans, you will want to refer to work you have done for previous exercises, especially Exercises 3.9, 3.10, and 4.3. After completing your lesson plans, evaluate them yourself, modify them, and then have the modified versions evaluated by three peers, using corresponding Exercise 5.3.

After completion of these two exercises, 5.2 and 5.3, you are ready to proceed in the development of the remainder of the lessons for your ITU.

INDIVIDUAL NOTES

EXERCISE 5.3

Evaluating Lesson Plans for My ITU

Instructions.   You may duplicate blank copies of this form for evaluation of the lessons you developed previously. Have one or both (to be agreed upon by your group) of your lesson plans evaluated by at least three of your peers and instructor. For each of the following items, evaluators should check either "yes" or "no" and write instructive comments. Compare the results of your self-evaluation with the evaluation of the others.

No   *Yes*

1. Are descriptive data adequately provided?   _____   _____

Comments _____

_____

_____

2. Are the goals clearly stated?   _____   _____

Comments _____

_____

_____

3. Are the objectives specific and measurable?   _____   _____

Comments _____

_____

_____

4. Are objectives correctly classified?   _____   _____

Comments _____

_____

_____

5. Do objectives include higher-order thinking?   _____   _____

Comments _____

_____

	No	*Yes*

6. Is the rationale clear and justifiable?   _____   _____

Comments _____

_____

_____

7. Is the plan's content appropriate?   _____   _____

Comments _____

_____

_____

8. Is content likely to contribute to achievement
    of objectives?   _____   _____

Comments _____

_____

_____

9. Given the time frame and other logistical
    considerations, is the plan workable?   _____   _____

Comments _____

_____

_____

10. Will the opening likely engage students?   _____   _____

Comments _____

_____

11. Is there a preassessment strategy?   _____   _____

Comments _____

_____

12. Is there a proper mix of learning activities for
    the time frame of the lesson?   _____   _____

Comments _____

_____

	No	Yes

13. Are the activities developmentally appropriate
    for the intended students?   _____   _____

Comments _____

_____

_____

14. Are transitions planned?   _____   _____

Comments _____

_____

_____

15. If relevant, are key questions written and key
    ideas noted in the plan?   _____   _____

Comments _____

_____

_____

16. Does the plan indicate how coached practice will
    be provided for each student?   _____   _____

Comments _____

_____

_____

17. Is adequate closure provided in the plan?   _____   _____

Comments _____

_____

_____

18. Are materials and equipment needed identified
    and are they appropriate?   _____   _____

Comments _____

_____

_____

	No	*Yes*

19. Is there a planned formative assessment, formal or informal? _____ _____

Comments _____

_____

20. Is there a planned summative assessment? _____ _____

Comments _____

_____

21. Is the lesson coordinated in any way with other aspects of the curriculum? _____ _____

Comments _____

_____

22. Is the lesson likely to provide a sense of meaning for students by helping bridge their learning? _____ _____

Comments _____

_____

23. Is an adequate amount of time allotted to address the information presented? _____ _____

Comments _____

_____

24. Is there a thoughtfully prepared and relevant student assignment planned? _____ _____

Comments _____

_____

25. Could a substitute who is knowledgeable follow the plan? _____ _____

Comments _____

_____

EXERCISE 5.4

A Self-Check on Developing Interdisciplinary Thematic Units

Instructions.   Now that you have completed this guide, check yourself on this final list. In the appropriate square to the right of each item, write in

3   *if you have acquired definite readiness or awareness about the item*

2   *if you have a comfortable level of readiness or awareness*

1   *if you are still uncomfortable with the item; need more work and information*

0   *if you have little or no awareness or knowledge about it*

Share the results with your instructor if you are working in a group.

	3	2	1	0
	aware	somewhat aware	need work	no awareness

When developing an ITU for an integrated curriculum, I reflected on the following related knowledge and skills:

Introduction to an Interdisciplinary Thematic Unit (Chapter 1)

1. I am aware of the concept of integrated curriculum and can recall related terms such as thematic instruction, multidisciplinary teaching, and holistic education.

2. I am aware of some of the theoretical origins of instructional styles and their relation to integrated curriculum.

3. I am knowledgeable about the spectrum of integrated curriculum and where some of my teaching efforts can be located on the spectrum.

4. I am aware of the role of an effective teacher in an integrated curriculum.

5. I am aware of ways to provide diversity and a multiculturalistic perspective in the curriculum.

	3	2	1	0
	aware	somewhat aware	need work	no awareness

6. I am aware of features of class management in active inquiry.

7. I am familiar with organizational change for curriculum integration.

8. I know of ways to use technology and community resources as instructional resources.

9. I am familiar with examples of Internet sites for teachers and students.

10. I am aware of various steps in developing an ITU.

11. I am familiar with the advantages and limitations of an integrated curriculum.

12. I can locate and use informational sources about ITUs.

13. I recall information from a teacher interview about an ITU.

Initiating an Interdisciplinary Thematic Unit (Chapter 2)

14. I have gained knowledge about selecting a theme for an ITU.

15. I can identify criteria for selecting a theme.

16. I can select documents for theme resources.

17. I am familiar with the national curriculum standards.

18. I am aware of ways to select a theme.

19. I can investigate specific questions and resources for an ITU.

20. I am familiar with problem-solving inquiry.

	3	2	1	0
	aware	somewhat aware	need work	no awareness

21. I am familiar with the experiences in the learning experiences ladder.

22. I am knowledgeable about scope and sequence of curriculum material related to an ITU.

23. I know ways to use the community as a resource.

Developing Objectives and Learning Activities (Chapter 3)

24. I feel confident about writing objectives for lessons in an ITU.

25. I am knowledgeable about the components to writing criterion-referenced behavioral objectives.

26. I can recognize objectives that are measurable.

27. I can classify instructional objectives in the cognitive, affective, and psychomotor domains.

28. I am familiar with the use of student logs, portfolios, and journals.

29. I can select an activity to initiate an ITU.

30. I can help students assume roles as a way to introduce them to various disciplines.

31. I am familiar with a question map to initiate an ITU.

32. I can select a culminating activity for the closure of an ITU.

Assessment of Student Learning (Chapter 4)

33. I am familiar with several purposes of assessment.

	3	2	1	0
	aware	somewhat aware	need work	no awareness

34. I am knowledgeable of several principles that can guide an assessment program.

35. I am familiar with the meaning of *authentic* assessment.

36. I know the advantages and limitations of authentic assessment.

37. I can record and evaluate student verbal and nonverbal behaviors.

38. I am familiar with the use of student journals, writing folders, peer conferencing, teacher-student conferences, and conference logs in assessing student learning.

39. I am familiar with examples of scoring rubrics for assessing students.

40. I am aware of the value of using portfolios for assessing students and their work.

41. I feel comfortable using checklists for student assessment.

42. I can maintain records of student achievement.

43. I feel comfortable grading and marking student achievement.

44. I feel comfortable determining grades for students.

45. I know several purposes for testing.

46. I can construct a brief test that has assessment items that measure against the objective(s).

47. I am familiar with the meaning of the term *content validity.*

48. I am aware of different types of assessment items.

	3	2	1	0
	aware	**somewhat aware**	**need work**	**no awareness**

49. I can prepare formative and summative assessment items for my ITU.

Completing Your ITU: Lesson Planning and Sample Units (Chapter 5)

50. I am familiar with a sample interdisciplinary lesson plan.

51. I am aware of suggested elements for writing a lesson plan.

52. I can suggest changes for a sample "lesson that failed."

53. I can prepare lesson plans for an ITU.

54. I can evaluate lesson plans for an ITU.

55. I am familiar with ITUs prepared by educators.

Totals (165 is perfectly aware)

FOR FURTHER READING

Bozeman, W. C., & Baumbach, C. J. (1996). *Educational technology: Best practices from America's schools.* Larchmont, NY: Eye on Education.

Ellis, A. K., & Stuen, C. J. (1998). *The interdisciplinary curriculum.* Larchmont, NY: Eye on Education.

Five, C. L., & Dionisio, M. (1996). *Bridging the gap: Integrating curriculum in upper elementary and middle schools.* Portsmouth, NH: Heinemann.

Kellough, R. D., & Roberts, P. L. (1998). *A guide for elementary school teaching: Planning for competence* (4th ed.). Upper Saddle River, NJ: Prentice Hall.

Korithoski, T. (1996, February). Finding quadratic equations for real-life situations. *Mathematics Teacher, 89*(2), 154–157.

Light, C. (1996, Spring). Illuminated medieval newspaper: Cross curriculum research for world history. *Social Studies Review, 34*(3): 36–39.

Loewen, J. W. (1996). *Lies my teacher told me: Everything your American history textbook got wrong.* New York: Touchstone Books.

McFaden, D. et al. (1996, February). Redesigning the model: A successfully integrated approach to teaching and learning. *NASSP* (National Association of Secondary School Principals) *Bulletin, 80*(577), 1–6.

Monroe, B. (1996, February). Teaching extended class periods. *Social Education, 60*(2), 77–79.

Nagel, N. G. (1996). *Learning through real-world problem solving: The power of integrative teaching.* Thousand Oaks, CA: Corwin Press.

Nowicki, J. J., & Meehan, K. P. (1997). *Interdisciplinary strategies for English and social studies classrooms: Toward collaborative middle and secondary school teaching.* Boston: Allyn & Bacon.

Post, T. R. et al. (1997). *Interdisciplinary approaches to curriculum: Themes for teaching.* Upper Saddle River, NJ: Prentice Hall.

Provenzo, Jr., E. F. (1998). *The educator's brief guide to the Internet and the world wide web.* Larchmont, NY: Eye on Education.

Roberts, P. L. (1998). *Multicultural friendship stories and activities for children, ages 5–14.* Lanham, MD: Scarecrow Press.

Rosen, C., & Bartels, D. (1996, Spring). Trade and exploration: A re-presentation. *Social Studies Review, 34*(3), 30–34.

Rottier, J. (1996). *Implementing and improving teaming: A handbook for middle level leaders.* Columbus, OH: National Middle Schools Association.

Schurr, S. et al. (1996). *Signaling student success: Thematic learning stations and integrated units for middle level classrooms.* Columbus, OH: National Middle Schools Association.

Shabbas, A. (1996, Spring). Living history with medieval banquet in the Alhambra Palace. *Social Studies Review, 34*(3), 22–29.

Thomas-Vallens, M. (1996). *A literature unit for "Dragon's Gate" by Laurence Yep.* Huntington Beach, CA: Teacher Created Materials.

SELECTED INTERNET SITES

Telementoring Young Women in Science, Engineering, and Computing
(http://www.edc.org/CCT/telementoring). This site is a mentoring program for young women.

United Nations' CyberSchool Bus
(http://www.un.org/Pubs/CyberSchoolBus/). This site provides curriculum units and projects, databases on U.N. member states, and global trends.

Windows to the Universe Project
(http://www.windows.umich.edu). This site provides information on recent earth and space research and discoveries.

APPENDIX

PLANNING MASTER 1.1

Overview of Teacher Interactions—A Self-Check Exercise

Instructions. The purpose of this exercise is to gain insight into a teacher's perceptions of an ITU experience and identify the behaviors that other teacher candidates include in their interactions in the classroom. Share your examples with others. Do you agree with all of the examples given? Why or why not?

The Teacher Interacts **Your Examples**

Centering learning on students _____

_____

_____

_____

_____

_____

Guiding students _____

_____

_____

_____

_____

Facilitating unit groups _____

_____

_____

_____

_____

_____

PLANNING MASTER 1.1
Continued

The Teacher Interacts

Demonstrating, reading aloud

Assessing and evaluating

Others selected by the group

Your Examples

_____

_____

_____

_____

_____

_____

_____

_____

_____

_____

_____

_____

_____

_____

_____

_____

_____

_____

PLANNING MASTER 1.2

Overview of Student Interactions—A Self-Check Exercise

Instructions. The purpose of this exercise is to identify student behaviors that other teacher candidates expect to see in their interactions during an ITU experience. Share your examples with others.

Your Examples

Learning in groups
_____
_____
_____
_____
_____
_____
_____

Selecting topics
_____
_____
_____
_____
_____
_____

Discussing, choosing, researching
_____
_____
_____
_____
_____
_____

PLANNING MASTER 1.2

Continued

Your Examples

Reading, responding, reporting

_____

_____

_____

_____

_____

_____

Scripting and bookmaking

_____

_____

_____

_____

_____

_____

Others suggested by the group

_____

_____

_____

_____

_____

_____

_____

PLANNING MASTER 2.1

Is This Theme One That Has

A Self-Check Exercise

Instructions. The purpose of this exercise is to provide a guide for your selection of a theme for an ITU. Respond independently to the following features about theme selection and then share your responses with those of your classmates. My selected theme is _____. Is this theme one that has:

	Yes	No

1. A connection to documents
Comments:

_____

_____

_____

_____

2. Background from teachers' experience
Comments:

_____

_____

_____

_____

3. Value, worth, and substance
Comments:

_____

_____

_____

_____

PLANNING MASTER 2.1
Continued

	Yes	No

4. Proper length; not too short or too long
Comments:

_____

_____

_____

5. Available materials and resources
Comments:

_____

_____

_____

6. Application to real world
Comments:

_____

_____

_____

7. Active learning, interest, and motivation for students
Comments:

_____

_____

_____

8. Other features you want to add

_____

_____

_____

PLANNING MASTER 2.2

Planning a Field Trip Related to ITU—A Self-Check Exercise

Instructions. The purpose of this exercise is to provide a guide for your study of how to plan for a field trip with a student group. Independently read the following features about planning a field trip and decide which features you would or would not discuss with the students in your classroom. Which features did you add? Delete? Share your reasons for your decisions with your classmates.

	Discuss	Do Not Discuss

Student-Teacher Decisions
Pre-learning

What do we want to find out?

Trip conduct

Alternate plan for bad weather

Trip Mechanics
Where we'll go

Name of contact person

Pre-trip visit by teacher

PLANNING MASTER 2.2

Continued

	Discuss	Do Not Discuss
Transportation plans		
Time to arrive/depart		
What will be needed (lunch, clothing, money)		
Permission needed		
Adults going		
Provisions for first-aid		
Restroom location(s)		

Features I want to add:

PLANNING MASTER 3.1

Classifying Cognitive Objectives—a Self-Check Exercise

Instructions. The purpose of this exercise is to assess your ability to classify cognitive objectives. For each of the following cognitive objectives, identify by the appropriate letter the highest level of operation involved: K (knowledge), C (comprehension), AP (application), AN (analysis), S (synthesis), and E (evaluation). Check your answers and then discuss the results with your peers. Your understanding of the concept involved is more important than whether your score is 100%.

_____ 1. Given a picture of examples of styles in classical Greek architecture, the student will recognize the style of a column as being Ionic, Doric, or Corinthian.

_____ 2. Given an information retrieval chart, the student will recognize the roles of Greek citizens.

_____ 3. After reading detailed instructions, the student will participate and make a hand puppet.

_____ 4. The student will create a verse using a four-line stanza.

_____ 5. The student will explain his or her critical appraisal of an essay on a selected topic or theme.

_____ 6. Given a selection of colors, the student will correctly identify by name the ones shown.

_____ 7. The student will be able to recognize faulty logic in campaign advertising.

_____ 8. Given the political and economic facts, the student will identify a reasonable hypothesis concerning the causes of a recent altercation, riot, gang battle, or belligerence between groups.

_____ 9. The student will devise a method to prove that a ray bisects an angle.

_____ 10. Given an Internet website, the student will locate information related to the theme or topic of an ITU.

Answer key

1. C	6. K
2. K	7. E
3. AP	8. AN
4. S	9. S
5. E	10. K

PLANNING MASTER 3.2

Classifying Psychomotor Objectives—a Self-Check Exercise

Instructions. The purpose of this exercise is to assess your ability to classify psychomotor objectives. For each of the following cognitive objectives, identify by the appropriate letter the level ranging from simple gross locomotor control to the most creative and complex level that requires fine locomotor control and originality: MO (moving), MA (manipulating), CO (communicating), and CR (creating). Check your answers and then discuss the results with your peers.

_____ 1. Given a jump rope, the student will successfully jump the rope five times without missing.

_____ 2. Given appropriate materials, the student will plant and successfully grow flower seeds.

_____ 3. Listening to a teacher-read story, the student will demonstrate active listening skills including asking questions and giving responses.

_____ 4. The student will write/create a brief musical jingle.

_____ 5. Given a microscope (magnifying glass), the student will correctly grasp and carry the scope (glass) to his or her desk.

_____ 6. Given a musical instrument of choice, the student will play the C scale.

_____ 7. The student will be able to describe his or her feelings about the extinction of animals in the rain forest areas.

_____ 8. Given appropriate art materials, the student will replicate an environment for a favorite animal that is endangered or faces extinction.

_____ 9. The student will correctly grasp a baseball bat when batting.

_____10. Given an item to observe, the student will accurately draw/sketch what is observed through the microscope/magnifying glass.

Answer key

1. MO	6. MA
2. MA	7. CO
3. CO	8. CR
4. CR	9. MO
5. MO	10. CO

PLANNING MASTER 3.3

Classifying Affective Objectives—a Self-Check Exercise

Instructions. The purpose of this exercise is to assess your ability to classify affective objectives. For each of the following objectives, identify by the appropriate letter the major level involved from least internalized to most internalized: REC (receiving), RES (responding), VAL (valuing), ORG (organizing), and INT (internalizing). Check your answers and then discuss the results with your peers. Your understanding of the concept involved, and the idea that some overlap occurs from one level to another, is more important than whether your score is 100%.

_____ 1. Given directions, the student will recall the ones for enrichment activities in the classroom.

_____ 2. Given a selection of books related to a topic or theme, the student will read at least one for enrichment.

_____ 3. The student will support actions against race, sex, or gender discrimination.

_____ 4. The student will form judgments about proper behavior/actions in the classroom.

_____ 5. Regarding assignments, the student will practice independently.

_____ 6. Given a group discussion, the student will listen and describe the ideas of others.

_____ 7. The student will protest against discrimination.

_____ 8. The student will adhere to a personal work ethic.

_____ 9. The student will act according to a defined code of behavior.

_____ 10. Given an Internet website, the student will read information for enrichment.

Answer key

1. REC	6. REC
2. RES	7. VAL
3. VAL	8. ORG
4. ORG	9. INT
5. INT	10. RES

PLANNING MASTER 4.1

Learning Assessment Checklist—A Self-Check Exercise

Instructions. The purpose of this exercise is to provide a guide for your development of a learning assessment checklist for your students. Independently read the following items and decide if you would include each on a checklist that you would develop for your students who are studying an ITU in your class. Which ones did you decide to include and why? What deletions, if any, did you make? Share your responses with others in your group.

STUDENT _____ **DATE** _____

TEACHER _____ **TIME** _____

	Yes	No
1. Can identify theme, topic, main idea of the unit	_____	_____
2. Can identify contributions of others to the theme	_____	_____
3. Can identify problems related to the unit of study	_____	_____
4. Has developed skills in (check all that apply):	_____	_____

_____ Applying knowledge

_____ Assuming responsibility

_____ Classifying

_____ Categorizing

_____ Decision making

_____ Discussing

_____ Gathering resources

_____ Inquiry

_____ Justifying choices

_____ Listening to others

_____ Locating information

_____ Metacognition (thinking about one's own thinking)

_____ Ordering

_____ Organizing information

_____ Problem identification

_____ Problem solving

_____ Reading text

_____ Reading maps and globes

_____ Reasoning

PLANNING MASTER 4.1

Continued

_____ Reflecting   _____ Thinking

_____ Reporting to others   _____ Using resources

_____ Self-assessing   _____ Working with others

_____ Sharing   _____ Working independently

_____ Studying   _____ Others unique to the unit

_____ Summarizing

Additional features added:

Additional teacher and student comments:

GLOSSARY

affective domain the area of learning related to the learner's attitudes, feelings, interests, personal adjustment, and values; can include the way a learner receives or responds to or values stimulus, organizes a system of values, and demonstrates consistent beliefs and behavior.

aligned curriculum refers to the matching of objectives, instruction, and assessment.

anticipated measurable performance refers to the student performance that indicates that the objective has been achieved.

assessment the process of determining what students have learned through instruction. Some educators consider it a relatively neutral process that can include collecting objective data from measurement sources and information from anecdotal records, teacher observations, and value judgments. Also see *evaluation.*

assignments a lesson plan feature that identifies what students are instructed to do as a follow-up to the lesson; can be homework or in-class work that gives students an opportunity to practice and enhance what is being learned.

authentic assessment the use of procedures that are compatible with instructional objectives. Also known as accurate, active, aligned, alternative, and direct assessment.

behavioral objectives statements of learning expectations that identify what the learner should be able to do after instruction; each contains four components that reflect the learner, the overt behavior, the conditions, and the level of performance. See also *performance objectives* and *terminal objectives.*

behaviorism a learning theory that focuses on a student's changes in behavior as an indication of learning.

block class scheduling a procedure that gives a teacher and students large blocks of time in the school program; it facilitates individualized instruction and grouping of students to meet needs and abilities.

brainstorming a strategy of instruction that facilitates the students' flow of ideas without peer judgment/criticism.

career portfolio a collection of samples of students' work that will document their abilities to move forward to another grade level, to a work environment from a school environment, or to postsecondary education. See also *portfolio.*

CD-ROM (compact disc read-only memory) found on a compact disc; contains encoded information.

character education relates to instruction in regard to development of values such as honesty, kindness, respect, and responsibility.

class management a process for building an environment for student learning; includes techniques for intervening and responding to student misbehavior.

closure a way to bring a lesson to an end.

coached practice a lesson plan feature that details ways that the teacher intends for students to interact in the classroom; also referred to as the "follow-up" and includes individual practice, dyad practice, small-group work, and conferences or mini-lessons during which students receive guidance and coaching from the teacher and their peers.

cognitive domain the area of learning related to the learner's intellectual skills; can include knowledge, comprehension, application, analysis, synthesis, and evaluation.

cognitive-experimentalism the theory postulating that learning is interaction with the environment through discovery and inquiry; the learner constructs new perceptions that lead to behavioral changes.

compact disc (CD)   a disc on which a laser has enscribed information digitally.

concept map   a visual representation of concepts and their relationships. For example, words related to a key word are written in groups (or categories) around the key word and the groups are labeled.

conceptual knowledge   type of learning that refers to meaningful, higher levels of thinking.

constructivism   theory postulating that learning entails the construction or reshaping of mental schemata and that mental processes mediate learning.

cooperative learning   type of instructional strategies that involve small groups of learners working together and assisting one another in the educational tasks; emphasizes support for one another rather than competition.

cooperative teacher-student log   entries written daily by the students before leaving their class, period, or school about what was learned that day. In some classes, the teacher responds to the entries.

covert behavior   the behavior of the learner that is not observable outwardly.

criterion   a standard used to judge behavioral performance.

criterion-referenced assessment   refers to assessing the progress of a student toward meeting learning objectives.

criterion-referenced grading   refers to determining student grades on the basis of preset standards.

criterion-referenced objective   identifies standards and/or guidelines for learning behaviors through the components of audience, behavior, conditions, and performance level.

critical thinking   refers to a student's ability to identify problems, to propose and test resolutions, and to arrive at conclusions based on the collected data.

curriculum   the plans for teaching and learning in school and nonschool environments in formal (overt) and informal (hidden) formats that lead to the development and acquisition of selected content.

curriculum standards   recommendations about the content that students should have (knowledge) and performances that they should be able to achieve (processes).

decision making   includes a planning or preactive phase, a teaching or interactive phase, an analyzing or reflective phase, and an application or projective phase.

direct instruction   instruction that involves presenting information to the students, giving examples, and applying the information to the learners' experiences; it is teacher centered.

discovery   involves learning in which the students identify a problem, develop hypotheses, test the hypotheses, and arrive at a conclusion. See also *critical thinking*.

effective teaching   engaging students in high rates of academic learning through hands-on and minds-on meaningful instruction, cooperative and collaborative interactions, clear communication, monitoring progress, and a thematic curriculum in which students participate.

empowerment   involves students' learning to think better of themselves and their own individual capabilities.

evaluation   often a subjective process that considers the results of a student's assessment; often based on standards, criteria, a rubric. See also *assessment*.

formative evaluation   refers to evaluating a student's ongoing learning during a study.

goal   (educational) a desired instructional outcome that can be broad in scope.

goal   (teacher) a desired instructional outcome that a teacher hopes to accomplish.

hands-on learning   active student learning and learning by doing.

hidden curriculum   unwritten rules of behavior, attitudes, and values that students must accept to succeed in school.

independent inquiry   an instructional strategy that permits students to self-select topics for study, set the goals, and work alone to attain them.

individualized learning   a process that is student self-paced during which an individual assumes responsibility for learning as he or she studies, practices, and receives feedback; sometimes accompanied with specifically designed learning guides, modules, or instructional packages.

inquiry   involves learning during which the student designs the processes to resolve the problem. See also *discovery*.

inquiry learning   refers to study during which the student designs the processes to be used in resolving a problem of study; requires higher levels of cognition.

instruction   arranged plans that lead to experiences that help students develop understandings and changes in behavior.

integrated curriculum   an organization of the curriculum that combines discipline/subject matter that historically has been taught separately. Similar terms include integrated studies, thematic instruction, holistic education, multidisciplinary teaching, interdisciplinary curriculum, and interdisciplinary thematic instruction.

interdisciplinary teaching team   a collaboration of two or more teachers who represent different disciplines or subject areas and who teach the same students in a way that combines subject matter formerly taught separately.

interdisciplinary thematic unit (ITU)   a study developed around a theme that connects or relates to two or more disciplines.

introduction   a lesson plan element that includes the process used to prepare students mentally for the lesson; also called the set, initiating activity, or the stimulus.

journal   usually a notebook that contains a student's writing and entries about what is being learned in the ITU and personal writing about the student's interests and experiences. See also *life-writing journal, thinkbook,* or *learning log.*

junior high school   includes students in grades 7 through 9 or 7 and 8 who keep a schedule and study a curriculum similar to a high school schedule and curriculum.

learning   experiences that lead to the development of understandings and changes in behavior.

learning center   located in a special area of the classroom; contains materials and activities designed for students who work independently to learn content.

learning log   a student's journal or notebook that contains a student's writing. See also *journal.*

learning style   the manner in which a student learns best in a given situation.

lesson conclusion   a lesson plan feature that is the planned process of bringing the lesson to an end, thereby providing students with a sense of completeness and, with effective teaching, accomplishment and comprehension by helping students to synthesize the information learned from the lesson. See also *closure.*

lesson development   a lesson plan section that details the activities that occur between the beginning and the end of the lesson and the transitions that connect the activities.

lesson extender   a lesson plan feature that identifies a plan for what to do if the students finish the lesson and time remains.

life-writing journal   a student's notebook that includes personal writing about the student's interests and experiences. See also *journal.*

longitudinal portfolio   a collection of samples of student work that relate to specified goals/objectives over a period of time such as the duration of an ITU. See also *portfolio.*

magnet school   a school that specializes in a selected academic area perhaps as a theme, such as international studies, language arts, mathematics, or science.

mastery learning   refers to students achieving one set of competencies and then moving on to the next set after assessment.

meaningful learning   results when connections are made between prior or former knowledge and remembered experiences and a new experience.

measurement   a descriptive and objective process that includes the collection of quantifiable data about specific behaviors including tests and statistical procedure.

metacognition   students' understanding of their own thinking.

middle school   a campus and buildings for students in grades 5 through 8; other organizational plans serve grades 6 through 8 or grades 7 and 8.

minds-on learning   refers to learning in which the student is thinking about what is being learned (i.e., intellectually active).

multicultural education   part of the curriculum designed to address the students' understanding of attitudes, behaviors, facts, and generalizations related to their ethnic backgrounds and to the backgrounds of others; helps students to eliminate acts of racism and other biases and to recognize and appreciate contributions made by all members of society.

multilevel instruction   the use of several learning/teaching levels in the same group or classroom; learners work on different tasks leading to the same objective or on different objectives. Also referred to as *multitasking.*

multiple intelligences   refers to a theory of different intelligences such as interpersonal, intrapersonal, kinesthetic, linguistic, logical/mathematical, musical, and spatial.

multitasking   see *multilevel instruction.*

multitext reading   refers to the use of several reading sources reflecting various reading levels for different students; students can read different books leading to the same objective or can work on different objectives.

norm-referenced assessment   refers to individual student performances that are judged relative to the overall performance of a group; for example, grading on a bell curve.

overt behavior   observable behavior of a student.

peer tutoring   an instructional strategy during which one peer, as a tutor, helps another peer to learn.

performance assessment   a specific type of student response is assessed and lends itself to assessments that are authentic.

performance objectives   expectations that describe what students should be able to do on completion of instruction. See also *behavioral objectives* and *terminal objectives.*

portfolios   a collection of samples of student work related to an ITU, progression to another grade level, the requirements of a study, or the teacher's objectives. See also *selected work portfolio, longitudinal portfolio,* or *career portfolio.*

preassessment   refers to a diagnostic judgment of what students know or think they know prior to the instruction.

problem-centered interdisciplinary thematic unit (ITU)   an arrangement of learning experiences when the theme represents a problem, in part or as a whole, to be solved.

procedural knowledge   type of learning that refers to the accumulation of pieces of information.

procedure   a statement, perhaps listed in steps, that tells the learner how to accomplish a task.

project-centered teaching   a teaching method that provides for multilevel instruction through activity projects that engage the learners; students can do different activities simultaneously to accomplish similar or different objectives.

psychomotor domain   the area of learning where the learner develops and becomes proficient in skills of moving, manipulating, communicating, and creating.

reliability   the accuracy with which a technique consistently measures a procedure.

romanticism-maturationism   theory postulating that learning entails adding new ideas to a subconscious store of old ones in the student's mind.

rubric   an educational outline of the criteria used to assess performance of students.

schema   the mental construct through which students organize their perceptions of knowledge and situations (plural; schemata).

schemata map   a visual or graphic representation of a learner's knowledge about a concept and connected relationships. Words related to a key word are written in groups around the key word and the categories are labeled.

school restructuring   a collection of activities that change basic assumptions, practices, and relationships in the organization, leading to improved learning.

secondary school   usually a campus and buildings to serve students for any arrangement of grades 7 through 12.

selected work portfolio   a collection of samples of student work as required or recommended by the teacher. See also *portfolio.*

spectrum of integrated curriculum   a visual depiction of a range of experiences that reflects from least integrated instruction through most integrated instruction.

summative evaluation   the assessment of learning of students after instruction is completed.

teaching team   refers to two or more teachers who work together to provide instruction to the same group of learners. They can teach together simultaneously or alternate instruction.

terminal objectives   a term often used to distinguish between instructional objectives that are intermediate and those that are final, or "terminal" to an area of learning. See also *performance objectives,* or *behavioral objectives.*

thematic unit   refers to the instruction of a study built on a central theme or concept.

theme   the message, the point, or the main idea that underlies a study through an interdisciplinary unit. The theme can be a brief word, broad phrase, or concept such as "changes," "patterns," or "migrations."

thinkbook   a student's notebook that includes personal reactions to material related to the study. See also *journal.*

timetable   a lesson plan feature that serves simply as a planning and implementation guide.

topic   subject matter relating to a theme under study.

validity   the degree to which a measuring instrument actually measures that which it is intended to measure.

whole language learning   a point of view that focuses on meaning through language production, risk-taking in learning, independence in producing language, and use of a variety of print materials in reading and writing situations.

CHILDREN'S BOOK INDEX

NAME INDEX

Aardema, V., 213
Abbott, J., 29
Abbott, S., 119
Abilock, D., 166
Accorsi, W., 188, 212
Agne, R. M., 31
Airasian, P. W., 29
Allen, T. B., 213
Ambrose, R., 145
Ancona, G., 212
Anderson, J., 212
Arredondo, D. E., 31
Asimov, I., 212

Baker, K., 80
Barbour, N. E., 145
Barron, J. B., 108
Bartels, D., 248
Bauer, C. F., 224
Baumbach, C. J., 248
Beam, J., 213
Beane, J. A., 108
Benedetti, P., 122
Betts, F., 63
Bishop, R. S., 111, 145
Bloom, B. S., 70, 72, 108, 164
Bolognese, D., 213
Borwood, B., 30
Bowen, G., 212
Bozeman, W. C., 248
Branstad, B., 213
Braunger, J., 30
Brebeuf, Father J. de, 212
Briggs, L. J., 108
Brookhart, S. M., 145
Brooks, J. G., 29
Brooks, M. G., 29
Brophy, J. E., 108
Brown, C. S., 158
Bruner, J., 3, 5, 29, 30

Bryan, B. M., 78
Buchman, R., 222
Bulla, C. R., 212
Burden, P. R., 30
Burrett, K., 108
Bush, G., 37

Caine, G., 3, 29, 108
Caine, R. N., 329, 108
Cantlay, S., 226
Carington, S., 220
Carr, J., 30, 63
Carroll, J. M., 30
Chow, O., 212
Christian, M. B., 212
Clark, D. C., 30
Clark, J. H., 31
Clark, S. N., 30
Coate, J., 30, 31
Cohen, J. L., 78
Combs, A. W., 4, 5, 29
Conley, D. T., 30
Conrad, P., 78
Costa, A. L., 30

Danielson, C., 30, 63
Darras, K., 66
Davenport, M. R., 30
Davida, K., 168
Davis, G. A., 29
DeCorse, C. B., 30
Denenberg, D., 212
Dever, M. T., 63
Dewey, J., 4, 5, 29
Dickinson, T. S., 31
Dionisio, M., 248
Doig, L., 30
Dunlop, V., 146
Dunn, R., 3, 29
Dwyer, C., 30

Dybdahl, C. S., 63

Earley, E. J., 117, 145
Early, L. M., 145
Ellis, A. K., 248
Ennis, R. H., 108
Erb, T. O., 31
Erickson, H. L., 29

Fersh, S., 108
Fisher, L. E., 212
Fisk, C., 146
Five, C. L., 248
Fleischman, P., 212
Fradin, D., 212
Freud, S., 5
Fritz, E. I., 212
Fritz, J., 188

Gagné, R., 5, 108
Gallagher, S., 30
Garcia, E., 30
Gardner, H., 3, 29
Gibbs, L. J., 117, 145
Giboney, N., 220
Glazer, S. M., 158
Gondree, L. L., 145
Good, T. L., 108
Goodrich, H., 145
Guskey, T. R., 145

Hackman, D. G., 145
Haladyna, T. M., 145
Hall, A., 30
Ham, J., 33
Ham, S., 33
Hansford, S., 145
Hargreaves, A., 145
Harris, D., 63
Harrow, A. J., 73, 108

SUBJECT INDEX